CRITICAL THINKING

THE BASICS

Critical Thinking: The Basics is an accessible and engaging introduction to the field of critical thinking, drawing on philosophy, communication and psychology. Emphasising its relevance to decision-making (in personal, professional and civic life), academic literacy and personal development, this book supports the reader in understanding and developing the knowledge and skills needed to avoid poor reasoning, to reconstruct and evaluate arguments, and to engage constructively in dialogues.

Topics covered include:

- the relationship between critical thinking, emotions and the psychology of persuasion
- the role of character dispositions such as open-mindedness, courage and perseverance
- argument identification and reconstruction
- fallacies and argument evaluation.

With discussion questions and exercises and suggestions for further reading at the end of the main chapters, this book is an essential read for students approaching the field of critical thinking for the first time, and for the general reader wanting to improving their thinking skills and decision-making abilities.

Stuart Hanscomb is a Lecturer in Philosophy and Communication at the School of Interdisciplinary Studies, University of Glasgow, UK.

THE BASICS

Available:

AMERICAN PHILOSOPHY
NANCY STANLICK

ANIMAL ETHICS
TONY MILIGAN

ARTIFICIAL INTELLIGENCE
KEVIN WARWICK

BIOETHICS
ALASTAIR CAMPBELL

**EASTERN PHILOSOPHY
(SECOND EDITION)**
VICTORIA HARRISON

EVOLUTION
SHERRIE LYONS

FOOD ETHICS
RONALD SANDLER

FREE WILL
MEGAN GRIFFITH

**HUMAN GENETICS
(SECOND EDITION)**
RICKI LEWIS

METAPHYSICS
MICHAEL RAE

PHENOMENOLOGY
DAN ZAHAVI

PHILOSOPHY (FIFTH EDITION)
NIGEL WARBURTON

Forthcoming:

CONSCIOUSNESS
KEITH FRANKISH

ENVIRONMENTAL ETHICS
BEN DIXON AND MAHESH ANANTH

GLOBAL JUSTICE
CARL DEATH

LOGIC (SECOND EDITION)
J.C. BEALL

PHILOSOPHY OF MIND
AMY KIND

CRITICAL THINKING

THE BASICS

Stuart Hanscomb

LONDON AND NEW YORK

First published 2017
by Routledge
2 Park Square, Milton Park, Abingdon, Oxon OX14 4RN
Simultaneously published in the USA and Canada

by Routledge
711 Third Avenue, New York, NY 10017

Routledge is an imprint of the Taylor & Francis Group, an informa business

© 2017 Stuart Hanscomb

British Library Cataloguing in Publication Data
A catalogue record for this book is available from the British Library

Library of Congress Cataloging in Publication Data
Names: Hanscomb, Stuart, author.
Title: Critical thinking : the basics / Stuart Hanscomb.
Description: 1 [edition]. | New York : Routledge, 2016. | Series: The
basics | Includes bibliographical references and index.
Identifiers: LCCN 2016023190| ISBN 9781138826236 (hardback) | ISBN
9781138826243 (pbk.) | ISBN 9781315739465 (ebook)
Subjects: LCSH: Critical thinking.
Classification: LCC B105.T54 H363 2016 | DDC 160—dc23
LC record available at https://lccn.loc.gov/2016023190

ISBN: 978-1-138-82623-6 (hbk)
ISBN: 978-1-138-82624-3 (pbk)
ISBN: 978-1-315-73946-5 (eBook)

Typeset in Bembo Std and Scala Sans
by Book Now Ltd, London
Printed and bound by CPI Group (UK) Ltd, Croydon, CR0 4YY

CONTENTS

BOXES

ACKNOWLEDGEMENTS

My thanks go primarily to Benjamin Franks for his numerous helpful suggestions and comments during the writing of this book.

Also to those students, GTAs and staff who contributed so much to T&C, A-R-T, and CTC.

And to Tim Ewing (at http://timemit.deviantart.com/) for the cover image.

INTRODUCTION

WAKING UP TO BAD ARGUMENTS

My husband says I'm argumentative. He's wrong though, and here are three reasons why ...

(Sacha T. Burnstorm, pers. comm.)

I wake up this morning to be told on the news that a culture that forces people to get up early and start work at 9 is a form of 'torture'. I hit the snooze button and wonder if an appeal to human rights could save me from having to give my 9 a.m. lecture. Unchangeable bodily rhythms and the idea that we're better suited to 10 or 11 o'clock starts seem very important, but even if the hypothesis is correct, have our lives thus far really been 'torture'? Sleep deprivation is a well-known method of cruel and unusual punishment, but anyone who has endured it might be rightly dubious of classifying an early start in this way. It's good for headlines though.

I shuffle to the kitchen and put the kettle on. Soon my 3-year-old son appears, yawning, looking for his breakfast. 'Would you like brown flakes or yellow flakes?' I ask, knowing this is what's called a 'false dichotomy'. There are several other cereal options but this keeps things simple. As wilful as he can be, he seems content to have his options framed in this narrow way first thing in the morning. Hopefully this isn't a form of torture.

Cycling to work, I take a route past a big field of cattle. There is a hedge that I can see over, and the sight of my moving head seems to spook one of the animals. He starts to run with me, parallel to the road along the side of the hedge. As he passes other cattle, they start galloping as well and before long I have caused a stampede. After about 20 seconds the original runner slows to a halt and the others do the same. They herd again, snorting and steaming, looking agitated, and possibly slightly embarrassed.

I have picked up speed and become aware of my reluctance to use the smallest and largest gear cogs (first and sixth) on my bike. Brief reflection shows me that this is conditioned response caused by the disintegration of the gear mechanism on my previous (ancient and dilapidated) bike, which meant that the use of these gears ran a high risk of the chain falling off. There is no reason to think that would happen with my new bike, but the learning has transferred itself and I limit myself for no reason.

Most animals and toddlers are not what we would call 'critical thinkers', but nor are we much of the time. This series of events is no exaggeration. Poor reasoning and the absence of reasoning on occasions where it would serve us well are everywhere. Life is typically fast-paced and mistakes will happen, but even when things are slowed down (for example, drafting a speech rather than being interviewed on the radio), we think erroneously in predictable ways.

Adding to our vulnerability is that bad arguments are often persuasive – entertaining even – impeding our ability and motivation to put them in their place. Professional persuaders (working in, say, politics or marketing) know two important things:

1. our critical thinking capabilities are not what they might be, and
2. the particular forms of persuasive communication that make us less likely to pay attention to, or even look for, poor reasoning, and that are therefore more likely to win us round to their point of view.

Arguments based on dubious, partial or irrelevant claims can be remarkably effective if they target our cognitive and emotional biases.

0.1 WHAT IS CRITICAL THINKING?

This is a book about how to avoid reaching the wrong conclusion in everyday, professional and academic contexts. The fundamental subject matter of critical thinking is the reasoning we apply in a wide variety of circumstances, and its aims are twofold:

1. to improve our ability to reason and generate strong arguments;
2. to improve our ability to assess the strength of the arguments used by others.

Since we should assess our own arguments by the same standards we use to assess the arguments of others, then these aims are very closely aligned. Also, a substantial part of our overall argument on an issue is an assessment of the arguments of others. As the nineteenth–century philosopher John Stuart Mill put it:

> When we turn to ... morals, religion, politics, social relations, and the business of life, three-fourths of the arguments for every disputed opinion consist in dispelling the appearances which favour some opinion different from it.
>
> (1962, p. 163)

ARGUMENTS

Although later chapters will provide more technical and detailed information about the structure and components of arguments, the basic concept of an argument is quite straightforward. There is little disagreement among academics as to what they are, and below are some examples of definitions:

> An argument is an attempt to prove or establish a conclusion. It has two major parts: a conclusion and the reason or reasons offered in support of the conclusion.
>
> (Ennis, 1996a, p. 2)

> By 'argument' we mean a claim, together with one or more sets of reasons offered by someone to support that claim.
>
> (Johnson and Blair, 2006, p. 10)

[Arguments are] characterized by a particular structure, where one or more statements ... are given in support of a conclusion.

(Tindale, 2007, p. 1)

'T o give an argument' means to offer a set of reasons or evidence in support of a conclusion.

(Morrow and Weston, 2011, p. xvii)

BOX 0.1   WHAT IS AN ARGUMENT?

These definitions state that an argument is comprised of:

1. *A claim being asserted* that we want other people to believe is true.
2. *Reasons offered in support of this claim* through which we try to convince other people that this claim is true.

Here is your initial piece of critical thinking terminology. While the claim being asserted is simply referred to in critical thinking as a **conclusion**, a reason offered in support of a conclusion is known as a **premise**. Someone might assert that we should not eat meat. We ask for their reasons and they say that it is better for our health, for the environment, and is less cruel to animals. Whether or not we think this is convincing, they have unquestionably presented us with an argument. That we should not eat meat is the conclusion, and the health, environmental and animal welfare benefits are the premises.

This meaning of argument, then, does not refer to 'having an argument' or a 'having a row' with someone, as in a bad-tempered **dialogue** based on a disagreement. If we are 'having an argument' with someone, then arguments (in the sense of conclusions with supporting reasons) will be put forward or implied, but the two uses of the word are clearly very different.

The context in which arguments are put forward is, though, one of disagreement. The reason for offering an argument is usually to provide the other person with reasons for believing something which you want them to believe, but which they do not currently believe. (I say 'usually' here because 'preaching to the converted' can involve arguments, but in these cases they are used to re-enliven people's beliefs, often with the intention of encouraging action rather than just verbal agreement.) Not all conversations involve arguments, but many do. We talk to each other for a number of reasons – to entertain and be entertained, to inform and find out information, to offer and seek explanations – but an important purpose of conversation is to express our view on an issue. Often when we do this, the other person will ask why we hold this view and our response will usually take the form of an argument.

DEFINING CRITICAL THINKING

Definitions of critical thinking tend to correspond with this definition of arguments. If an argument is a conclusion plus premises (reasons given in support of the conclusion), then critical thinking is the process of identifying what the argument is that is being put forward, and determining whether or not the premises justify accepting the conclusion (in other words, assessing whether it is a good argument or not).

Robert Ennis, author of one of the most influential textbooks on the subject, defines critical thinking as: 'reasonable reflective thinking focused on deciding what to believe or do' (1996b, p. 166). Ennis' reference to 'doing' as well as 'believing' indicates critical thinking's emphasis on deliberation and decision-making. It is very much an applied area of study that intends to teach knowledge and skills that have a clear practical application.

American philosopher John Dewey is often credited as being the originator of critical thinking as a field of study. In his book, *How We Think*, Dewey defines what he calls 'reflective thinking' as: 'Active, persistent, and careful consideration of a belief … in the light of the grounds which support it' (1910, p. 6). 'In some cases,' he says:

> a belief is accepted with slight or almost no attempt to state the grounds that support it. In other cases, the ground or basis for a belief is deliberately sought and its adequacy to support the belief is examined. This process is called reflective thought; it alone is truly educative in value.

> (Ibid., p. 2)

Dewey's choice of words – 'active', 'persistent', 'careful' – indicate the emphasis critical thinking places on a responsible and effortful marshalling of our thoughts. Instead of passively accepting what appears right on the surface, or what we've always believed, we *actively* consider whether something should be believed or not. The 'stream or flow' of ideas that pass through our mind becomes a 'chain, or thread' (ibid., p. 3) – we impose on them an order that allows us to assess whether they should be believed or acted upon.

How, then, do we bring order to our unruly thoughts and become critical thinkers (or better critical thinkers)? There are three aspects to this:

1. Theoretical knowledge about arguments, rationality, and all of the other elements covered in books like this one.
2. Practice – *a lot of practice* – in applying this learning to examples of arguments and exchanges between people that involve arguments and counter-arguments.
3. Self-reflection on how we form our beliefs and how we interact with others.

Advice with respect to how this book can facilitate the second of these can be found at the end of this chapter (and I would urge you to read this section carefully, since to get the most from this subject, it is vital to combine what textbooks offer with external experiences and materials).

With respect to the third point, although critical thinking is about avoiding errors in our reasoning and assessing the quality of arguments, in a very important sense, it is also about *us*. It is about us as human beings, vulnerable to biases in our thinking, to moods and emotions that cloud our judgement, and to character dispositions that entrench these tendencies. And it is about us as individuals with a desire to know more about our own particular strengths and weaknesses and how to eliminate, mitigate, and improve upon them.

This book, then, is about how we can improve our thinking so that we become better disposed to making good judgements, and it is also therefore about self-knowledge: greater awareness of the aspects of psychology and character that are relevant to constructive deliberation and improved decision-making. Put another way, critical thinking can contribute to self-improvement, and knowing about the self can help improve critical thinking. This book considers the importance of critical thinking as part of the wider question of how to live well.

0.2 CRITICAL THINKING AND THE SPIRIT OF PHILOSOPHY

Critical thinking's historical origins can be identified in two foundational features of Western philosophy: (1) commitment to truth (even in the face of social and political pressures to remain ignorant); and (2) the individual's development of virtues associated with wisdom and sound judgement (with self-knowledge among the most prominent). In what is often taken to be the seminal work of modern philosophy, René Descartes opens his *Meditations* (originally published in 1641) with the following resolution:

> It is some time ago now since I perceived that, from my earliest years, I had accepted many false opinions as being true, and that what I had since based on such insecure principles could only be most doubtful and uncertain; so that I had undertaken seriously once in my life to rid myself of all the opinions I had adopted up to then, and to begin afresh from the foundations.
>
> (1968, p. 95)

Descartes is expressing not just a desire for truth, but recognition that the search for it must involve self-examination. In the eighteenth century, Enlightenment thinking championed reason over superstition and tradition in politics and ethics as well as science. Reason was regarded not just as the route to the truth, but as a virtue that benefits the individual and society. Through reason comes progress, and to be willing to apply rational thinking to all issues is to take responsibility for one's destiny; to grow up. In *An Answer to the Question: What is Enlightenment?* (originally published in 1784), Immanuel Kant emphasised 'release from … self-incurred tutelage. Self-incurred is this tutelage when its cause lies not in lack of reason but in lack of resolution and courage to use it without direction from another' (1963, p. 3).

These are examples of great philosophers and scientists challenging established knowledge, such as religious dogma and ancient scientific assumptions. Most of us are not going to be the authors of world-changing theories, but the lesson from philosophy for most individuals concerns the attitude we take to our own lives and the issues that define them. At bottom this is the importance of *taking responsibility* for our beliefs; of thinking them through rigorously, testing them out where possible and taking 'ownership' of them. In this vein, the nineteenth-century philosopher Søren Kierkegaard observed in *The Present Age* (originally published in 1846):

> There are handbooks on everything, and generally speaking education will soon consist of knowing letter-perfect a larger or smaller compendium of observations from such handbooks, and one will excel in proportion to his skill in pulling out the particular one, just as the typesetter picks out letters.
>
> (1979, p. 104)

His complaint concerned how, in an age proud to define itself as progressive in terms of social and scientific advances, individuals come to see themselves as embodying this progress without themselves needing to put the work in; without, as Cardinal Newman put it in *The Idea of a University* ([1852] 1982, p. 101) 'making the objects of our knowledge subjectively our own'. This is a product of concentrated thought about aspects of our world, whether novel or taken for granted; and it is to understand the value of questions like: 'What exactly does this claim mean?', 'What can we infer from it?', 'How do I know it is the truth?', 'Why is it important to know about?', and 'What difference might knowing about it make to my life?' While critical thinking is not proposing the impossible task of understanding everything, it is proposing that there are dispositions or attitudes we can develop that make us less susceptible to error; that enable us to ask the right questions and, perhaps most importantly, to have a reflective awareness of what we, as individuals, do and do not know.

Features of what is now called 'critical thinking' are foundational to the mood and practice of modern philosophy, but the prototypical critical thinker is the ancient Athenian, Socrates (469–399 BCE). He did not write anything, but his ideas, personality and philosophical approach, as presented in Plato's dialogues, are hugely influential. Socrates (like his pupil Plato, and Plato's pupil Aristotle) was concerned about the level of ignorance he encountered in those around him, including teachers and statesmen. More importantly, he was exercised by people's ignorance of their own ignorance. For example in the *Apology*, after engaging a politician with a reputation for wisdom in dialogue, he concludes:

> It is only too likely that neither of us has any knowledge to boast of; but he thinks he knows something that he does not know, whereas I am quite conscious of my ignorance ... I am wiser than he is to this small extent, that I do not think that I know what I do not know.
>
> (Plato, 1993, p. 42)

He then reports on talking with a poet and a craftsman, and in both cases finds that because they know about their particular art or skill, they then assume that they 'have a perfect understanding of every other subject' as well (ibid., p. 43). This is an unwarranted generalisation which implies a lack of appropriate humility, or at least self-knowledge.

For Socrates, this attitude was created and indulged by improper education; in particular, an over-emphasis on the practice of **rhetoric**. Through being effective in various forums (such as politics and law), rhetoric had tended to relegate and obscure both the nature and value of truth, and the frames of mind needed to attain it. Rhetoric (or oratory) in ancient Greece was the art of persuasive public speaking, and can be more broadly defined now as the art of persuasive communication. Socrates viewed it as the 'knack' of winning over uninformed audiences by 'pandering' to them; presenting versions of reality which are superficially pleasing at the cost of true understanding. In the *Gorgias*, he compared rhetoric to cookery, which

> puts on the mask of medicine and pretends to know what foods are best for the body, and, if a doctor or a cook had to compete before an audience of children ... with the job of deciding which of them is the better judge of wholesome and unwholesome foodstuffs, the doctor would unquestionably die of hunger.
>
> (Plato, 2004, p. 32)

In this analogy, the people of Athens are the children (a prelude to Kant's 'tutelage' metaphor), the orator is the confectioner and the philosopher is the doctor. The weakness in the comparison is that, unlike children, the people of Athens should know better; they are, to an extent, allowing themselves to be taken in by the more palatable illusions of the speech makers. Not least of these illusions is the belief that their opinions are the right ones, especially if supported by those who deliver a version of them with confidence and eloquence.

Attaining true wisdom (rather than the superficial appearance of it) requires the painful or disquieting knowledge of our ignorance and a commitment to 'examining life' that is hard, if ultimately rewarding. For Socrates, being able to think independently and competently is a fundamental component of living well and being happy, and he saw himself as a living reminder of this fact in Athens. Famously he gave the state little option but to kill him for his troubles, but in his own defence, he argued in the *Apology*, 'If you put me to death, you will not easily find anyone to take my place.' He depicted his city as

> a large thoroughbred horse which because of its great size is inclined to be lazy and needs the stimulation of some stinging fly; and all day long I never cease to settle here, there, and everywhere, rousing, persuading, reproving every one of you.
>
> (1998, p. 54)

We do not need to be agitators in this way to be critical thinkers, but the horse and fly metaphor can also represent our attitude to ourselves; *we need to be our own fly*. As we have seen, critical thinking is a form of 'rousing', helping to improve our error-prone habits of thought and action.

The method of the fly is **dialogue**: the exchange of views – of explanations and arguments – between two (or more) people. (For the sake of simplicity I will assume it to be a two-person discussion.) A lot will be said about the nature and importance of dialogues in Chapter 2, but aspects on its significance for Socrates will be briefly discussed here. A dialogue can be two people with opposing views trying to convince each other of the rightness of their particular view; or it can be one person attempting to persuade an uncommitted person. Socrates' dialogues usually take the latter form, with him questioning someone who believes they know something with the aim of testing the firmness of the grounds of that belief. While Descartes in his *Meditations* engaged in a kind of internal dialogue to establish what he should and should not accept as true, Socrates' method was interpersonal.

Socrates also saw himself as a 'midwife', assisting the person, through philosophical discussion, to realise the status of their beliefs. The vital point of the midwifery metaphor is that the individual is not handed the truth (for example, as something to be learned by rote), but is encouraged to reason their way to it. Most of us will know from experience what this kind of clarity feels like; we, in a sense, remind ourselves of why we know what we know. Alternatively we discover that we do not know what we thought we knew, and through reasoning come to appreciate our ignorance. It must be said that reading many of Plato's dialogues can leave us with the impression that Socrates did not always help people achieve this, but the principle stands and remains basic to educational practices advocated by philosophy. Rather than passive absorption, dialogue is active, and rather than dependence on the wisdom of another, it emphasises independence of thought. As we have seen, these are basic to Dewey's definition of critical thinking.

There is an asymmetry in many of Socrates' dialogues – he the sceptical enquirer, the other person claiming to know something. Teachers and peers can play this role, but very often dialogues are symmetrical, with both parties having diverging convictions about the matter at hand. Under these conditions the risk is that competition and emotion interfere with truth-seeking. That aside, holding a constructive dialogue is not simply a matter of common sense. For these reasons, as we will see in the next section, strains of critical thinking have placed great emphasis on understanding and promoting the art of dialogue.

The spirit of philosophy, as exemplified by Socrates, can be summarised in terms of four archetypes:

- *The critical thinker:* questioning assumptions about the way the world is.
- *The seeker:* of ultimate truths (even if this is the realisation that there can be no such truths), and of happiness or an otherwise fulfilling life.

- *The reflector:* self-understanding with respect to what one wants, what one wants to want, and the tendencies we have that hinder our chances of achieving these insights.
- *The rebel/agitator:* challenging the assumptions and practices of others with the aim of improving society.

Socrates was all of these things, and other philosophers will embody all or some of them. The perspective of this book is that critical thinking as a discipline should not be isolated from these other characteristics. While it is not my view that being a critical thinker is the sole component of a fulfilling life, it is nevertheless vitally important to that end. As already highlighted, self-understanding will be improved by the approach I am taking, and other virtues that can be seen as basic to human fulfilment are typically associated with an ideal critical thinker. The ethical and democratic value of being a critical thinker will be explained soon and also addressed throughout the book.

Before moving on to outline modern approaches to critical thinking, I will say something about the status of rhetoric in the later dialogues of Plato, and in the writings of Plato's pupil, Aristotle. They came to recognise that rhetoric is something to be studied – an art or skill (*technê*) – and not merely natural eloquence enhanced by rote learning and imitation. Part of learning rhetoric is to understand the ways in which people are susceptible to persuasion (what we now refer to as the **psychology of persuasion** or the psychology of influence). Many of Aristotle's insights in *The Art of Rhetoric* are supported by modern research, including how emotions function to bias judgements, the persuasive power of familiar maxims and metaphors, and the importance of the speaker's authority and likeability (or at least the appearance of these things). From the critical thinker's point of view, an appreciation of the ways in which we can be unconsciously influenced matters because it allows us to be on our guard against these processes, and because of how these influences are able to explain some of the errors we make in our judgements.

As we shall learn about in Chapter 2, it is now very well known in psychology and communication that arguments alone are rarely enough to make us change our behaviours. Plato and Aristotle knew this too. While Aristotle emphasised the value of rhetoric as compensating for the limited intellect or attention span of audiences (1991, pp. 75–6), Plato (through the voice of the teacher of rhetoric, Gorgias) makes the point that:

> It has often happened that I have gone with my brother and other doctors to visit some sick person who refused to drink his medicine or to submit to surgery ... and when the doctors could not persuade him I have succeeded, simply by my use of the art of oratory.
>
> (Gorgias, 2004, p. 18)

In the *Phaedrus*, Plato insisted that although knowledge of psychology ('the nature of the soul') is relevant to the business of rhetoric, the most persuasive speakers are those who also have some depth of knowledge of the topic they are speaking about. Moreover, if the philosopher is going to offer any degree of approval of the practice, consideration must be given to the ends to which it is put; the improvement of society or merely the self-advancement of the speaker. In short, for Plato, rhetoric is best taught and best practised by philosophers.

0.3 THE HISTORICAL AND ACADEMIC CONTEXT OF CRITICAL THINKING AS A DISCIPLINE

There are two main places from which critical thinking emerges as a discipline: philosophy and education. As we have seen, the spirit of philosophy and the spirit of critical thinking are closely related, but the analysis of arguments and reasoning is specific to the branch of philosophy known as logic (the others are metaphysics, epistemology and values (ethics and aesthetics)). Logic is primarily interested in what is called 'validity' (see Chapter 4 for a discussion of this concept), or the rules that govern our assessment of inferences. An inference is the step we make in reaching a conclusion on the basis of certain premises. A simple example would be inferring that someone is married because they wear a wedding ring or, with greater certainty, that an object is considered (by some) to be a work of art because it is on display in an art gallery.

If, then, logic in general is the study of arguments and reasoning, **informal logic** is the study of arguments and reasoning as employed in real-life contexts rather than in abstraction (which can be known as 'formal logic'). It is interested in the kinds of arguments people use in their professional and daily lives, how effective these are, the mistakes that are made, and how we can avoid making these mistakes. To an extent it is possible to represent these arguments in schematic (abstract) forms, but a more complete understanding of them requires contextual knowledge about the topic under discussion, the audience the argument is directed at, and certain characteristics of the person presenting the argument. It is these considerations that informal logic seeks to make explicit, and in so doing it offers a systematic approach to understanding and evaluating everyday arguments. This involves skills concerning comprehension and interpretation (working out what the person's overall point is and the reasons they are providing (or implying) in support of it), and of assessing the strength of the inference. Both comprehension and assessment involve an understanding of typical forms of reasoning and typical mistakes in reasoning (**fallacies**); an understanding that is enriched by a range of empirical considerations, most notably, the psychology of cognitive biases and their motivational underpinnings.

It was traditional logic's disinterest in this wider context that led to informal logic asserting itself as a highly distinctive sub-discipline in the mid-to-late twentieth century. Early examples of this paradigm are Stephen Toulmin's *The Uses of Argument* (1958), C.L. Hamblin's *Fallacies* (1970), and Michael Scriven's *Reasoning* (1976). Of greatest influence, however, have been Anthony Blair and Ralph Johnson, whose textbook *Logical Self Defense* was first published in 1977, and who launched the first journal devoted to the discipline – *Informal Logic Newsletter* – in 1978.[1]

Also in the latter part of the twentieth century the more explicitly interdisciplinary field of **argumentation** developed. Of particular importance was the attention it paid to dialogues: their categorisation and an analysis of the norms and rules that should govern them if they are to be constructive. Here the work of philosopher Douglas Walton and the theory of pragma-dialectics (developed at the University of Amsterdam by Frans van Eemeren and Rob Grootendoorst in the 1980s) have been influential in their analyses of the components and rules of what they term 'critical discussions' – dialogues in which participants with differing views on an issue present arguments to one another in the hope of reaching a resolution. These join a number of theories which emphasise the interpersonal and wider social aspects of argumentation:'rhetorical argumentation' (Perelman and Olbrechts-Tyteca, 1969), 'feminist argumentation' (Nye, 1990), 'coalescent argumentation' (Gilbert, 1997), and 'cooperative argumentation' (Makan and Marty, 2001). These approaches to argument and reasoning have closely aligned informal logic with rhetoric and applied communication, and it is noteworthy that many have sought to create alternatives to competitive ('adversarial') models of dialogue.

More recently, there has been growing interest in the links between critical thinking and psychology, and in particular the now extensive and quite well-understood range of biases that condition judgement and decision-making. If there are identifiable kinds of widespread mistakes in reasoning that are consistently revealed in informal argumentation – for instance, seeing causal relationships where they do not exist, making hasty generalisations, or determining the quality of an argument by reference to irrelevant attributes of the arguer – then it is reasonable to expect that there are underlying cognitive biases that predispose us to make these errors. Researchers in the fields of philosophy and psychology have tended to follow parallel paths in their investigations of reasoning, but convergence is now happening that is substantially enriching the interdisciplinary field of critical thinking.

The motivation of these philosophers is to make logic useful and have a direct, practical application to daily life so that someone who took a course in it would not only be better at logic, but better deliberators among worldly affairs, and better academics and learners. Similar desires inspired the education–oriented 'critical thinking movement' in the USA in the 1980s. Prime movers such as Richard Paul and Robert Ennis (who were also instrumental in developing informal logic) were critical of the standards and standing of critical thinking in American school curricula and sought, with some success, to raise its profile and generate materials and techniques for its teaching. 'Our overemphasis on rote memorization and recall of facts,' says Richard Paul:

does not serve us well. We must exchange our traditional picture of knowledge and learning for one that generates and rewards active, independent, self-directed learning so that students can gather and assess data rigorously and critically. We need to abandon methods that make students passive recipients of information and adopt those that transform them into active participants in their own intellectual growth.

(1995, p. 45)

Along with significant emphasis on its role in a healthy democracy, Paul stresses the importance of **critical thinking dispositions**. 'Weak' approaches to critical thinking teach only the skills of argument analysis, but a 'strong' approach seeks to foster habits of thinking and dispositions (character traits) – such as reduced egocentricity – that have a deeper, more holistic effect on the individual's development. To use higher education scholar Ronald Barnett's expression (1997), students become 'critical beings' rather than just people able to argue. Dialogical context – arguments encountered and analysed along with counter-arguments in unfolding debates and discussions – Paul also sees as crucial for nurturing this 'strong' conception of critical thinking (see Paul, 1984a). Having one's beliefs subject to open-minded and respectful questioning, along with a critical stance towards the positions of others, encourages personal insight and responsibility. It is part of what John Dewey called a 'community of inquiry', and 'schools that model themselves on such a community,' says educationist Deanna Kuhn,

foster not just the acquisition of knowledge, but the acquisition of reason and judgement – the sine qua non [essential condition] for participation in a democratic society, as well as for realization of a fulfilled individual life.

(1991, p. 298)

In *The Skills of Argument* (1991) – an empirical investigation into people's explanations of various social phenomena (such as failure at school) – Kuhn theorizes a progressively sophisticated way of understanding the status of knowledge and how it is achieved. 'Absolutist' thinkers presume that there are clear answers agreed upon by the experts, while 'multiplist' thinkers recognise divergent views but assume there is no way of reconciling these. Faced with this barrier, they are liable to fall back on whatever first-hand experience they have for explaining the phenomenon in question because, according to this perspective, what you believe in the end comes down to a matter of subjective opinion. 'Evaluative' thinking, on the other hand, sees how progress can be made by assessing divergent opinions towards a conclusion based on the relative strengths of competing theories. This perspective is correlated with critical thinking, and it is clear why this is the case. If you think that knowledge is just there to be discovered by those with the skills or experience, or that it is just a matter of opinion and that multiple opinions have 'equal legitimacy' (ibid., p. 184), then argumentation is not likely to be seen as valuable. So, a deepening appreciation of the complexity of branches of knowledge along with the progress they have made helps establish the value of argumentation. And as Kuhn points out, 'people must see the point of argument, if they are to engage in it' (ibid., p. 201).

0.4 CRITICAL THINKING AND ETHICS

In this section I will address two issues associated with the ethical consequences of critical thinking. The first is linked with its protective function, and concerns critical thinking's potential for empowering individuals faced with the agendas of others, and the need to be appropriately self-determining. Value is placed on knowing ourselves and choosing the direction of our lives to the extent that this is possible; to be, as Harvey Siegel has it, *rational and self-sufficient* (1988, pp. 55–61). Arguing for the virtues of critical thinking in this respect can quickly elide with a generalised view of what constitutes an ideal education in a modern liberal democracy.

Siegel offers a further reason for the ethical value of critical thinking in education: 'democratic living'. He says:

> Democracies rely for their health and well-being on the intelligence of their citizens. ... [S]uch intelligence, if it is to truly be of benefit, must consist in part of the skills, attitudes, abilities and traits of the critical thinker. It is not simply an intelligent citizenry, but a critical one, which democracy wants.
>
> (Ibid., p. 60)

The argument goes that democracy is a good thing, and to maintain this good thing, individuals need to be able to deliberate effectively when engaging with the fast-moving, multi-faceted, multi-opinioned, bias-laden debates that help define modern democratic living. Although clearly informed by knowledge of a range of issues and disciplines, being a democratic citizen is not itself a specialist subject to be learned as one would learn chemistry or history. The judgements a democratic citizen needs to make, however, are significantly assisted by the knowledge, self-knowledge, and know-how of critical thinking.

The second ethical consequence of critical thinking I wish to discuss is less favourable, and concerns its place in the increasingly instrumental approach to education that is now dominant in many western countries. When discussing its ethical qualities Siegel says, 'Critical thinking is no rubber-stamp friend of the *status quo*; indeed it is an enemy of the unjustifiable *status quo*' (ibid., p. 55). But rather perversely, some now see it as part of an 'unjustifiable *status quo*' within education. If you read the rhetoric of most universities in English-speaking countries, there is surprisingly little mention of the value of learning for its own sake – of finding out about and being fascinated by the world – and a lot about how students will graduate with transferable skills, be highly employable and 'equipped for the workplace'. If we are to understand the modern aims of higher education through the lens of what are called 'graduate attributes', then the emphasis on learning for the sake of something else is striking. A well-respected British university lists the following 16 attributes found in graduates:

- knowledgeable in their subject area;
- competent in applying their knowledge and skills;
- information literate;
- a skilled and ethical researcher;
- a critical, analytical and creative thinker;
- an entrepreneurial problem solver;
- someone who sees the big picture and understands the importance of context;
- experienced in working with clients, communities and partners outside the university;
- an active citizen who respects diversity and has the cultural agility to work in multinational settings;

- a flexible team worker;
- an independent learner;
- an efficient planner and time manager;
- an accomplished communicator;
- skilled in the use of IT;
- professional and adaptable;
- a well-rounded individual, reflective, self-aware and self-motivated.[2]

These entries, and the balance between the instrumental and non-instrumental, are fairly typical across Anglophone universities. 'Knowledgeable in their subject area' is at least top of the list, but is quickly overwhelmed by the other 15 items, and there is no further reference to characteristics such as enthusiasm for one's subject, love of learning, or students' motivation to attain an ever-deeper understanding of the world around them.

The important point for our purposes is that critical thinking appears on virtually all of these lists and is thus implicated in an instrumentalist turn in higher education. If you are not worried about this development, then there is no ethical issue, but if you are, then critical thinking needs to be careful how it situates itself in this setting.

My view is that this is a genuine concern. Transferable skills such as critical thinking are certainly important, and of course many students will want to know where their degree might lead them and how it can take them there, but it is a matter of balance. We need to avoid the implication that university is only for a certain type of person; not all students will have or want a clear idea of future directions and are primarily at university to learn things about subjects they care about. But perhaps more importantly, for most students, love of learning and deep immersion in the subject matter of their degrees will be a possibility even if they enter higher education with a broader instrumental agenda. The trouble with this hefty emphasis on graduate attributes and measuring the value of a degree in terms of employability or financial rewards is that the 'finding out about the world' aspect is liable to be diminished or even forgotten. Understanding learning for the sake of a career and all that this implies is easy for most people to understand and accommodate, but the value of a deep engagement with the knowledge an academic discipline brings is more abstract and not always so easy to truly appreciate. So in the context of global capitalism and the marketisation of higher education, it needs to be preserved.

It is not controversial to suggest that one facet of an emancipated person from an educational perspective is their love of learning for its own sake and being fascinated by the world (Peters, 1973). Certain modes of critical thinking, however, conflict with this type of passivity. To the extent that critical thinking is the asking of questions in order to further comprehension, then there is no tension between it and an immersion in the world. But it also wants the learner to, in a sense, take command of the situation through their scepticism. They are encouraged to be active in the sense of being *responsible* for making evaluations, but in an important, if unusual, sense of the phrase, this stress on self-consciousness places the weight of the world on their shoulders. A book teaching critical thinking is not going to reject this perspective, but a balance is needed, and my belief is that a full appreciation of critical thinking and what it is to be a critical thinker accommodates this balance.

It is relatively straightforward to synthesise elements of the discipline of critical thinking as a whole – especially if we incorporate the more dialogical and non-adversarial approaches – to generate a set of skills and attitudes that corrects corporate and other superficial appropriations. As Chapter 4 will demonstrate, of foundational importance to the art of critical thinking is the ability to reach the heart of the matter without over-simplification; the truth of what the other person is trying to communicate. This is not the same as speculating about symbolic and other underlying meanings, or writing exegeses of literary or arcane prose, but rather putting in order and tidying up messages than are intended to have unambiguous, if often complex, content. Critical thinking first requires open-minded and generous reading or listening, and not until this is achieved can we hope to offer an evaluative response.

0.5 THIS BOOK'S APPROACH I: OVERVIEW OF CONTENTS

In this book I seek to synthesise the most enlightening and useful elements of these approaches. Chapter 1 seeks to explain rationality with a particular emphasis on the psychology of judgement and decision-making, and the role of emotions in argumentation. Chapter 2 concentrates on **critical thinking dispositions** and the nature of **constructive dialogues**. These opening chapters involve, in part, critical thinking about critical thinking. Towards explaining what I take to be its most valuable features, alternative approaches to critical thinking's subject matter and teaching are considered and assessed. The conclusions I reach then shape the remainder of the book where the focus is on the skills of argument analysis.

Chapter 3 looks at the nature of arguments and explains the art of argument reconstruction – setting out the essential structure and content of arguments expressed in natural language so that they can be better understood and responded to. Chapters 4–7 are concerned with a range of argument forms and their associated fallacies. These include arguments from authority, ad hominem arguments (those attacking the person rather than what the person has to say), causal reasoning, generalisations, and arguments from analogy. In each case my analysis will include discussions of the persuasive (or rhetorical) potential of these argument forms and fallacies; the psychological biases that predispose us to them; their relationship with (the absence of) certain critical thinking dispositions, and their impact on attempts to generate constructive dialogues. Chapter 8 explains some further fallacies that are important to know about, and the book's final chapter, the Conclusion, includes some reminders of how critical thinking is not just about assessing the arguments of others, but how we construct and reflect upon our own arguments as well.

The book also contains a Glossary that provides definitions of key words and phrases used in critical thinking. These key words and phrases appear in bold in the text.

0.6 THIS BOOK'S APPROACH II: USE OF EXAMPLES

The examples used in critical thinking books usually involve general subject matter – statements and arguments that do not require specialist knowledge. Up to a point the strength of an argument is determined by the form it takes (for instance, an argument containing a contradiction is very likely to be a weak one; as is one that appears to jump to a conclusion without providing sufficient premises), but mostly it is the combination of the form of the argument employed and the context and subject matter of that argument that decides its quality. This means that in order to do critical thinking properly, we need to know something about the issue being discussed. Topics that fall under 'current affairs' and 'general knowledge' thus serve two purposes: first, their familiarity allows for a deeper understanding of the kind of work that critical thinking does; and, second, they can serve to illustrate how you should go about applying critical thinking to the subject matter and situations (academic, professional, personal) that you have significant knowledge of and responsibility for.

With this in mind I will make a few points about the examples and exercises found in this book:

1. For the various argument forms discussed, I will provide examples and, where necessary, relevant background information will be provided. These will come from a combination of academic and non-academic sources, but in all cases I have tried to make them as interesting or as topical as I can. I should also point out the unusual approach to referencing used in this book. As a general rule, texts relevant to the ideas I am discussing will be shown as Harvard references with the full reference given in the bibliography. Texts that serve only as examples of these ideas are fully referenced via the endnotes, but do not appear in the bibliography.
2. Since context (including dialogue) is so important for the proper understanding and assessment of arguments, then students and other readers will gain far more from applying their learning to extended examples rather than brief and isolated ones. The upshot of this is that critical thinking is best learned through materials and experiences that no textbook by itself can hope to provide.

However, remedies are not so hard to find:

1. If you are learning critical thinking in university or at school, then you and your teacher can select your own examples. These could

come from subjects being studied alongside critical thinking, or perhaps more profitably from the current affairs of the place and time you find yourself in. Students of critical thinking should get into the habit of seeing patterns of argument and reasoning errors in the world around them, and taking responsibility for finding examples is an ideal way of helping to establish such a habit.

2. A similar point goes for those of you interested in critical thinking but who are not currently in formal education. Apply what you learn here to the information and conversations you encounter at work and in other areas of your life.

3. Extended arguments and argument-based narratives can be found in various media, including documentaries, political speeches, and works of fiction. As you will see, I have my favourites, including Al Gore's global warming documentary, *An Inconvenient Truth* (Davis Guggenheim, 2006), Martin Luther King's *Letter from Birmingham Jail* (1963), a particular section of the film *The Last King of Scotland* (Kevin MacDonald, 2007), and Naomi Klein's treatise on climate change and global capitalism *This Changes Everything* (2014). But there are endless possibilities, and I can very happily guarantee that the ideas and skills you will learn about in this book will give you insight into, and the tools to analyse, any text you choose that involves argumentation and rhetoric.

Perhaps unexpectedly the extended text I have found to be the most effective for teaching and learning critical thinking is the film *Twelve Angry Men* (written by Reginald Rose in 1957, originally as a TV drama, but later made into a film by Sidney Lumet). Since I will make many references to it in the book, I will briefly explain the story. Set in New York, a jury of 12 men have to reach a unanimous verdict on a murder case in which a 16-year-old is accused of killing his father. If he is found guilty, he will face capital punishment. On the surface, the case seems open and shut – the boy is clearly guilty – but one member of the jury (Juror 8, played by Henry Fonda) is unwilling to return a guilty verdict before there has been at least some discussion of the case. He persuades the other 11 men to revisit the evidence, and as they do, it starts to become apparent that the things are not as clear-cut as they had seemed. The ensuing drama is, in effect, an extended piece of argumentation in which Juror 8 battles with the prejudices, poor reasoning and the under-developed dialoguing skills of most of the rest of the jury. From a critical thinking perspective the beauty of the film lies not just with Juror 8's ability to formulate and challenge arguments, but with his capacity to stay calm, tolerate uncertainty, not jump to conclusions, and remain independent from the pressure of the majority (which often takes the form of personal attacks and bullying). In the process, countless arguments are presented by both sides, and many of these are representative of the argument forms and fallacies that will be discussed in this book.

Twelve Angry Men provides richness of context, and in so doing brings the subject matter of critical thinking to life. Reasoning, reasonableness and their opposites are put into sharp focus by the highly recognisable behaviour of the characters. And the situation is not trivial; life and death pivot on certain protagonists' abilities to think critically. It is old, it is in black and white, it is heavy on dialogue, light on 'action', but it is a great film by any standards and one I urge you to watch as a teacher or student of critical thinking.

I shall conclude this opening chapter with an extended definition of critical thinking as explored in this book:

BOX 0.2   DEFINITION OF CRITICAL THINKING

The aim of critical thinking is to make us better deliberators and decision-makers through knowledge, techniques and a frame of mind that do the following:

1. help us identify the sorts of questions we should be asking before making significant decisions;
2. teach us about the pitfalls associated with reasoning in terms of:

    i. weak arguments and their associated psychological biases;
    ii. features of unconstructive dialogues;
    iii. dispositions that make us prone to poor reasoning and unconstructive dialogues.

FURTHER READING

- Good primary sources for understanding the Socratic spirit and his critique of rhetoric are Plato's *Apology* and *Gorgias* (multiple editions are available). A good secondary source is David Melling's *Understanding Plato* (1987), Chapter 5.
- For a very good discussion of the wider contexts of argumentation, including chapters on non-European and feminist perspectives, see Berrill's *Perspectives on Written Argument* (1996).

NOTES

1 Known just as *Informal Logic* since the mid-1980s.
2 University of Sheffield (2016) 'The Sheffield Graduate Attributes'. Available at: www.sheffield.ac.uk/sheffieldgraduate/studentattributes

RATIONALITY, COGNITIVE BIASES AND EMOTIONS

Reflective thinking is always more or less troublesome because it involves overcoming the inertia that inclines one to accept suggestions at their face value.

(John Dewey, 1910, p. 13)

I think I am smart unless I am really, really in love, and then I am ridiculously stupid.

(Taylor Swift, *The Guardian*, 30 May 2015)

Learning to think critically makes us more rational. Traditionally the discipline of critical thinking does this through an analysis of arguments, including forms of fallacious (or erroneous) arguments that we typically encounter and generate in argumentation. It is also interested in what causes us to make the kinds of mistakes we do, and part of the answer comes from an understanding of the psychology of judgement and decision-making. This chapter is an introduction to aspects of this field of study, and its subject matter will remain relevant throughout the book. Here it will be addressed under four main headings: Rationality, Heuristics and biases, Emotions, and Framing.

1.1 RATIONALITY

In an investigation of critical thinking, two forms of rationality are important to distinguish: 'cognitive' and 'practical' (or 'functional'). Cognitive rationality refers to the grounds on which we hold our beliefs. Beliefs that are inconsistent with the weight of evidence presented, or which contradict other beliefs held by the individual, are prime examples of cognitively irrational beliefs. So, for instance, Leonard's denial that his wife might be having an affair despite her acting out of character, displaying signs of guilt, 'staying late at the office', coming home smelling of aftershave, her loss of interest in sex (with him), and the reports of friends who've seen her out with another man, is a likely case of cognitive irrationality. My Uncle Vance's claim to hate all pets, but loving my brother's dog would also appear to be cognitively irrational.

Practical rationality refers to the decisions we make and the actions we take rather than to any beliefs that underpin them. A course of action is rational in this sense if it is consistent with achieving our goals. If Annie wants to pass her exam, it is not rational to forsake the necessary revision for a night on the Jägermeister with her pals, but if Megan has finished her exams, wants to unwind with friends and likes Jägermeister, then such a night could well be a rational decision. So, Annie could have the cognitively rational belief that she needs to revise in order to pass her exam, but because of some form of denial, or perhaps weakness of the will, makes the practically irrational decision to go out with friends.

Practical rationality requires self-understanding – knowing what our wants are, and how these wants are prioritised – but it also requires an accurate appreciation of how the world is in relevant respects and of what needs to be done in order to achieve certain ends. In this respect, it is reliant on cognitive rationality, but many practically rational decisions are also made in the absence of cognitive rationality.

TWO SYSTEMS

Cognitive psychologists will agree that decisions are influenced by different forms of information processing, and from our own experiences we know the difference between reasoned deliberation and quicker decisions that involve little or no concentrated thought. There is less agreement, however, on how we categorise these modes of thought; for instance, whether there are discrete systems of fast and slow thinking, or a continuum running from automatic decision-making through to decisions based on explicit and abstract reflection.

The more traditional view (found in what are called 'dual-process theories') is that humans have two 'modes of thinking', typified by what Amos Tversky and Daniel Kahneman (1974) call **System 1** and **System 2** thinking. I will work with this terminology in this book, but it should be acknowledged that a more nuanced categorisation (or a continuum) could turn out to be more accurate. For our purposes, the general distinction between relatively unreflective and relatively reflective thinking that the System 1/2 model points to is uncontroversial. And it is this general distinction that matters for understanding how critical thinking can provide insight into, and help us manage, the ways we process information towards making decisions. They are described in this way:

> *System 1* operates automatically and quickly, with little or no effort and no sense of voluntary control.
>
> *System 2* allocates attention to the effortful mental activities that demand it, including complex computations. The operations of system 2 are often associated with the subjective experience of agency, choice and concentration.
>
> (Kahneman, 2012, pp. 20–1)

We spend most of our lives operating in System 1 mode, which is well adapted to quick decision-making amidst routine activities in familiar environments. The more that System 1 can handle, the more energy we have for mustering System 2 to attend to the unfamiliar and to tasks that require concentrated attention. Among the examples of System 1 thinking offered by Kahneman are routine driving on an empty road, understanding straightforward sentences, and familiar arithmetic like 2 + 2. In contrast, System 2 is required for more precise or unexpected driving manoeuvres, more complex or unfamiliar sentences or problems to be solved. All critical thinking goes on in System 2.

These two ways of engaging with the world should be familiar to us from everyday experiences. In System 1, we are in the flow of things, letting our previous experiences guide us through the situations we encounter. In System 2, we step out of the flow and become analytical and reflective. The importance of dialectics for Socrates and Plato was that it maintains our reflective concentration. Rhetoric, on the other hand, panders to the forms of quick thinking that are basic to System 1.

1.2 HEURISTICS AND BIASES

System 2 is slow, and reasons in ways that critical thinking seeks to understand and improve. System 1 is quick and employs what are called **heuristics**. A heuristic is tool for quick decision-making; a rule of thumb that is applied to certain types of situation that, although lacking precision, makes better than chance judgements. Every day we encounter a vast range of circumstances that require decisions, and there is simply not the time to think all of them through in detail. Many will not require such thought because they are routine and predictable, but some demand our effortful concentration. Ideally there would be the right balance between these types of decision so that we have the energy we need when we need it, but that is not the way it tends to be. Instead we make choices about what we attend to, and this leaves a number of decisions that would benefit from System 2 engagement in the hands of System 1. System 1 will then get these right sometimes, and not others, but whatever the case, it seems that we need to rely on it to take up the slack.

There are a couple of ways in which knowledge of heuristics is important for critical thinking:

1. Understanding the various heuristics we use can improve our self-knowledge and motivate us to become less vulnerable to their negative influence. It can, for example, contribute to a form of self-awareness (referred to in Chapter 2 as 'metacognition') in which we are more alert to their likely presence in certain situations and therefore able to employ strategies to avoid or mitigate their bias.

2. They can themselves be educated by the practice of critical thinking. We have, for example, an authority heuristic that inclines us
towards those beliefs and decisions that are held and advocated
by apparent experts on the matter at hand. However, our criteria
for detecting expert authority in someone can be more or less
crude, and learning about both what constitutes such authority,
and the ways in which we tend to be tricked into seeing authority where it does not exist, can educate our quick as well as our
slow responses. It can, in other words, make our heuristics more
intelligent.

Since they systematically privilege some potentially relevant information over other potentially relevant information, heuristics are, by
their nature, biased ways of thinking. However, their bias (meaning
'unfair preference') can be justified to the extent that it has the practical advantages mentioned. There are cognitive biases, however, which
do not have an obvious heuristic value. These can take the form of
predictable mistakes in fast and slow reasoning that are no more than
logical errors, or distortions of reality that are the product of deeper
motivations. We might say, then, that all heuristics are biases, but that
not all biases are heuristics. Unfortunately the language used to identify them is not particularly consistent, and nor is it always that clear
when a particular bias has a heuristic function. For these reasons, I
will treat them in a similar fashion, and the remainder of this section
is devoted to descriptions of some of the main heuristics and biases
that help explain our vulnerability to fallacious arguments.

THE CONFIRMATION BIAS

The confirmation bias (sometimes referred to as the 'my side bias')
is a strong cognitive default in which we seek out, attend to and
remember evidence and arguments that confirm our current beliefs
at the expense of those that disconfirm them. Scientists know that
in order to keep a theory alive, finding evidence which is consistent
with it is only part of the story. We must also know what disconfirming evidence would look like, and seek this out as well. Everyday
thinking, however, tends to neglect this requirement. Philosopher
Bertrand Russell observed:

> If a man is offered a fact which goes against his instincts, he will scruti-
> nise it closely, and unless the evidence is overwhelming, he will refuse to
> believe it. If, on the other hand, he is offered something which affords a
> reason for acting in accordance to his instincts, he will accept it even on
> the slightest evidence.[1]

In her empirical study of informal reasoning, Deanna Kuhn found
that participants' previously expressed theories about why some individuals drop out of school significantly limited their interpretation
of new information on the topic. Despite being aware of a wider
range of causes, new data was typically comprehended in a way that
confirmed people's pre-existing beliefs ('it says pretty much the same
thing that I think'). Kuhn says:

> Although such subjects have reflected, probably accurately, on the relation
> between one theme contained in the evidence and their own beliefs, they
> have imposed their own beliefs on the evidence to such an extent that it
> has prevented them from accurately representing what the evidence in
> fact consists of.
>
> (1991, p. 231)

In order to protect ourselves from the confirmation bias, we need
to develop the habit of looking for disconfirming evidence, but this
habit will be all the harder to acquire if we do not also become aware
of the range of other biases that contribute to it.

THE SELF-SERVING BIAS

The confirmation bias is a variation on a pattern that is common to
many heuristics – seeing and interpreting events and ideas in a way
that preserves a coherent, but over-simplified, view of the world. And
since our world views are also partly the product of the other biases
and heuristics discussed in this section, its effect can be significantly
distorting. Richard Paul sees critical thinking as a corrective to ego-
centric and sociocentric biases because:

> There are deep-seated tendencies in the human mind to reason in order
> to maximise getting what we often unconsciously want. This typically

involves using cognitive and affective processes to maintain self-serving or pleasant illusions, to rule out or unfairly undermine opposing ideas ... and otherwise to distort or 'misinterpret' our experience to serve our own advantage.

(1984b, p. 5)

The 'pleasant illusions' Paul refers to have become known as the **self-serving bias** (Taylor and Brown, 1988): an automatic and systematic tendency to over-estimate those features of ourselves and the world that are core to our sense of self-esteem and our motivation to succeed. These include our positive attributes (traits and abilities); the amount of control we have over events that affect us, and how bright our future will be in comparison to the futures of our peers. A generalised bias that serves these illusions sees us taking too much credit for successes and not enough responsibility for our failures.

Not everyone is subject to these self-serving illusions, but it seems that the majority of us are. The implication of this research is that we are not particularly good at dealing with reality square on, and in many respects it is an example of the capacity for self-deception that has historically been seen as basic to the human condition. One of the most comprehensive contemporary approaches to self-deception has been the psychotherapeutic analysis and categorisation of **ego defences**. These are ways in which we distort reality in order to keep painful truths away from full consciousness, and one of the most common is **rationalisation**. To rationalise is to provide a reason for why something happened that (1) is not the real reason; (2) we unconsciously know it is not the real reason, but (3) does the job of protecting us, at least temporarily, from the real reason. We protect ourselves because the real reason makes us uncomfortable. Often others will know that we are rationalising because the reason given is not that plausible, or they have insight into our motivations. In the moment, however (and perhaps for longer) the person rationalising cannot afford to see the truth, and so they allow themselves to be taken in by their contrivance.

Novels, dramas and films are full of examples of rationalisations, and because they are so common in everyday life, they are usually quite recognisable. The plots of the UK comedy series *Peep Show* are almost entirely based on absurd situations caused by rationalisations;

and in stark contrast to his seemingly ultra-realist partner, the character Martin Hart (played by Woody Harrelson) in the first series of *True Detective* likes to take comfort from them. At one of his lowest points, he justifies an extended affair with an attractive younger woman by claiming that it is a release from the pressures of work and therefore done for the benefit of his family. An almost saintly act of self-sacrifice, I'm sure we can all agree.

COGNITIVE DISSONANCE, COMMITMENT AND CONSISTENCY

In a classic study in social psychology (Lerner and Simmons, 1966), participants who had been told they were taking part in an experiment about 'cues of emotional arousal' found themselves observing a peer receiving painful electric shocks in another lab experiment. They were then asked to rate these people in terms of positive and negative attributes. There were six separate conditions under which this observation was made, and these varied in terms of how unpleasant the situation was for the person receiving the shocks. For example, in the 'known reward' condition, observers were told the person was halfway through the experiment and that they (the observers) could decide whether this subject should continue receiving shocks, or should be subject to a neutral condition, or to a reward condition (being paid 25 cents for each correct answer). They voted (anonymously) and were told that the reward condition had won. At the other end of the spectrum, observers had no control over proceedings and were told that the person was only halfway through the experiment, and so would be continuing to experience painful shocks.

Counter-intuitively, the results showed that the better the circumstances were for the subjects receiving shocks, the more highly rated they were in terms of attributes. Those suffering the worst experimental conditions and over which observers could have no influence, were rated the least favourably. This looks like kicking someone when they are down, and in a sense it is, but Lerner and Simmons hypothesised that this perception is motivated by a 'just world belief'. This is the seemingly quite widespread and often unconscious idea that the world is fair and that people 'get what they deserve'. So, on observing participants' suffering as a result of nothing but bad luck, the observers' just world view can only be maintained by reaching the conclusion that somehow (because they are not particularly good people compared to the others), the participants deserve it. 'Derogation of the victim' is not uncommon – consider some of the public opinion and media coverage of the Syrian refugee crisis of 2015–16 – and 'just world belief' could be at least part of the explanation.

For our purposes, this is an example of **cognitive dissonance**, a term coined by psychologist Leon Festinger in 1957 referring to the discomfort we feel when there is a contradiction between what the evidence is showing us, and some deeply held belief about our self or the world. Faced with this tension, we are prone to maintain the belief at the cost of altering the reality we are faced with. In this case, a just world belief is sustained by appraising the person as someone who is deserving of their unfortunate fate.

Cognitive dissonance is an aspect of a broad set of theories, now well established, that point to a profound need for consistency between our various beliefs, our beliefs and our actions, and our actions and our self-image. Once we commit to something (a cause, a belief, a course of action) 'we will encounter personal and inter-personal pressures to behave consistently with that commitment' (Cialdini, 2007, p. 57). 'Personal pressure' because most of us desire the character integration and rationality that consistency is so central to; 'interpersonal pressure' because our need to rely on people being true to their word makes us highly condemning of promise-breakers. For this reason, public declarations or pledges are extremely power-ful techniques for ensuring that intentions are carried out.

The strength of this need for consistency is demonstrated by a range of persuasion techniques which induce compliance in people with respect to a trivial commitment, and then use this to leverage more significant, but apparently consistent, behaviours. Known as the 'foot-in-the-door' technique, if I answer 'yes' to the telesales person's trivial question 'Would you like a better deal on your gas and electricity?' I am now implicitly committed to the conversation (by being willing to give an answer), and explicitly committed to being open to hearing about the details of this 'better deal'.

A more serious example of where small commitments can land us is found in the Milgram experiments, discussed in Chapter 5.

To avoid being trapped by the consistency heuristic, we need to be careful what we commit to, both in terms of promises made and the views we hold. In Chapter 6 (Section 6.2) we will consider how absolutist statements and arguments can, through the need for consistency, force us to defend unacceptable or implausible positions.

RECIPROCATION

According to anthropologists, rules of **reciprocation** – a fair balance between what we receive and what we give – are found in all cultures. Even if it is in the form of a 'thank you', a favour done merits something in return. Anyone who has not received the required murmur of gratitude for holding a door open for someone else, or the raised hand of acknowledgement from the driver of the car you have made way for in traffic, will know how sensitive we are to this norm.

In **Caveman Logic** (2009), Hank Davis tells the story of a non-religious friend whose wife underwent tests on symptoms that could have meant a terminal condition. When he found out the condition was treatable, he immediately headed for the hospital chapel and wrote 'thank you' in the message book. 'He did not write "Thank you God",' Davis recounts. 'He did not pray. He simply, as he put it to me, felt an irresistible urge to say "Thank you" … A gift had been received and some circuitry had been triggered in him' (ibid., p. 49).

Persuasion specialists know that an unsolicited gift in a charity appeal envelope or as you step into shop will increase the likelihood of you giving or buying. A variation of this tactic is known as the 'door-in-the-face' technique. Unlike 'foot-in-the-door', 'door-in-the-face' begins with a large request rather than a trivial one. A refusal is expected though, and once this happens, the guilt we (irrationally but irresistibly) feel at having to say no to someone makes us much more likely to accept their next (more reasonable) offer. As a naïve youth, I was stopped in the street by someone who turned out to be from a local cult. We chatted a while and then he asked if I wanted to buy one of the cult's publications, for £10. That wasn't going to happen, but he swiftly produced a pamphlet for 50p, and that was me, sold, and on my way. (Also at work here is the 'contrast effect', which you will learn about below.)

In the world of negotiation, there is something known as a 'reciprocal concession'. Early on in *Twelve Angry Men* Juror 8's 'not guilty' vote means that a stalemate has been reached. On the one hand, none of the other jurors seem willing to talk about the case, but, on the other, a unanimous verdict is needed. Juror 8 makes an offer: the jury will have another secret ballot, and if the outcome is still 11-1, he'll change his vote to 'guilty', but if there's one more vote for 'not guilty', then they must agree to discuss the case further. The riskiness of this offer from Juror 8's perspective is plain to see, so the relatively small concession of agreeing to a ballot is hard for the rest of the jury to say no to.

THE REPRESENTATIVENESS HEURISTIC

The **representative heuristic** attempts to provide quick answers to questions like 'What's the probability of individual X belonging to group Y?', or 'What the probability of event P being the cause of event Q?'. It does this by making reference to what a *typical* member of group Y, or a typical cause of Q is like. If one of the answers available is representative of the type in question, this is what it will pick. So, if I enter a university laboratory to take part in an experiment and I am expecting to be met by two people – the experimenter and another volunteer – my representative heuristic will tell me that the person in the white lab coat is the one running the experiment. If asked whether someone whose hobby is fox hunting is more likely to be politically left- or right-wing, this heuristic will guide me to answer 'right'. If rain is forecast in the UK, it will lead me to conclude that it is more likely to be caused by a band of cloud moving in from the west rather than the east.

However, as helpful as this aid to quick thinking can be, it can also lead us to make some predictable mistakes. One concerns stereotypes, a definition of which is an inaccurate generalisation about core features of a particular category. Representativeness only has a chance of providing the right answer if our idea of the typical group member or causal factor is accurate in the first place. (More will be said about stereotyping when we discuss generalisations in Chapter 6.)

The other kind of mistake caused by the representative heuristic is the overlooking of other critical questions we should be asking in certain situations. A famous example used by Tversky and Kahneman (1983) is the 'Linda Problem', which goes like this:

> Linda is 31 years old, single, outspoken, and very bright. She majored in philosophy. As a student she was deeply concerned with issues of discrimination and social justice, and also participated in antinuclear demonstrations. Please [indicate] the most likely alternative:
>
> a) Linda is a bank teller
> b) Linda is a bank teller and is active in the feminist movement

The correct answer must be a) because b) contains the same information along with another claim about Linda, making is necessarily less likely. However, most of us immediately give answer b) because it typifies the kind of person Linda seems to be in a way that just being a bank teller very much does not.

In this instance, the representative heuristic causes us to overlook the conjunction rule (that the likelihood of X + Y is smaller than X by itself), and thus to commit the conjunction fallacy. Tversky and Kahneman also claim that representativeness is behind the common fallacy of 'base rate neglect'.

BASE RATE NEGLECT

Base rate neglect (or sometimes 'background' rate neglect), is a remarkably widespread fallacy. It refers to situations in which, when making a judgement about a particular person or event, we overlook relevant background information. Another famous example from Tversky and Kahneman involves 'Steve' who (with one or two adjustments to the original) we are told is: 'quite shy, not especially sociable, but with a few close friends. He has a need for order and structure and a passion for detail' (1974, p. 1124). Asked if, for example, Steve is more likely to be a librarian or a salesperson, most of us will assume the former. However, this overlooks: (1) the fact that there are many more salespeople than librarians; and (2) that there is nothing in this description of Steve that precludes him from being a salesperson. Our representative heuristic causes us to jump to the conclusion that he is a librarian because his personality is what we see as typical (or stereotypical) of this profession. In doing this, though, we neglect other considerations that are relevant to answering the question.

My parents used to live in a small rural town that was quite arty and, because many of the younger people would leave to study and find work in cities, it had a relatively old population. Sam, who lives in this town, plays in a band, enjoys the occasional mosh pit, and is partial to illegal stimulants. Is it more likely he is in his twenties or his fifties? Our representative heuristic says twenties, but because of base rates, it is considerably more likely he is in his fifties.

Ignoring or suppressing base rates can be used to persuasive effect. A story that has made the news more than once in recent years is that eating a small daily amount of processed meat increases our chances of contracting colorectal cancer by 18 per cent. This sounds scary for bacon roll eaters like me, and all the more so because news sources are in no hurry to provide the absolute figures. The background rate is that 6 in 100 people contract bowel cancer, and for those who consume 50g or more of processed meat a day (about two slices of bacon), this goes up to 7 in 100. This is less scary, and it will not change my diet, whereas an 18 per cent rise from 30 in 100 to about 35 might.

Supporters of Scottish independence quite often use the argument that Scotland has only had a representative government in the UK Parliament for 34 out of the past 68 years. This sounds like quite a serious problem with the union until you realise that it must be true of many regions of England and Wales as well. Without a system of proportional representation, it is an unavoidable outcome, but the statistic presented in isolation can present a distorted perspective of democratic norms.

Base rate neglect describes the error of taking a statistic or other piece of information out of its comparative context in such a way that it makes it look more significant than it is. We neglect to ask the critical question 'What is the norm in this situation?', and instead make a judgement based on what is generally representative of high, low, good, bad, and so on. A 50 per cent price rise appears dramatic, and normally is. However, a 50 per cent rise in the price of lollipops from 10p to 15p (assuming your entire diet is not based on them) is probably not a cause for outrage because the base rate is so low.

Background rate neglect is quite a common error, and to an extent we are used to arguers being called out on it in dialogues. A development of this is the fallacy of suggesting false background rates in order to minimise or normalise a situation that is in fact *not* trivial or normal at all. In a speech relating to the Charleston church shooting in June 2015, President Obama addressed just this fallacy:

> Let's be clear: at some point, we as a country will have to reckon with the fact that this type of mass violence does not happen in other advanced countries. It doesn't happen in other places with this kind of frequency.[2]

THE AVAILABILITY HEURISTIC

The **availability heuristic** (also named and studied by Tversky and Kahneman) judges the likelihood of an occurrence on the basis of how readily it comes to mind. Availability is a fairly reliable measure of likelihood because common occurrences are often those that come to mind with greater ease. I do not follow German league football, but if asked whether Borussia Dortmund or Bayern Munich has won their top division the most times in the past thirty years Bayern Munich would immediately present itself as the answer, and it would be the right one. Bayern's presence in the Champions League and the number of German internationals who have played for them mean they make an impression on my memory that other German club sides do not.

However, the availability heuristic can also predict certain kinds of mistake. In a study where participants were asked to guess the relative likelihood of different causes of death, most would rate things like accidents or tornadoes as significantly more likely than less 'available' causes such as asthma, strokes or diabetes.[3] The reverse is true (for example, at the time asthma caused 20 times more deaths than tornadoes) but factors such as news worthiness, vividness, and emotional impact mean that they come to mind more readily, skewing our judgements. You would imagine that a contemporary study in the UK (and possibly elsewhere) would reveal similarly exaggerated ideas about the frequency of child abductions and terrorist attacks.

A piece of advice given to young medics making diagnoses is 'If you hear hoof beats, think horses not zebras.' More vivid and dramatic causes will more easily come to mind, but these will not be representative of their relative likelihood in comparison to more mundane explanations.

ANCHORING AND THE CONTRAST EFFECT

The **anchoring** and **contrast effects** are examples of how the contextualising of information can influence our perceptions and interpretations. Anchoring happen when our judgement of a quantity (or other value) is biased by an initial piece of information. Asked, for example, to estimate the exact length of the Mississippi River (which is around 2,300 miles), experimental participants who had previously been asked if it was 'more or less than 200 miles long' guessed on average that it was around 1000 miles, while the average estimate of participants who had previously been asked if it was 'more or less than 20,000 miles long' was much larger – around 8,000 miles (McElroy and Dowd, 2007). A likely explanation is that the initial figure is interpreted as a plausible (if extreme) answer, and the individual's subsequent deliberations keep this in mind (are 'anchored' to it). Anchoring is known to be a pervasive and powerful phenomenon in a range of real-life as well as laboratory settings. In negotiations there can be an advantage in making the first move because even a demand expected to be excessive will have a disproportionate influence over the range of prices (or whatever is at stake) that is considered to be acceptable. When two academics grade a student's assignment, a more objective assessment is made if the second marker is ignorant of the first marker's grade. Remaining ignorant is one way to counter the anchoring effect, and but where this is not possible, a disciplined mind is required, for example, undertaking prior research into acceptable price ranges in a negotiation situation.

The contrast effect refers to the influence of nearby comparators with contrasting qualities. Any parking ticket I've received in the UK first declares that you must pay a substantial fine (say, £70), but then goes on to state that if you pay within two weeks. this will be reduced to half that amount. £35 is still a lot of money to pay for overrunning a meter by ten minutes, but it looks much more reasonable when you've just been threatened with a £70 fine.

The contrast effect is commonly used as a sales and fund-raising tactic ('If you cannot afford £100, could you then donate £10?'), but it has a psychologically protective function as well. In a study looking at the coping mechanisms of women diagnosed with breast cancer, a downward comparison was typically employed. For example, those requiring a lumpectomy would be thankful they were not like those facing a mastectomy; and those needing a mastectomy in later life could at least be grateful they were not one of the younger women who required this treatment.[4] Finding a perspective from which we can regard our situation as better than it might be is a means by which the contrast effect can help us come to terms with difficult or tragic circumstances. In his address to the people of Newtown after the Sandy Hook shooting in 2012, President Obama began with a piece of scripture emphasising the temporary nature of our earthly lives in comparison to God's eternal perspective. Under the circumstances it is hard to see what else he could have done by way of consolation.

AUTHORITY AND LIKEABILITY

When making quick judgements (in comparison to slow ones), we are significantly more influenced by the characteristics of the people presenting the arguments. In *The Art of Rhetoric*, Aristotle suggests three means of persuasion: (1) *pathos*, referring to the emotions aroused in the audience; (2) *logos*, meaning the speaker's arguments, and (3) *ethos*, the good character (or the apparent good character) of the speaker. In recent research, two features of the speaker's (or writer's) character have been shown to be especially persuasive: (1) the extent to which we perceive them as an authority; and (2) how likeable we find them.

Forms of authority will be considered at length in Chapter 5, but to illustrate the heuristic power of perceived expert authority, consider an experiment investigating the effects of mood on how we engage with arguments. It is known that being in a happy mood will incline us to System 1 thinking more than a neutral mood will. In this experiment a happy mood was induced in half of the participants (by rewarding them with money for a prior task), and the other half remained in a neutral state. Everyone was then asked to listen to a speech about acid rain and to evaluate it in terms of how it had changed their attitude towards the topic. Half the participants listened to a speech containing strong arguments, half to one containing weak arguments. Also, half were told that the speech had been written by an expert, the rest were told it had been written by a non-expert. The results showed that not only was there far less discrimination between strong and weak arguments by the happy group, but that their beliefs about expertise had a far greater influence on their assessment of the speeches. For the neutral group, expert source had no significant impact on how arguments were rated, whereas for the happy group it led to a much higher reported attitude change (Worth and Mackie, 1987).

The social psychology literature on likeability indicates a number of factors that will increase our chances of liking someone, including how physically attractive they are, their ability to make us laugh, and how much they like us. Of pronounced importance is how trustworthy (or reliable) they are, and their degree of perceived similarity to us. Similarity can thus act as a heuristic. Short of time and information about a product or course of action, its being promoted or modelled by someone whom I identify with can serve as a short cut to deciding in its favour; if it works for them, it might work for me too. More will be said about the role of identity in argumentation and persuasion under **referent power** in Chapter 5 (Section 5.5).

SOCIAL PROOF

I used to hitchhike a lot in my twenties. Often I'd be the only person standing at a service station or a roundabout thumbing a lift, but when there were other hitchers waiting as well a phenomenon I noticed was how, when a driver stopped to pick up one of us, other drivers would very quickly stop as well. We could all be waiting for an hour with no one taking the bait, then two or three cars would stop in rapid succession. My suspicion was that **social proof** was the reason. Under conditions of uncertainty, such as what to order from an unfamiliar curry house, what an acceptable volume of speech is in a particular public library, or indeed the appropriateness and safety of picking up hitchers in modern Britain, the behaviour of other people becomes an important (if you will excuse the pun) rule of thumb.

Basing judgements on social proof can, of course, be unreliable. For example, in the phenomenon known as '**groupthink**' (Janis, [1972] 1982), social proof contributes to a range of problems affecting collective decision-making. Groupthink describes a set of processes of social influence that cause a group of otherwise rational and intelligent people to make very poor decisions. Irving Janis' theory was based upon mid-twentieth-century US foreign policy disasters such as the Bay of Pigs fiasco in Cuba, and the escalation of the Vietnam War, but aspects of his highly detailed analyses can readily be applied to group or committee decision-making in a wide range of contexts. It is easy to see, for example, how the confirmation bias can be exaggerated in group deliberations. If certain information and points of view are shared by the majority of members, these will tend to gain more traction in discussion at the expense of information and points of view held by individual members only. It could be the case that, put together, these individually held views amount to a strong counter-argument, but a collective confirmation bias obscures this potential.

Of particular relevance to social proof is the phenomenon of **pluralistic ignorance**. Imagine you are sitting on a high-powered committee that needs to decide on an important and urgent matter, and that you are feeling unsure about a piece of information, an argument, or a decision about to be made. If you are reluctant to admit your ignorance, or to give the appearance of lacking conviction, then you will quite likely (while maintaining a calm demeanour) look to similar-minded colleagues and try to ascertain their position on the matter. You scan the body language of several, and since they show no obvious signs of dissent, you go with what seems to be the majority view. What, though, if they are feeling the same way and looking to you and the others for the same signs? Under these conditions, ignorance is mutually interpreted as assent to whatever direction the deliberations are heading in. The result of these and other predictors of groupthink (such as the presence of a dominant group leader intolerant of dissent, a strong sense of identity or similarity among group members, and a crisis situation in which emotions are running high) can be an inadequate evaluation of alternative courses of action and more than likely a poor decision.

1.3 EMOTIONS

Emotions are typically seen as being irrational and getting in the way of critical thinking. There is some truth in this, but perhaps not as much as we are inclined to think. In contemporary research emotions are often viewed as forms of heuristic, assisting our more immediate judgements, and they can also be viewed as 'intelligent' in a deeper sense as well. It is through these understandings that the role of emotions in arguments will be illuminated, providing us with the necessary tools for assessing what are called 'appeals to emotion'.

EMOTIONS AS IRRATIONAL

Emotions can be seen as cognitively rational when they are based on accurate beliefs and judgements about the world. There are plenty of occasions when we regard an emotional response as rationally justified, or where it would be irrational for a person not to feel a certain way. About grief, philosopher Martha Nussbaum says:

> If a person believes that X is the most important person in her life and X has just died, she will feel grief. If she does not, this is because in some sense she doesn't fully comprehend or has not taken in or is repressing these facts.
>
> (1990, p. 41)

Anger is, generally speaking, justifiable when: (1) something frustrates us – i.e. stops us from getting what we want; and (2) this is unfair or unjust. So, if someone at work gets an undeserved promotion at our expense; or when we witness or read about a legal or political injustice, it is rational to be angry.

However, would we also not want to say that emotions can be significantly irrational? For example, someone crying inconsolably for a whole night after seeing *Romeo and Juliet*, the 'red mist' of uncontrolled rage; phobias; obsessive jealousy, or the dizzy disproportionate rollercoaster of romantic love. Our emotions appear to make us think and do crazy things, but it is important to ask whether it is the emotion *per se* that is irrational, or the belief that causes it that is irrational. As philosopher Robert Solomon once put it: 'Emotions are not irrational; people are irrational' (2003, p. 235).

Considering the biases and heuristics that have been the subject matter of this chapter, this cannot be denied. For Solomon, the emotions we feel when we are being cognitively irrational simply correspond to these biases. So, when a small failure is pointed out to him, it is the narcissist's false belief that he is generally superior to others that causes his excessively strong reaction of anger. However, in a sense, the emotion – the strong reaction – is not the culprit, but rather the distorted belief which underpins it.

This is fine as far as it goes, but it does not seem to explain a number of features of emotions, including the effects they have on our perceptions and judgements once we are experiencing (or undergoing or *in* the grip of) them. Very strong emotions can lead to what is been called 'cognitive incapacitation': a situation in which we are unable to think clearly. Strong emotions in particular are associated with:

- Exaggerated (disproportionate) thoughts and behaviour, such as our perceptions of the other as 'perfect' or 'the one' when under the spell of romantic love. In this chapter's epigraph, Taylor Swift appears to concur. Attention tends to be narrowly focused and judgements tend to be black and white.
- Inappropriate or muddled thoughts and behaviour.

We find an example of this second type of distortion in a scene from Rose Tremain's novel *Music and Silence*. Set in 1629, land-owner George Middleton is throwing a New Year's Eve party, and he is a very happy and relieved man. He is deeply in love with his fiancée Charlotte, and has recently recovered, against the odds, from an operation to remove gall stones. In the kitchen the waiting coachmen, now sloshed, have consumed a batch of the guests' mince pies, and George

> knows nothing of all this, but he would nevertheless approve it, because there is nothing, on this night, of which he is able to disapprove. Even those neighbours of whom he is not particularly fond. When he looks at them hopping in a jig or endeavouring to bow gracefully in a minuet his heart

forgives them their futile and irritating habits, their habitual disputatious-
ness, their past attempts to marry him to their ugly daughters. Indeed, he
finds that he *loves* them. He even loves their *daughters*. He and Charlotte
pass from table to table and hands reach out to them, and they seize these
hands with an unconcealed show of affection. '[Charlotte]', says George,
'you have enabled me to adore the world!'

(Ibid., p. 299)[5]

Recall Solomon's view that 'Emotions are not irrational; people
are irrational.' Should we say that George Middleton is irrational to
want to survive surgery and to marry Charlotte; or to feel relieved
after the operation? If not, then what is irrational? Presumably it is
the effects of the emotion itself; an example of what is called the
'transferral of affect' where the feeling expands beyond its rational
origins and attaches itself to irrelevant and inappropriate objects and
events.

Strong emotions tend to distort and impede rational thought,
but mild emotions and mood states have distorting effects as well.
Experiments have shown that a person's emotional frame of mind
will affect their subsequent judgements. For example, if individuals
are induced into a positive or negative mood and then asked to make
judgements on crime or political figures, their mood will condition the judgements they make.[6] This effect is sometimes referred to
as 'emotional framing', and is a valuable persuasion technique (for
more on framing in general, see Section 1.4). If a speech-maker finds
an angle on a topic that will predictably induce, say, anger in her
audience (e.g. terrorist threat), she can then use the resulting mood
to elicit the response she wants to promote other issues that would
be less persuasive were the audience not already in an angry frame of
mind. For example, in many countries, immigration is a controversial topic that is associated with a range of emotions, including anger,
fear, pride, and compassion. If a politician is anti-immigration, then
he will want to play on anger and fear, and he will gain an advantage
if he can introduce the topic to an appropriately primed audience.
To put it another way, emotions and moods embody a confirmation
bias; when under their influence, we are, often quite unconsciously,
inclined to seek out features of our surroundings that confirm our
feelings.

EMOTIONS AS HEURISTICS

If emotions cause irrationality in the cognitive sense, they can also assist more habitual forms of decision-making by serving as heuristics (referred to sometimes as the '**affect heuristic**'). In recent decades, Antonio Damasio's (2000) 'somatic marker' theory has been highly influential. The idea is that our initial response to many situations is an emotional one – broadly positive or negative – and this 'feeling of what happened' then serves to guide our attention and the judgements we make.

Whereas in the last section this was viewed as problematically biased and something which leaves us vulnerable to manipulation, Damasio's position is that, through helping to capture and then focus our attention, emotion is a vital component of rational action. I'm in the kitchen cooking and I hear my 3-year-old son screaming in the garden. My fear-based response is immediate; I drop the spoon and I'm out the back door to see what's going on. When I see that he's not hurt (and that's immediate as well), my compass quickly switches and I see his younger brother walking on his sandcastle. Previous experience has mellowed any potential irritation at my son's extreme reaction and instead empathy is triggered and suitably understanding words and actions follow. The situation is sorted.

Notice a couple of things about this, quite typical, situation. First, I do not have a great deal of control over my thoughts and actions, which is fine when the range of causes and effects I'm encountering are familiar, but not so helpful when a situation has quite a few novel features. Second, and in accordance is a basic theme of this book, it is important to appreciate the kinds of situations in which emotions as heuristics are valuable guides to behaviour, and those in which they are less so. Discussing the heuristic function of feelings in what is generally an excellent textbook on emotions, Oatley, Keltner and Jenkins use this example:

> [M]any of the judgements we make are often too complex to review all the relevant evidence. For instance, a comprehensive answer to the question of how satisfied you are with your political leader might lead you to think about current environmental policy, the state of health care, unemployment and inflation rates, what is being done about global warming …

> Given this complexity of so many important judgements, we often rely on a simpler assessment based on our current feeling, asking ourselves 'How do I currently feel about this person?'
>
> (2006, p. 265)

It is quite possible that what they have in mind here is someone being asked this question in a street survey, in which case, one's feelings used as a heuristic might be a reasonable basis for a response. In other circumstances, however – such as a focus group or when deciding who to vote for – feelings should be applied far more cautiously. For instance, the general warmth I might feel towards the current leader of a particular Scottish political party can function as a starting point for investigating what is behind this, and the same goes for my antipathy towards other leaders and parties. The heuristic becomes a hypothesis that can lead me to both look closely at track records and policy promises, and also at my own prejudices. Overall, though, if I am willing to fully investigate voting options, then heuristics need to be put aside and I need to be dealing with the evidence on its own terms rather than on the basis of a system designed to find coherence with existing schemas. By putting them aside I am able to make a less biased judgement, and I'm also able to educate my heuristics. When I return from my reflections back to the world, as it were, my 'gut reactions' are better informed.

By itself then, what's been called the 'affect heuristic'

> appears at once both wondrous and frightening: wondrous in its speed, and subtlety, and sophistication, and its ability to 'lubricate reason'; frightening in its dependency upon context and experience, allowing us to be led astray or manipulated – inadvertently or intentionally – silently and invisibly.
>
> (Slovic *et al.*, 2007, p. 1349)

EMOTION AND REFLECTION

Emotions are intelligent; they are generated by what is currently important to us, and they can also serve as reminders of what we might otherwise overlook, or not look closely enough at. It is in this respect that they play a valuable role in critical thinking.

As we have seen, being in a particular affective state will attune us to features of a situation that are consistent with that feeling; anger at injustice, sadness at tragedy, fear at threat, and so on. Handled rightly, emotions can assist critical thinking by directing and holding our attention so that we are better able to attend to relevant details of the premises we are confronted with. In philosopher Michael Brady's words, they 'motivate a reassessment or reappraisal' of the events that have given rise to them (2013, p. 14). For example, feeling pity motivates empathy, such that the pitiful image or vignette engenders a deeper and more persistent empathetic engagement with the full story behind the argument. As a consequence, we are better able to know whether the pity is justified.

However, even if the pity is justified, true stories are rarely straightforward, and the risk is that only one dimension is revealed by the emotion-led argument, no matter what the accuracy of one's new, emotionally motivated understanding. In September 2015, images of the drowned 3-year-old Syrian refugee Aylan Kurdi featured on news media across the world, and had a galvanizing effect on attitudes towards the Syrian refugee crisis in some countries.

The image of the dead body – dressed like any other little boy – on the beach and in the arms of a policeman, was unbearable, particularly for anyone who has children of this age. There was some controversy about papers printing the image but the *Independent* in the UK justified it in this way:

> The Independent has taken the decision to publish these images because, among the often glib words about the 'ongoing migrant crisis', it is all too easy to forget the reality of the desperate situation facing many refugees.[7]

Indeed, so the emotion prompts a more empathetic engagement with the severity of the situation that drives people to take such risks. And this degree of understanding is a vitally important aspect of what we need to know in order to reach an informed decision about how Europe (say) can best respond to the crisis, and therefore what a given individual should be doing (who to donate money to, who to lobby, and so on). However, it is only one aspect, and the risk of emotion-led reflection is that the 'availability' it affords distorts the argument.

How, then, are we to counter this risk of imbalance? A couple of suggestions are these:

1. Where the situation lends itself to this, a balance of emotion-led reflections can help. In the Syrian case, several emotions will be relevant to different facets of the situation; as well as compassion for the refugees, there might be forms of personal and national guilt, anger towards Assad and IS, and fear of the effects of mass migration. This is a somewhat risky approach, however, since it assumes that all important aspects will be emotionally compelling, and that enough relevantly detailed stories will be accessible.
2. Part of the answer might be developing an intellectual appreciation of this kind of bias – as is the intention here. But knowing in this abstract sense is rarely enough to influence behaviour, especially when up against the kind of engagement emotions bring. In support of this, we need a range of what have been called 'epistemic virtues', and what are referred to in this context as **critical thinking dispositions**'. These include the ability to be flexible in our thinking, to detach ourselves from what is currently compelling (or our personal commitment) and assume a less biased perspective motivated by the desire for truth and objectivity. Chapter 2 will discuss various critical thinking dispositions, and their relevance to different types of argument will be a theme of this book.

ARGUMENTS APPEALING TO EMOTIONS

There is a category of arguments known as 'arguments from emotion' or 'appeals to emotion'. In theory, this could include any emotion you care to name, but analysis is weighted towards those which are more common or 'basic', and those which have tended to be associated with rhetorical techniques: appeals to fear, pity, guilt, pride, anger (or indignation), and humour (or amusement).

Unlike other argument forms that will be covered in this book, appeals to emotion tend not to have a clear structure, but instead piggy-back on other types of argument. For example, **slippery slope arguments** (see Chapter 6) gain much of their persuasive traction from inducing fear in audiences. Also, the subject matter of most arguments will involve emotions to some extent; usually we stand to lose or gain something depending on whose conclusion is right or accepted, and what we lose or gain can cause us to feel fear, guilt, anger, pity, joy, pride, and so on.

For this reason, the preceding discussion of emotions is important preparation for formulating, receiving, and assessing arguments. We are constantly vulnerable to error if we lack self-awareness and allow strong feelings to cloud our judgement. And this is especially important since some of those who try to persuade us will seek to undermine our critical thinking in just this way. With this in mind the key distinction we need to make when assessing the emotional effects of arguments is between those arguments that aim to generate emotion in order to persuade, and those that generate emotions only as a natural consequence of the subject matter under discussion.

In 2014, Tania Clarence was sentenced to an 'indefinite hospital order' (confinement to a psychiatric hospital) rather than prison after killing her three children, all of who suffered from the severely disabling condition of spinal muscular atrophy. Details of the case show that Ms Clarence had been under extreme pressure since their births and was suffering from depression. It was a tragic case and Jim Sturman QC, defending Ms Clarence, said a hospital order would be the 'just and compassionate' sentence and, importantly for our purposes, that 'anybody who reads the evidence cannot fail to be moved'. What is implied here, however, is not that being moved by the events will bias our judgement, but that being moved is an appropriate response to the circumstances. The pity we feel is an accurate measure of the tragic nature of the case, and the tragic nature of the case has a profound bearing on how it is understood legally (and morally).

Put another way, when the defence lawyer explains the circumstances of the killing, he is offering premises that are relevant to the conclusion (that Tania Clarence is not responsible for her actions). These premises arouse pity in us, but the lawyer's aim is not to use this pity to get away with a poor argument, it is a *natural consequence of the subject matter under discussion*. The lawyer's reference to being 'moved' becomes a short-hand for a rightful judgement of the case.

As another kind of example, consider the difference between the student who asks for an extension for their assignment deadline because of tragic family circumstances, and the student who burst into tears in my office before telling me that he cannot submit his essay because his computer broke, losing all his files. Of course, this second example might not be designed to be manipulative, but for the sake of argument let's assume it is. Let's assume that he knows that this is a poor excuse (whether or not it is true), but that if he is able to generate pity in me from the start, I will be suitably softened up. 'Softened up' here means my pity for him makes me more receptive to the tragic facets of his situation, and therefore more likely to be biased in his favour when making a judgement on an extension.

In order to better protect ourselves from the problematic influence of emotions in arguments, we need to ask these questions:

Q1: Is this an issue that has generated strong emotions in me?
Q2: Is the arguer attempting to cloud my judgement on the issue by invoking strong emotions instead of presenting strong arguments?
Q3: Do the emotions arise as a natural consequence of the subject matter of the argument?
Q4: If so, are the emotions generated representative of a balanced view of the issue?
Q5: If so, is it the strength of the argument (including insights assisted by the emotions evoked), rather than the feelings themselves (i.e. the affect heuristic) that leads me to accept or reject the conclusion?

1.4 FRAMING

A generalised idea that can be applied to most examples of persuasive communication is **framing**. The basic meaning of framing is captured by expressions like 'frame of reference', or 'frame of mind'. In communication, it refers to a way of looking at things, of putting an 'angle' or 'spin' on a particular issue. In essence, it involves emphasising some aspects of the matter at the expense of others.

Whereas some might say that my Uncle Vance is an alcoholic, others would say he's a 'party animal'. In his Autumn Statement in 2015, the UK Chancellor of the Exchequer, George Osborne, backed down on tax credits cuts after pressure from the Lords and from the general public. The opposition said this was a 'U-turn', his supporters said it demonstrated how he is flexible and prepared to listen.

All heuristics and biases frame situations because they are systematically selective in what they lead us to take from them. Another form of framing is the use of figurative language. Metaphors, analogies and allegories try to explain or illuminate some aspect of the world by comparing it with something recognisable to an audience. Arguments from analogy work in a similar way, and this will be the subject matter of Chapter 7.

Broadly speaking, there are two purposes to which framing is put:

1. It can serve the audience's needs by helping to make sense of something new by comparing it with something the audience is currently familiar with; a basic educational process. In Naomi Klein's book, *This Changes Everything* (2015), analogies with the anti-slavery, women's and civil rights movements form a central argument for why rapid and radical change to the economic system that sustains climate change is in fact achievable. Alternatively, framing can provide a way of coping with a situation. For example, I have always felt that it is healthier for students to see exams as a 'challenge' rather than something to be scared of or just to 'get out of the way'. (See also the contrast effect, above.)
2. Or framing serves the communicator's needs by deliberately obscuring aspects of reality in order to gain an audience's approval. This is how propaganda operates; 'Successful ideologies,' says philosopher Mary Midgeley,

> commonly make their impact by hammering at a single image, or small group of images, which expresses one side of the truth so vividly that they fill the reader's imagination, making it hard to remember that there is any other.[8]

Things become more interesting when both sets of needs are relevant. In his *Letter from Birmingham Jail*, Martin Luther King is attempting to convince an audience, otherwise sympathetic to his cause, of the value of non-violent civil disobedience. He has been accused of being an 'extremist', a label he at first rejects, but then accepts with a caveat.

He lists various radicals and law-breakers from history and the Bible – such as Jesus, Paul, Lincoln, and Jefferson – who are foundational to American values. He then reframes the issue: 'the question is not whether we will be extremist, but what kind of extremists we will be'. He has selected his argument and the examples he uses with great care; these are extremists for 'love' rather than extremists for 'hate'. It is by no means a balanced picture, but at the same time it will provide a potentially helpful angle for an educated audience to engage with his argument. Unlike propaganda, it is part of a respectful dialogue.

1.5 ARGUMENTATION AND RHETORIC

Rhetoric, as explained in the Introduction, is the art of persuasive communication. Arguments also aim to persuade, but a good way to distinguish between the two is, whereas arguments appeal to System 2 thinking, rhetoric appeals to System 1 thinking. As we have seen, though, arguments were one of Aristotle's three routes to persuasion, and most rhetorical communication (such as rousing political speeches and sales pitches) do involve arguments. However, the quality of the rhetoric is assessed on how persuasive it is, rather than how strong the arguments are, and weak arguments are not discouraged so long as the intended audience is convinced by them. It is for this reason that it is important to learn about fallacies (weak arguments that have the appearance of being strong), and to understand our cognitive frailties as we have been doing in this chapter. These two sets of information will help protect us from forms of persuasive communication that benefit from keeping System 2 asleep in the back.

It should also be recognised that rarely (if ever) can argumentation be entirely free from rhetoric, from what I will call '**System 1 candy**'. Features of its content or source will be persuasive in ways that do not directly relate to the essence of the point being made, and so on all occasions, we need to maintain vigilance. We have already seen two ways in which this occurs: one in the section on arguments from emotion (for example, the unavoidability of pity in the Tania Clarence case), and the other in the section on framing regarding Martin Luther King's careful choice of analogies. We should also bear in mind that all arguments have a source and a medium and these will rarely be persuasively neutral (think of authority and like-ability, and see as well the 'halo' and 'horn' effects to be discussed in Chapter 5).

When we are practising argumentation rather than rhetoric, it would be wrong to use these features of arguments to gain an advantage, but awareness of them can be used more legitimately if it means the difference between someone listening to your argument and someone switching off. In their book on 'principled negotiation', Fisher and Ury make a helpful suggestion along these lines:

> In talking to someone who represents a construction company, you might say, 'We believe you should build a fence around the project within forty-eight hours and beginning immediately should restrict the speed of your trucks on Oak Street to fifteen miles an hour. Now let me tell you why ...' If you do, you can be quite certain that he will not be listening to the reasons. He has heard your position and is no doubt busy preparing arguments against it. He was probably disturbed by your tone or by the suggestion itself. As a result, your justification will slip by him altogether. If you want someone to listen and understand your reasoning, give your interests and reasoning first and your conclusions or proposals later. Tell the company first about the dangers they are creating for young children and about your sleepless nights. Then they will be listening carefully, if only to try to figure out where you will end up on this question. And when you tell them, they will understand why.
>
> (1991, p. 29)

This is not about obscuring or twisting the truth, but rather a suggestion for how we compose our arguments in certain situations so that they are heard.

EXERCISE

From what you have read in this chapter, draw up a list of things we could do to protect ourselves from the dangers of heuristics and biases. This will include ways to prevent poor decision-making in groups; protection from those who will deliberately deploy persuasion techniques in order to influence us, and ways to assist the management of our emotional responses to arguments. Some recommendations have been explicitly included in the chapter and some are implied, but there will be others that you will be able to think of yourselves on the basis of the chapter's content.

FURTHER READING

- Further investigation of biases and heuristics can be guided by the in-text references in this chapter; most notably Kahneman (2012), whose focus is on judgement and decision-making; and Cialdini (2007) who explores how heuristics are exploited by professional persuaders.
- For methods of debiasing, see Larrick (2004), and for an evaluation of dual process theories of reasoning, see Osman (2004).
- Hank Davis' *Caveman Logic* (2009) is primarily an argument for the dangers of heuristic reasoning. In contrast, Gerd Gigerenzer, Peter Todd, *et al.*'s *Simple Heuristics that Make Us Smart* (1999), argues that they have more value than we have tended to assume.
- For a review of the anchoring effect, see Furnham and Boo (2011).
- For a recent analysis of groupthink, see Baron (2005).
- A very good philosophy book on emotion and rationality is Brady (2013).
- And a good psychology source is the chapter 'Emotions and Cognition' in Keltner, Oatley, and Jenkins (2013).

NOTES

1 *Roads to Freedom* (London: Routledge, 1996), p. 116.
2 For a transcript, see www.theguardian.com/us-news/2015/jun/18/obama-on-charleston-ive-had-to-make-statements-like-this-too-many-times.
3 Slovic *et al.*, as cited in Kahneman (2012), p. 138.
4 Discussed in Brown (1986), pp. 165–7.
5 Reproduced by permission of The Random House Group Ltd.
6 For an experiment along these lines, see DeSteno *et al.* (2004).
7 A. Withnall, (2015). Available at: www.independent.co.uk/news/world/europe/if-these-extraordinarily-powerful-images-of-a-dead-syrian-child-washed-up-on-a-beach-dont-change-europes-attitude-to-refugees-what-will-10482757.html
8 *Wisdom, Information and Wonder* (London: Routledge, 1991), p. 48.

2

CRITICAL THINKING AND DISPOSITIONS

It is not enough to have a good mind, rather the main thing is to apply it well.

(René Descartes, *Discourse on Method* [1641] 1968)

My husband says I'm overly sensitive to criticism. BUT WHAT DOES HE KNOW? WHO IS HE TO CRITICISE ME? HE'S LUCKY I DON'T DIVORCE HIM!

(Sacha T. Burnstorm, pers. comm.)

Learning about heuristics and biases is not the same thing as learning to think in ways that avoid their negative effects. Critical thinking is something that we need to *do*, not just *know about*. However, the doing is particularly challenging because of the automaticity of System 1 thinking. We need to develop the habit of critical thinking in order to counteract the powerful tendency to think quickly in situations where thinking slowly would be more beneficial. The skills of critical thinking thus aim to instil more constructive habits of *thought*.

A further level is added, though, in which these skills are motivated by **dispositions** to think critically. To be a critical thinker in this sense is having what Ennis calls an 'inclination' to think critically.

According to this approach, we do not just 'do' critical thinking, but 'become' a critical thinker. 'Becoming' a critical thinker, however, does not mean some cultish, full-blooded transformation in your personality, as seems to be suggested by some theorists. Harvey Siegel, for example, says that 'when we take it upon ourselves to educate students so as to foster critical thinking, we are committing ourselves to nothing less than the development of a certain sort of person' (1988, p. 41). Learning critical thinking can certainly change the way we approach our beliefs about ourselves and the world, and the ways in which we make decisions, but this is usually about shifts in emphasis and the nurturing of existing dispositions rather than the emergence of dominant traits or attitudes. Even if creating 'a certain sort of person' is possible, this will not be a desirable profile for many of us, but this should not stop us attempting to develop and enhance critical thinking dispositions. For each individual, these tendencies will merge with the rest of their personality so that no two critical thinkers will be recognisably 'alike' in any generalised sense. Instead, what we would expect are similarities in certain dispositions they exhibit in deliberations and other situations in which arguments are exchanged.

Two further points should be highlighted before proceeding. The first is that we must be careful not to see these dispositions as simply enabling critical thinking in a practical sense, but as motivating it as well. Critical thinking is valued, and should we find we are not thinking critically on an occasion in which we should, then we are moved by this omission; disappointed in ourselves, perhaps angry.

The second point concerns the distinction between encouraging dispositions that will tend to make us better critical thinkers, and seeing critical thinking as a discipline that will foster these dispositions. Writings in this area tend to be framed in terms of the former, but the latter is implied as well. Therefore, answers to Robert Ennis' question, 'What dispositions does an ideal critical thinker possess?' (1996b) tell us: (1) which characteristics we need to develop in order to have a readiness for, or be predisposed towards, thinking critically; and (2) which characteristics can be acquired as a result of learning critical thinking knowledge, values and skills. These will, of course, be mutually reinforcing, but from an educational point of view, the second should be the primary aim. Education will develop dispositions in students, whether this is intended or not, but this largely occurs as part of the intellectual and social practices they are being inducted into, rather than as a separate aim. For this reason, teaching critical thinking dispositions in order to be a better critical thinker seems to put the emphasis in the wrong place. Instead, the knowledge, skills and values of critical thinking are taught, and we then expect certain dispositions to develop out of this culture.

There have been a number of attempts to formulate lists of critical thinking dispositions, including those by Richard Paul (1995, Chapter 13), Robert Ennis (1996a, pp. 368–9), and Peter Facione (2006). The discussion that follows is informed by several of these, and by other scholars interested in what are known as 'epistemic virtues'. Dispositions (or virtues) tend to be highly interdependent, so that possessing one requires possessing many others as well. Any list of critical thinking dispositions has the potential, therefore, to be very long indeed. To avoid this, I will focus on the ones that I believe have the most direct influence: love of truth, open-mindedness, flexibility, modesty, self-knowledge, meta-cognition, and what I'm calling 'dialogical dispositions'. Where appropriate, however, I will also indicate related or complementary dispositions.

2.1 LOVE OF TRUTH

According to Ennis (1996a, p. 9), ideal critical thinkers will 'care that their beliefs are true, and that their decisions are justified; that is, care to "get it right" to the extent possible, or at least care to do the best they can'. The critical thinker has a commitment to the value of truth, and thus to the appropriate processes for reaching the truth. A 'justified' belief here refers to one that is established on the basis of rational enquiry – the use of reason and evidence. It is important to recognise that we can have a love of truth, but not a commitment to rational enquiry as a means of attaining it. Instead we could regard notions like faith, feeling or intuition as roads to truth. In some domains (e.g. religious and spiritual beliefs), this might be appropriate, but even here the critical thinker would need to provide an argument for why these domains require a different type of knowledge.

One thing we need to be aware of, in ourselves and others, is the desire to be right posing as the desire for truth. Many of the dispositions discussed below have a bearing on this distinction. The desire to be right implies competitiveness rather than love of truth, and it will leave us especially vulnerable to the **confirmation bias** and other ego-defensive biases that serve the self rather than objective knowledge. Juror 4 in the film *Twelve Angry Men* is the reasoned voice of the guilty vote in that he is intelligent, calm, and willing to look at the evidence on its own merits. But unlike Juror 8, he seems to also have excessive pride in being *right*, and it is arguably this need that dampens his inquisitiveness and makes him unwilling to go to the lengths of Juror 8 in scrutinising the arguments put forward by the prosecution.

2.2 OPEN-MINDEDNESS

Since seeking truth requires us to listen to the views and reasoning of others, and an appreciation of the fallibility of our own beliefs and convictions, then open-mindedness must be a fundamental disposition of the critical thinker. Open-mindedness is a corrective to the confirmation bias. It does not mean that we should have no opinion on an issue in order to deal with it fairly, but it does mean that we are able to bracket – put aside – this opinion in order to more objectively assess its worth. Instead of looking for premises that support a conclusion already reached, we should be looking closely at what premises present themselves and what conclusion these should then lead us to. This is what John Dewey calls the 'attitude of suspended conclusion' (1910, p. 13), or as Johnson and Blair (2006, pp. 50–1) put it: 'To engage in [argumentation] … is to admit in principle the possibility that your premises do not constitute good grounds for your conclusion (even though at the moment you think they do).'

A good critical thinker understands the limitations of her individual perspectives and the value of other perspectives (and thus the value of dialogue) as a way of opening her mind. Often other people will have positions and arguments that we had not thought of before listening to what they are saying. Open-mindedness entails a willingness to change one's mind, either in the direction of another's view, or towards a new conclusion not previously considered by the discussants. But, says physicist David Bohm in his book *On Dialogue*,

> such communication can lead to the creation of something new only if people are freely able to listen to each other, without prejudice, and without trying to influence each other … If, however, two people merely want to convey certain ideas or points of view to each other, as if these were items of information, then they must inevitably fail to meet. For each will hear the other through the screen of his own thoughts, which he tends to maintain and defend, regardless of whether or not they are true or coherent.
>
> (2004, p. 3)

Open-mindedness is hard to achieve because we must bracket, not just our current belief in some abstract sense, but also the conviction that will typically accompany it. In order to truly *listen*, we need to be calm. And as already indicated, carefully attending to what the other is saying is a fundamental requirement for critical thinking.

2.3 FLEXIBILITY

In the passage from Bohm just quoted, he also states that each participant in a dialogue 'has to be interested primarily in truth and coherence, so that he is ready to drop his old ideas and intentions, and be ready to go on to something different, when this is called for'. The critical thinker recognises that beliefs are often provisional, open to being disconfirmed by subsequent evidence and argument. If open-mindedness is a willingness to change our mind, then flexibility of thought is the ability to do so. Both are challenging. In the case of flexibility, the firmness of commitment that is needed to act is psychologically opposed to the 'openness to being wrong' that critical thinking demands. For this reason many other philosophers writing in this field – such as Valerie Tiberius (2008, Chapter 3), and Douglas Walton (1992, pp. 267–70) – recognise and support the value of trying to be as flexible as possible in this way. The critical thinker must try to be highly tolerant of – to function well in the world in spite of – uncertainty.

Endurance is also required in circumstances where open-minded decisions need to be made. As we know, **System 2** thinking is energy-sapping, slows us down, and is characterised by John Dewey as 'mental unrest and disturbance' (1910, p. 13). Facing dilemmas, we need to have the fortitude to maintain what psychologist Irvin Yalom (1980, p. 312) calls 'simultaneous ambivalence'. This is the result of remaining clearly focused on the for and against of both (or all) the options available, rather than letting one of them dominate our attention and, therefore, that way incline us to a less troublesome, but biased, decision.

As well as the need for conviction, we must also recognise that a vital feature of a fulfilled life is substantial time spent being 'unreflectively absorbed by what we value' (Tiberius, 2008, p. 67). This is also a different psychological mode to critical thinking, and one that is similarly at odds with it. If both this type of absorption and reflective thinking are so important, then we can see how being 'ready' (to use Bohm's expression) to move between the two is also important.

2.4 MODESTY

Modesty (or humility) is primarily understood as possessing accurate perceptions of ourselves and the status of our beliefs in relation to others. The exaggerate pride in being right we identified in Juror 4 is the opposite of modesty. This is a person for whom it is important to see himself as better than others, whereas in the modest or humble person, we find a generalised sense of equality. They will thus bring an absence of egocentricity to a discussion that allows for more open debate.

Also, however, modesty is important for critical thinking for a slightly different reason. Critical thinking is empowering in terms of the insights it provides, and how it improves our ability to successfully interrogate the arguments of others. These are no mean abilities, and have the potential to create a sense of superiority in the learner. Modesty is a corrective to this. It will incline us, for example, to realise that critical thinking is just one among many important practices; that virtually anyone can become a better critical thinker if they commit themselves to learning it; and, perhaps most important of all, to recognise that if people are not schooled in this way, it does not follow that: (1) they are unintelligent; (2) they do not have worthwhile beliefs; or (3) they are not worthy or respect. (For more on this kind of issue, see the section, 'Don't be a smart arse', below.)

2.5 SELF-KNOWLEDGE

Knowledge of one's self in part comes from an appreciation of the strengths and frailties humans share, including the intellectual frailties that are of interest to critical thinking. It also comes from the actual content of what we believe and feel. This will include relatively superficial and practical knowledge, but also *deep personal attachments to values and worldviews* (such as religious, political and ethical beliefs) that can be an impediment to open-mindedness.

These attachments are part of what it is to be a person, and they will not always be something that critical thinking believes we should be prepared to bracket in the context of a discussion. That is a choice for an individual. However, what is important for critical thinking is that we are aware of what these deep-seated commitments are. One reason for this is that it allows us a clear choice about what we do and do not want to put out there for critical appraisal by others. A similar reason is that it permits us to assess which of our assumptions we want to question and which we do not. Also, foundational beliefs will permeate many of our other beliefs, so recognising what Walton refers to as 'dark side commitments' (1992, p. 255) will provide important premises in arguments concerning a very wide range of topics.

2.6 META-COGNITION

Closely related to self-knowledge is the disposition to be meta-cognitive. The most specific meaning of this term refers to an awareness of our thought processes, and is exemplified by ideas like 'alertness to loss of control of one's thinking', and 'the impulse to stand back and take stock' (Perkins *et al.*, 1993, p. 8). It is not about formal knowledge of our cognitive biases, but rather the disposition to monitor and assess the quality or mode of our thinking in different situations. An important aspect of this concerns knowing when to think critically and when not to. For example, Perkins *et al.* refer to the importance of the 'detection of complex thinking situations' (ibid., p. 8), which will include knowing when to switch from System 1 to System 2 thinking.

David Bohm discusses the 'blocks' we have that make us unaware of some of the contradictions in our beliefs, and therefore less open-minded. To assist in our understanding of these blocks, he suggests we become sensitive to mild emotional responses to ideas that we encounter. 'If one is alert and attentive,' he says,

> he can see for example that whenever certain questions arise, there are fleeting sensations of fear, which push him away from the consideration of these questions, and of pleasure, which attract his thoughts and cause them to be occupied with other questions. So one is able to keep away from whatever it is that he thinks may disturb him. And as a result, he can be subtly defending his own ideas, when he supposes that he is really listening to what other people have to say.
>
> (2004, p. 5)

With reference to ideas discussed in Chapter 1, we might call this the development of an intelligent affect heuristic.

We should not lose sight, however, of how these considerations are part of a broad sweep of activities and practices making up a life, including ones where meta-cognition is simply not welcome or necessary: painting for pleasure, unself-conscious dancing, and an evening with a *Breaking Bad* boxset come to mind. Many such occasions can be sought out and (reflectively) worked into the composition of one's life. It might require critical thinking and its associated dispositions to determine and facilitate these happenings, but many of the resulting experiences are then justifiably pressing meta-cognition's snooze button.

2.7 DIALOGICAL DISPOSITIONS

Critical thinking does not necessarily occur in the context of a dialogue, but it usually does. Written arguments (in academic journals, opinion pieces in news media, social media forums, and the like) are invariably a response to other arguments, and are responded to in turn. Arguments presented in spoken, and in particular face-to-face, dialogue can be some of the most persuasive, and are of course found in multiple professional, personal, political and legal settings. We present arguments to convince others of our position; arguments provoke questions and counter-arguments, and via this process the open-minded, flexible, self-aware person should be able to edge closer to the truth about the issue under discussion. Good quality dialogues are thus profoundly important, and so the ability to conduct them constructively has equivalent importance. In part, this is a matter of knowing and applying certain rules (see below), but there are also dispositions that facilitate this process and embody its value and significance. These include a genuine desire to listen to others' positions, and a desire to present your own position as clearly as possible. And this means providing not just your conclusion, but the reasons supporting that conclusion as well.

I will discuss some important dialogical dispositions – courage, staying focused, respect for others, and not being a 'smart arse' – before providing some basic rules for constructive dialogues.

COURAGE

One reason we might be reluctant to be clear about our reasons for holding the beliefs we do is fear of these beliefs being cast into doubt. This is one reason why an important dialogical disposition is courage. Another is that critical thinking is about independence of thought and thus taking responsibility for one's convictions, and this can sometimes mean standing alone in the face of significant social pressure to conform. *Twelve Angry Men* and the Milgram experiments (which will be discussed in Chapter 5) are dramatic examples of pressures associated with **groupthink** and forms of authority, but as we saw in Chapter 1, the underlying processes are common. Social media is a prime example; one academic researcher writes about how she came to the 2015 UK general election as a floating voter who raised questions about the policies on all sides, but who was confronted 'time and time again' by 'posts from my peers packed full of expletives implying that I was bigoted for even doubting the Labour or the Green economic approach'.[1]

There are two types of reprimand that the person challenging a group norm can face: one relating to the content of their opinion, the other to the process of speaking out itself. Speaking out can be perceived as problematic for a number of reasons, including 'rocking the boat' (destabilising an established, possibly hard-won, equilibrium). In certain circumstances or at certain times, critical thinking (or at least its expression) is not appropriate, and, depending on the exact context, 'boat rocking' could be one of them. However, as the previous discussion of the characteristics of groupthink demonstrates, this is often not a judgement call that is easy to make. It takes courage.

Another consideration that affects motivation for critical thinking is that it exposes us to the dark underbelly of existence. By this, I do not mean human deviousness or folly, but two of the fundamental existential concerns that continually and inevitably haunt us: that we must take responsibility for our decisions and that there is no preordained order to our lives (no final set of truths or essential self to be discovered). At a cultural level, Kant meant something like this when he described the Enlightenment as an emergence from a 'tutelage' that is 'self-imposed', not by an inability to reason, but by a lack of 'resolve and courage'. Critical thinking gains much of its significance from a profound freedom that comes with the understanding that existence has no ultimate answer or purpose. Words like 'active' and 'judgement' serve as reminders that in a very important sense our lives are what we choose to make of them. There is a freedom and excitement associated with this recognition, but also an anxiety, and it is this anxiety that can make critical thinking off-putting. It is strangely disquieting.

STAYING FOCUSED

In dialogues it is very easy to become side-tracked, so the critical thinker always tries to stay focused on the overall point of the discussion. Losing focus can happen by accident, but it can also be the aim of tactics employed by an arguer who feels they are losing, or who wants to end the discussion prematurely. **Fallacies** associated with losing focus include **ad hominem arguments** (see Chapter 5), **red herrings** (see Chapter 8) and **straw man arguments** (see Chapter 3).

Part of the art of staying on track is asking the right questions at the right times. Ennis (1996a, pp. 373–5) identifies various types of questions:

- 'Clarification questions' like:

  Would you say a little more about that?
  What do you mean?

- 'Main point' questions like:

  Let me see if I have this right. Is this your main point ...?
  I'm afraid I don't quite see what you're driving at. Could you say a little more about it?

- 'Reason-seeking' questions, or requests, like:

  Perhaps you could elaborate on why you believe that?

- And 'relevance' questions like:

  How does that support the conclusion?
  Are you assuming that ...?

Other terms for 'staying focused' might be persistence or perseverance, and it is noteworthy that John Dewey includes the former in his definition of critical thinking: 'Active, persistent, and careful consideration of a belief ... in the light of the grounds which support it' (1910, p. 6). Persistence is part of the courage discussed above, but it can also be valuable when faced with an absence of clarity or deliberate attempts to divert the discussion.

RESPECT FOR OTHERS

Among critical thinking scholars, there is some disagreement about whether respect, or care, for others should be counted as a critical thinking disposition. Peter Facione (voicing the view of the majority of scholars at the time) says:

> Good critical thinking has nothing to do with any given set of cultural beliefs, religious tenets, ethical values, social mores, political orientations, or orthodoxies of any kind. Rather, the commitment one makes as a good critical thinker is to always seek the truth with objectivity, integrity, and fairmindedness.
>
> (2006, p. 11)

'Integrity and fairmindedness' can of course be ethical dispositions, but what Facione has in mind here is their role in truth-seeking – in other words, as epistemic dispositions. Respect and concern for others – qualities that seems to be present in *Twelve Angry Men*'s Juror 8, but not in master problem-solver Walter White (from *Breaking Bad*) – are not, according to this view, part of the profile of the ideal critical thinker.

It is interesting though that, while recognising it is not a defining characteristic, Ennis sees the need to include 'care about the dignity and worth of every person' among his list of critical thinking dispositions. His reason is it would serve as a 'corrective' against critical thinkings misuse, implying that it is a powerful ability that has the potential to hurt (humiliate, disempower, oppress) others. However, I will argue: (1) that this is not enough of a reason to include it as a core disposition; but also (2) that there is another reason why we should regard respect and concern for others as having particular importance for critical thinking.

Critical thinking dispositions can indeed be used for unethical purposes, but this is true of most sets of practice-related dispositions, such as those relevant to being a good sports person or a good business person. The good sports person is not the same things as a good person more generally conceived, but if we want them not to use their talents and dispositions for ill-intent, then they need to also have virtues such as respect and compassion for others. So, in a sense, we would add this basic ethical disposition to all other lists of dispositions. A general respect for the welfare and dignity of others is a disposition we would hope to promote and instil in our children, whether or not we are promoting critical thinking; and most professions these days have ethical codes of conduct.

So, in this sense, the ethical dimension is relevant, but Ennis has not provided a reason why it should have *special* relevance for critical thinking, and to this extent Facione and others have a point. I believe, though, that there are some more specific reasons why care for others should be seen as, if not core, then as having greater importance to critical thinking than it has to other practices (such as sport). The reasons in question concern the functioning of constructive dialogues, and the first of these I will initially express in terms of **premises** and **conclusion**:

Premise 1:   Constructive dialogue is crucial for critical thinking.

Premise 2:   Constructive dialogue is less likely if we do not have concern for the welfare of the people we are in a dialogue with.

Conclusion: Therefore concern for the welfare of others is a disposition of an ideal critical thinker.

The initial premise has already been explained, but the second is in need of some elaboration. One reason constructive dialogue is less likely if we are not respectful towards other participants is that it could be an incentive for them to disengage. A person detecting signs of disrespect might leave the discussion entirely, or be reluctant to give it their full energy, or to be entirely open about their position and reasons for holding it.

This point brings us to a second argument for why concern for others is so important for critical thinking. The reasoning here is less about the functioning of the dialogical process, and more about our ability to understand the positions that others hold. It has already been established that open-mindedness is fundamental to critical thinking, but this is not just a matter of being able to detach ourselves from our commitments in order to objectively assess alternatives, it is also the ability to really *listen* to those alternatives with the right degree of attentiveness. Often the bases of people's beliefs are subtle and highly contextual, and in order to truly understand them, we need to be willing to devote time and energy, and a kind of selflessness, to others' belief systems. John Stuart Mill (1962, p. 164) felt strongly about this:

> Ninety-nine in a hundred of what are called educated men are in this condition; even of those who can argue fluently for their opinions. Their conclusion may be true, but it might be false for anything they know: they have never thrown themselves into the mental position of those who think differently from them, and considered what such persons may have to say; and consequently they do not, in any proper sense of the word, know the doctrine which they themselves profess ... [T]hat part of the truth which turns the scale, and decides the judgment of a completely informed mind, they are strangers to; nor is it ever really known, but to those who have attended equally and impartially to both sides, and endeavoured to see the reasons of both in the strongest light.

To be willing to do this, I would argue, we need to have a prior respect for the other as the holder of these beliefs. It is this respect that helps motivate careful and sustained listening. Also, to repeat the point made above, the person who suspects that this respect is not present will be reluctant to fully divulge their beliefs and the reasons supporting them. And since the whole point of critical thinking is to *scrutinise* beliefs, it is even more important that this is carried out against a background of trust: trust that others are doing it for the right reasons, and that they are aware that beliefs do not exist independently of believers.

BELIEFS AND BELIEVERS

'Argument, on this model,' says Michael Gilbert about his theory of 'coalescent argumentation', 'is among persons, not between theories' (1994, p. 112). Because many of our beliefs – and certainly many of those worth debating – are personal, then to enter into argumentation dialogues can be to run a significant risk. It is more than a matter of the possibility of finding out you are wrong in a way that is analogous to getting an answer on a test wrong; it is finding out that a belief that is central to your values and commitments is wrong. To take this on board can require quite a far-reaching re-evaluation of aspects of one's life. This is a risk we will be more likely to take if we feel that our partners in dialogue are appreciative of this fact, and correspondingly motivated to listen to us in a way that is underpinned by basic respect.

Sadly, the way that critical thinking is taught (and how its aims and methods are communicated), too often runs counter to this attitude. In his article 'Argument is War … and War is Hell' (1995), Daniel H. Cohen is critical of the adversarial, combative way in which argumentation tends to be understood. This, he says, runs the risk of creating 'not just able arguers, but *argumentative* arguers: proficient, pedantic and petty …' (ibid., pp. 180–1). Taking pleasure in argument for argument's sake, or seeing the aim as winning the argument rather than establishing truth, is all part of the dispositional profile of an adversarial approach. It is something that is readily apparent in the practice of formal debates, and in the way court cases in many countries are conducted.

In place of the 'war' metaphor, Cohen suggests a number of alternatives, including collaborative frames such as 'brainstorming' and the nineteenth-century American tradition of 'barn raising' (which is still practised by communities like the Amish). In place of listening in order to defeat, there is listening motivated by *inquisitiveness*. In place of 'me against you', there is 'me and you trying to sort out a problem, the solution to which we might not have been able to reach alone, and which could end up being a hybrid or synthesis of our initial, individual positions'.

A side-effect of this attitude to dialogues can be a kind of intimacy that, especially if reciprocated, is profoundly rewarding. The careful, respectful listening and thus opening up of the other's world is one reason for this. Another is that the sharing of ideas in a dialogue towards new, mutually generated, important insights is an excellent basis for bonding. Philosopher Bertrand Russell describes his meeting with novelist Joseph Conrad in a way that demonstrates this potential:

> We talked with continually increasing intimacy. We seemed to sink through layer after layer of what was superficial till gradually both reached the central fire. It was an experience unlike any other that I have known. We looked into each other's eyes, half appalled and half intoxicated to find ourselves together in such a region. The emotion was as intense as passionate love, and at the same time all-embracing, I came away bewildered, and hardly able to find my way among ordinary affairs.
>
> (Cited in Yalom, 1980, p. 396)

This is an example of what has come to be known as 'flow'; the experience of focused engagement with an intrinsically rewarding task that you are skilled at and in control of, but which is suitably challenging and provides immediate feedback. It is associated with an experience of timelessness (being lost in the moment); non-self-consciousness (the boundaries of the ego are more supple than usual), and calmness. According to the concept's originator – Mihaly Csikszentmihalyi (2002) – it can be elicited by a range of activities, including sport, creative work, and one-to-one social encounters.

A non-dialogical variation of flow is what Dewey (1910) calls 'wholeheartedness'. In contrast to the perseverance needed to maintain concentration in some deliberative situations, wholeheartedness is an intellectual absorption in a subject where 'the material holds and buoys his mind up and gives an onward impetus to thinking'. It is complex, reflective thinking with its own momentum, in which questions and ideas arise 'spontaneously'.

Overall, it can be seen that care for the well-being of others is an important disposition for a critical thinker to possess, but it should also be apparent that the practice of critical thinking, if encouraged in the right ways, can serve as a gateway to understanding and compassion. Critical thinking can thus be motivated not just by truth-seeking, but by connection and intimacy.

DON'T BE A SMART ARSE

Becoming a critical thinking can change a person in a couple of respects. On the one hand, they have, or have honed, the dispositions so far discussed, and, on the other, they have a vocabulary that is distinctive. In terms of exercising one's ability, one has to be aware that this can, as Ennis (1996a) puts it, 'intimidate and confuse' others who have not had this training, or who are not otherwise inclined to think in this way.

However, this does not mean that we should not engage people who are less inclined to think in this way in dialogue, or even 'push' them to do so, but it does mean that we should do this sensitively. We need to be careful with the language we use, and we must not believe that we are in some sense superior.

For Ennis, then, the ideal critical thinker will 'take into account others' feelings and level of understanding, avoiding intimidating or confusing others with their critical thinking prowess' (ibid.). In other words, *don't be a smart arse*. On the whole, we need to be very careful when using comedy routines as examples of arguments, because for the most part their intention is to entertain rather than to seek the truth. (It should be recognised, however, that there are genuine hybrids, such as Comedy Central's *The Daily Show*, and the work of people like Michael Moore, Mark Thomas and Dave Gorman.) However, I'm going to break this rule here and consider a story told by comedian Stewart Lee. It is an example that I believe is justified because the comedian's own published reflections seem to make it clear that this was a real event and that this is how he felt about it. During one of his shows, Lee is making a point about intolerance, and the context is a cab driver who says to him, out of the blue, 'All homosexuals should be killed.' Lee asks him for his reasons.

> And then there was a pause, because he'd never had to go to the next level of the argument, fraternising mainly with cab drivers ... where that was just accepted as a point.[2] ... after a moment he said 'Well, because homosexuality is immoral.'

Offering the example of the ancient Greeks, Lee then explains to him that 'morality is not a fixed thing' and therefore not the best basis from which to argue this point. The cabbie's response is: 'Well, you can prove anything with facts, can't you?'

Lee continues:

> For a minute I went, 'Yeah.' And then I thought, 'Hang on! That's the most fantastic way of winning an argument I've ever heard! ... I'm not interested in facts. I find they tend to cloud my judgement. I prefer to rely on instinct and blind prejudice.'[3]

As abhorrent as the cabbie's stated view is, Lee is being a smart arse because the argument he presents is going to derail him. It deals in historical facts and abstract concepts like moral relativism that the cabbie probably will not be familiar with. Lee is talking over his head, and so understood more charitably, the response 'you can prove anything with facts' should not be taken literally. Instead it should be interpreted along the lines of 'I don't understand what you're talking about', or 'displaying familiarity with technical terms and giving the appearance of clever arguments can fool some people, but not me', or perhaps simply, 'I know when I'm being patronised.'[4]

The virtue that has been called 'deliberative friendliness' captures the type of constructive approach that would mitigate smart-arsery. It has been defined as: 'the willingness to entertain discussion in a manner that does not unnecessarily offend or alienate interlocutors' (Aikin and Clanton, 2010, p. 415). It does not directly refer to the respect for others previously discussed, but to the style of one's engagement. This should be critical but encouraging, 'sporting' rather than 'quibbling and quarrelsome', and resolutely not one that 'takes any argumentative failure on the other's side to be evidence of cognitive asymmetry between the two' (ibid., p. 415).

In summary, the features of arguments and argumentation that arise from this aspect of the discussion of dispositions are these:

- Dialogues can be valuable for reaching mutually satisfying and edifying answers, rather than a win–lose framework.
- A recognition of the complexity and hard-to-get-at nature of the basis of many of the beliefs that we hold. This means that dialogues involving these issues need to be conducted with respect, sensitivity, and tolerance (including for apparent dogmatism).
- Increased or deepened knowledge of others will often be a result, and can be an additional aim, of argumentation.
- Increased or deepened self-knowledge will often be a result of argumentation, and can be an additional aim.
- Careful and sustained listening is privileged as a skill, and as a disposition (the desire to discover another's worldview).
- Sensitivity is required, not just to the complexity, subtlety and distinctiveness of the positions others hold, but to their style of thinking, vocabulary and conversational norms. These are not necessarily those of the critical thinker, but this is not the same as being unintelligent or uninformed. And even if someone is these things, that does not mean they cannot be engaged in some level of argumentation.

2.8 GUIDELINES FOR A CONSTRUCTIVE DIALOGUE

In addition to this analysis of dialogical dispositions, it might be helpful to provide a summary of rules of conduct (influenced by Ennis, 1996a; Walton, 2006; and the work of pragma-dialecticians such as Eemeren and Grootendorst, 2004) that should be followed in order to give dialogue the best chance of success. The person embodying critical thinking dispositions will be inclined to these ways of behaving, in which case, these guidelines can serve as a kind of summary of how the ideal critical thinker comes across when engaging in argumentation. It can also, however, function as a stand-alone checklist that has value regardless of underlying dispositions to conduct oneself in these ways.

1. The discussants should be allowed to speak freely – both in terms of expressing their view, and in terms of being critical of the views of other discussants.
2. If a discussant is asked to explain their viewpoint (for example, provide more clarity, or provide reasons why they hold that view), they must be prepared to do so. This is especially important since premises are often implicit. (See Ennis' list of 'clarification questions', above.)
3. Discussants have a duty to listen carefully to, and avoid misrepresenting, each other's views.
4. Unless the issue is about the person (or persons) involved, personal attacks (ad hominem arguments – see Chapter 5) should be avoided where possible. Often these are fallacious, but even when they are not, their emotive nature can cause the discussion to descend into a quarrel.
5. Discussants should address each other in a civil manner.
6. Discussants should follow basic rules of conversation such as turn-taking.
7. The discussion should usually only end when all the parties agree that they have said all that they need to say (including asking for clarifications and explanations from others), and that all the issues have been given due consideration (even if some of these are postponed to a later time). Also, note that dialogues should only start under at least implicit agreement by all parties that they want to enter into a discussion (or must enter into a discussion, as in the case of a jury).

EXERCISES

1. A particularly valuable exercise I have used in class involves watching (and/or reading) *Twelve Angry Men* and assessing the critical thinking dispositions of some or all of the characters in the play/film. The quality of the content of their arguments, and

in particular the way they interact with one another will serve as clues to the presence or otherwise of dispositions and behaviours that have been the subject of this chapter. The same approach can of course be applied to characters from other stories or from real-life contexts (such as political debates) as well.

2. A good way to loosen up our biases is through what is known as 'counter-attitudinal advocacy'. This means writing or speaking in favour of a position that you do not hold and/or to argue against a position that you do hold. Its effectiveness with respect to changing minds is well established in psychology and communication research (see Petty and Cacioppo, 1996, Chapter 8), but its weakness is that you can only get people to act in this way under particular circumstances. A critical thinking class is just such a circumstance, however. For example, class members' views on contentious contemporary issues can be sought and a debate organised in which the participants argue counter-attitudinally.

3. As an exercise in personal reflection (rather than class discussion), you might want to attend to the presence and development of your own critical thinking dispositions and behaviours as you work your way through this book and/or your critical thinking class. (For a discussion of the relationship between academic work and dispositions, see Hanscomb, 2015.)

FURTHER READING

- Aikin, S. F. and Clanton, J.C. (2010) Developing group-deliberative virtues. *Journal of Applied Philosophy*, 27(4), 409–24. This has particular relevance to avoiding the problems associated with groupthink that were discussed in Chapter 1.
- A very useful source of advice for constructive dialogues can again be found in Robert Ennis' *Critical Thinking* (1996a) (see 'Thinking Critically When Discussing Things with Others', 1996a, pp. 371–5).
- For a more in-depth look at the nature of dialogues (including 'Rules for a Critical Discussion'), see Walton (2006), Chapter 5.
- For an interesting discussion of flexibility, see Tiberius (2008) Chapter 3.

NOTES

1 Diana Beech, 'Attitude is everything', *Times Higher Education*, 21 May 2015.
2 He accepts in a footnote that he is stereotyping cab drivers.
3 *How I Escaped My Certain Fate: The Life and Deaths of a Stand-up Comedian* (London: Faber & Faber, 2011), pp. 80–2.
4 I should point out that Stewart Lee is not usually a comedian who mocks anyone vulnerable, such as inarticulate people. Much of what he says and seems to stand for is actively promoting fairness and non-prejudicial attitudes. (And of course, what astonished/angered him here is the cab driver's prejudicial statement.)

3

ARGUMENTS AND ARGUMENT RECONSTRUCTION

A physician cannot treat a disease ... properly without diagnosing it correctly. An attorney cannot advise a client properly without knowing the precise and full particulars of the client's situation. Nor can a reasoner evaluate an argument properly without a precise understanding of what the argument is.

(Johnson and Blair, 2006, p. 11)

In this chapter we turn our attention away from the arguer's biases and dispositions and towards the nature of arguments themselves. The majority of it is devoted to explaining argument reconstruction; the practice of extracting the essential content and structure of someone's argument from the everyday language in which it is expressed or implied. Here we will encounter concepts and techniques such as ambiguity and vagueness, straw man arguments, implicit premises, and the principle of charity. Prior to this, though, I will provide a reminder of what an argument is, and explain how the sentences which comprise the premises and conclusions must be what are called 'propositions' or 'statements'.

3.1 THE STRUCTURE OF ARGUMENTS

In the Introduction, it was explained how the identification and analysis of **arguments** are at the heart of critical thinking. An argument, you will recall, is comprised of:

1. A claim being asserted that you want other people to believe is true.
2. Reasons offered in support of this claim; i.e. to try to convince other people that this claim is true.

The point of offering an argument is to convince someone else of your point of view. This point of view forms the **conclusion** of the argument, and information (statements) offered in support of this are called **premises**. An argument can have any number of premises, and in the traditions of formal and informal logic, they are usually set out in this form:

> Premise 1:
> Premise 2:
> Conclusion:

For the sake of brevity, a premise is abbreviated to 'P' and a conclusion to 'C', so that we have:

> P1:
> P2:
> C:

This would be the structure of a simple two-premise argument, such as:

> Anything that intensifies racial discrimination should be outlawed. Capital punishment intensifies racial discrimination. Therefore capital punishment should be outlawed.

Set out formally, it would read:

> P1: Anything that intensifies racial discrimination should be outlawed.
> P2: Capital punishment intensifies racial discrimination.
> C: Therefore capital punishment should be outlawed.

Another example of a simple argument is:

> Isaac Newton was not a true natural scientist. This is so because anyone who believes in the principles of alchemy cannot be a true natural scientist, and Newton believed in the principles of alchemy.
>
> P1: Newton believed in the principles of alchemy.
> P2: Anyone who believes in the principles of alchemy cannot be a true natural scientist.
> C: Therefore Newton was not a true natural scientist.

Often arguments are more complex that this, involving many more premises (some of which might be 'implicit'), more than one conclusion, and what are known as 'sub-conclusions'. These variations will be looked at shortly.

3.2 PROPOSITIONS (STATEMENTS)

Premises and conclusions must be what are called **propositions** (or statements). A proposition is a sentence that makes a claim about something that can be (in theory) adjudged to be true or false. The majority of the things we say are propositions, from 'The primary cause of the American Civil War was slavery' to 'The running of FIFA is not unlike an organised crime syndicate' to 'I'm feeling hungry'.

Propositions are contrasted with other kinds of sentence, most commonly:

> Questions: ('Where's my drink?')
> Directives: ('Well, go and get me another one then!')

Directives are instructions or orders like 'pass the remote control', or 'take one tablet twice a day'. Both questions and directives, you will notice, cannot be true or false; they are not attempts to say things about the world. Because arguments are all about establishing truth and falsity, then their components must be sentences that can be evaluated in this way; in other words, they must be propositions.

When reconstructing arguments, part of the challenge can be converting rhetorical questions into statements. If my wife asks me if I would like to watch an episode of *Game of Thrones*, there is no statement implied in this; she is simply asking me a question to which I need to supply an answer. If, however, as another character is dispatched in a graphically drawn-out, gory and disturbing manner, she asks, 'Is that really necessary?', she is not expecting a reply, but implying a proposition. Her rhetorical question can be translated into a statement like '*Game of Thrones* would be just as good without quite so much gruesomeness', or '*Game of Thrones* would be even more engaging if the writers didn't feel obliged to shoehorn in plotlines that allow for horror rather than advancing the overall story.'

3.3 ARGUMENT RECONSTRUCTION

The skill of argument reconstruction and evaluation is one way in which many of the things learned in critical thinking are applied and practised. In this section you will be learning about the reconstruction part (which argument (or arguments) is (or are) being put forward), and the rest of the book will be relevant to the evaluation part – assessing the quality of the argument or arguments.

Argument reconstruction is a skill more than simply a demonstration of what you know, and like many skills it involves judgement because:

1. In each case you will be applying it to new arguments, and the forms these take across different types of communication vary considerably.
2. Quite often what people are saying is open to more than one plausible interpretation.

You will become better at making these judgements the more you become familiar with the subject matter of critical thinking, but more importantly, it is a matter of practice. As indicated, argument reconstruction is primarily a skill. There are a number of guiding principles and recommendations (that are set out below), but mastering it requires doing it, and doing it really quite a lot. This can be tedious for sure, but with perseverance your improvement will be very apparent, as will be the way in which this ability will transfer itself to improved questioning and comprehension in any aspect of life of which arguments are a part.

The basic aim of argument reconstruction is simple enough: *distil the essence of the argument that is being made*. It can be understood as a form of *summarising*. Critical thinking has been defined as minimising errors in our reasoning by improving our ability to generate strong arguments and evaluate the arguments of others. Since formulating our own arguments usually involves responding to the arguments of others, then the quality of these evaluations is of fundamental importance. But assessment can only be effective if the argument has been properly understood in the first place.

The truth of this is perhaps fairly obvious, but worth highlighting because its intellectual obviousness can mask how difficult it is to achieve in practice. Many of the reasons behind this difficulty were discussed in Chapter 1, and the interpersonal, ethical and epistemological significances of careful reading and listening were addressed in Chapter 2. In the language of argumentation, a misrepresentation of someone's position so that it is negatively distorted or caricatured is known as a **straw man argument**. Straw man (or straw person) arguments are so named because it is easier to push over (or otherwise bring down) a straw effigy than a real person. The metaphor represents the difference between, on the one hand, X's real position and, on the other, a weaker position ascribed to them by Y that is easier to argue against.

For example, in recent years, an argument by the right-of-centre UK Tory government against the left-of-centre Labour Party has been made along these lines: 'Labour are against our austerity measures, and say that the government should not be making cuts, so clearly they do not think that the budget deficit is a serious issue.' They do think it is serious, but they also believe that reviving the economy by avoiding cuts is the best way to reduce the deficit. It is easier to argue against a party who deny the importance of reducing the deficit than it is to argue against a party who not only have a different approach to reducing it, but one that is liable to be popular with a significant proportion of the electorate.

Sometimes, as in this case, a distorted version of an opponent's position is employed deliberately, but the straw man label also applies to instances where it is a mistake. From a dialectical point of view, being misrepresented is extraordinarily frustrating, and if due time or space is not allowed for us to make corrections to what others have said, then the dialogical process is liable to be derailed.

Controversial topics (such as abortion or immigration), and situations where lines are sharply divided (such as party politics) breed straw man arguments that are fuelled by emotion and competitive urges. They often happen under cooler conditions as well, though, sometimes because of inattention to detail. In all cases the confirmation bias is implicated (see Chapter 1), and the discussion in Chapter 2 about open-mindedness and paying careful attention to both the words and the circumstances of the other is important for avoiding unintentional straw man arguments. In particular, we need to avoid, where possible, hearing arguments second hand. As John Stuart Mill says, we should

> hear them from persons who actually believe them; who defend them in earnest, and do their very utmost for them. [We] must know them in their most plausible and persuasive form; ... must feel the whole force of the difficulty which the true view of the subject has to encounter and dispose of; else he will never really possess himself of the portion of truth which meets and removes that difficulty.

> (1962, p. 163)

Critical thinking scholars are fairly consistent in listing the tasks that need to be performed towards reconstructing arguments,[1] and in this tradition the rest of this chapter will help you develop and refine this skill under the following headings: identifying premises and conclusions; argument-friendly rewording; implicit premises and conclusions; and argument structure (sub-conclusions, re-ordering of premises).

IDENTIFYING PREMISES AND CONCLUSIONS

There are two methods for identifying the conclusion of someone's argument. The first is to read (or listen) carefully and ask yourself 'What point are they making?' In **dialogue**, if the overall point is not clear, it is crucial to get into the habit of asking people to clarify what they mean (which can be easier said than done if you think back to the discussion of **groupthink** in Chapter 1). With written arguments the responsibility lies with us to read, and if necessary re-read, what is presented in order to establish the overall conclusion.

Similarly with premises; once you have established the overall point, it is a matter of working out what is being said in support of that point. Not everything in the text in question will be relevant to the argument, and often it will not be presented in the best order or as clearly as it might be. As you will see, part of the argument reconstruction process is to tidy up these aspects leaving only what is (or what seems to be) relevant to the argument.

The second method is to look for **premise and conclusion indicators**. These are words that often function as precursors to premises and conclusions; for example, conclusions can often be identified by the presence of terms such as:

therefore
thus
so
hence
accordingly
in which case.

And premises can often be identified by terms like:

My reason is …
My evidence for this is …
This is so because …

The two methods can be used together, but for several reasons I am inclined to emphasise the first one. One reason is that reading and re-reading a passage help us to understand it more deeply, and not be tempted by the short-cuts that premise and conclusion indicators can provide. The second is that premise and conclusion indicators are not always present. For instance, if the conclusion is at the start of a passage (like the paragraph you are reading right now), it will not be prefixed by an indicator like 'therefore'. A further reason is that we find premise indicators in **explanations** as well as arguments. The difference between an argument and an explanation is that with arguments, the conclusion has not been agreed upon, whereas with explanations it is agreed that something is the case, and someone is then enquiring about what has led to this. So, I might explain that I was late for the meeting because of a puncture, or that Pluto is sometimes closer to the sun than Neptune because it has a more elliptical orbit than its neighbour. Notice that the word 'because' is used here as well, and with both arguments and explanations we are providing 'reasons'. Notice also that it is not always that clear whether something is an explanation or an argument if we are lacking the necessary context. In the latter example it could be that someone needs to be convinced of the fact that Pluto can be nearer the sun than Neptune.

ARGUMENT-FRIENDLY REWORDING

Part of the skill of argument reconstruction is to make what is presented both argument-friendly and as concise as possible without losing its meaning. Great care must be taken with this because premises and conclusions can contain subtleties, so that inattentive rewordings can lead to important nuances being lost in the edit. The rule for avoiding this is: *if in doubt, retain the original words.*

The three main aims of argument-friendly rewording are:

1. Translating information in the form of non–statements (such as rhetorical questions) into statements.
2. Condensing the argument where necessary through:

   i. using more efficient expressions;
   ii. leaving out material that does not contribute to the premises or conclusions.

3. Clarifying ambiguous and vague sentences.

The passage below is from Martin Luther King's *Letter from Birmingham Jail*. As you will recall from Chapter 1, the overall aim of the letter was to justify King's method of non–violent (but sometimes illegal) direct action against forms of white oppression in the southern states of America. The letter, though published in the press nationwide, was ostensibly written to members of the white clergy in Alabama who, though supportive of his cause, were critical of his methods. One of many arguments he makes is this:

> In your statement you asserted that our actions, even though peaceful, must be condemned because they precipitate violence. But can this assertion be logically made? Isn't this like condemning the robbed man because his possession of money precipitated the evil act of robbery? Isn't this like condemning Socrates because his unswerving commitment to truth and his philosophical delvings precipitated the misguided popular mind to make him drink the hemlock? Isn't this like condemning Jesus because His unique God-consciousness and never-ceasing devotion to His will precipitated the evil act of crucifixion? We must come to see, as federal courts have consistently affirmed, that it is immoral to urge an individual to withdraw his efforts to gain his basic constitutional rights because the quest precipitates violence. Society must protect the robbed and punish the robber.

It is immediately evident here that King's argument employs a series of rhetorical questions. Each, however, contains a relevant point, and so they need to be preserved in the reconstruction in the form of statements. Some of his sentences are quite wordy and can, arguably, be condensed; and the last sentence seems to be a rhetorical restatement of the conclusion that has already been expressed in the previous sentence (and in the second sentence of the passage). Taking these things into consideration, a reasonable reconstruction might be as follows:

P1: It is claimed that our peaceful actions must be condemned because they precipitate violence.

P2: To condemn our peaceful actions in this way is like condemning someone (e.g. the robbed man, Socrates, Jesus) for doing what is right (or what they are entitled to do) just because it provokes bad/misguided people to do wrong.

P3: It is wrong to condemn the robbed man/Socrates/Jesus.

P4: The federal courts have consistently affirmed that it is immoral to urge an individual to withdraw his efforts to gain his basic constitutional rights because this precipitates violence.

C: Therefore it is illogical and morally wrong to condemn non-violent protest because it precipitates violence.

This presents the essential structure of the argument (which is an argument from analogy; see Chapter 7) and an appeal to various authorities (see Chapter 5), but by condensing some of the premises, this version quite possibly loses the full implications of the examples he uses. For audiences familiar with the relevance of Socrates and Jesus to the point being made, this version might be adequate; and so too in a situation where the reconstruction aims only to reveal the argument's essential structure on an occasion when all parties are looking at the original passage at the same time. Otherwise, however, the detail King offers is important to include, resulting in the following reconstruction:

P1: To condemn our actions because they precipitate violence is like condemning the robbed man because his possession of money precipitated the evil act of robbery.

P2: This is like condemning Socrates because his unswerving commitment to truth and his philosophical delvings precipitated the misguided popular mind to make him drink the hemlock.

P3: And this is like condemning Jesus because His unique God-consciousness and never-ceasing devotion to His will precipitated the evil act of crucifixion.

P4: We do not condemn the robbed man/Socrates/Jesus.

P5: The federal courts have consistently affirmed that it is immoral to urge an individual to withdraw his efforts to gain his basic constitutional rights because this precipitates violence.

C: Therefore it is illogical and wrong to condemn the peaceful actions of the civil rights movement.

Premises 1–3 could be grouped into a single, very long, premise, but separating them in this way makes the argument easier to analyse. For example, we might want to contest the strength of King's analogy with the robbed man but be more satisfied with the Socrates and Jesus analogies.

In summary then: if they are to form part of the reconstruction, then questions and other non-statements *must* be re-worded; but if in any doubt as to whether significant re-wording or condensing of sentences might lose important content, then leave them in their original form.

Ambiguity and vagueness

An ambiguous sentence is one that has more than one possible meaning, for example:

> After the bar room brawl the tables were turned.

As this suggests, ambiguity, as the basis of puns, is a fertile source of humour:

> Did you hear that Jason was fired from his job at the orange juice factory? Apparently he was squeezed out.

Ambiguity can also cause serious problems. A colleague of mine came across this sentence in a child development textbook:

> 19 per cent of US children are poor, rates that climb to 30 per cent for Hispanic children, 32 per cent for Native-American children, and 34 per cent for African-American children.[2]

This can imply that these ethnic groups are not US children, whereas what the author intends to say is that '19 per cent of US children *as a total population* are poor ...' (This has since been corrected, by the way.)

In his *Guardian* newspaper column, Giles Fraser wrote a piece called 'Assisted suicide is the equivalent of a zero-hours contract with life'. He argued that the recent trend for suicide in the UK is a symptom of excessive individualism. Everything has become an individual choice (rather than a community responsibility), including when we die.

> Maud lives round the corner from me in south London. She remembers a time when everyone knew everyone else, and when there was genuine community solidarity. Nowadays people come and go, she says, and young people can't be bothered with the elderly. She is often lonely. 'Even the doctor came round to see me and asked me if I wanted to commit suicide,' she says.[3]

Some very black humour flirts with this example because I do not believe for a second that the doctor was offering Maud suicide as an option (as he might offer her forms of medication or counselling). In light of her loneliness or depression, I imagine he was trying to ascertain if she was a suicide *risk*. In this example it is hard to know whether it is the doctor, Maud, or Giles Fraser who has caused the mix-up. Let's hope it is Fraser, but either way, what we are presented with is ambiguous.

When teasing out the premises and conclusion of a person's argument, ambiguous sentences have to be disambiguated. In a dialogue we can ask the person for clarification, but if they are not available for questioning, we can either:

- do our best to suppose their intended meaning, applying the principle of charity (see below), or
- reconstruct more than one version of the argument, applying alternative meanings of ambiguous sentences in each case.

Sometimes, though, you might come across, not just words and terms with ambiguous meanings, but concepts which are indeterminate (Freeden, 2005). 'Democracy' is an example; no amount of disambiguation can overcome its complex and contested nature, and all a reconstruction can do is either stay with the original wording, or use the context of the argument to generate implicit premises indicating which aspects of this idea seem to be most relevant to the discussion (such as forms of equality, or human rights). With this latter strategy, however, we need to be highly sensitive to the provisional nature of the reconstruction and recognise that the way the term is used is something that is likely to have to be negotiated by the discussants.

If an ambiguous sentence is one which can mean more than one thing, a vague sentence lacks precision. In many contexts, an absence of precision is entirely appropriate; 'Give me a moment', 'I'll be there soon', 'Just give me a few potatoes.' My 4-year-old does not like vagueness. He recently asked me how long a 'moment' is, and he is also not too wild about his astronomy books saying that Jupiter has 'more than 60 moons'. I'm kind of with him on this one; it could mean about 62, or around 70, or over 100. Or it could mean they do not have a clue. Which is it?

The Intergovernmental Panel on Climate Change (IPCC) has been urged to change its style of reporting probabilities to the media because of a mismatch between the vague terms it was using and what these are taken to mean by the general public. For example, in statements like 'Anthropogenic influences have very likely contributed to Arctic sea-ice loss since 1979',[3] they use 'very likely' to mean >90 per cent certainty, but it has been found that the public's understanding of 'very likely' is >70 per cent certainty.[4] This represents a significant discrepancy that will not help the already tough task of communicating urgency and motivating climate-related behaviour change.

Vague statements can signal the beginning of a dialogue in which a relatively unformed belief about an issue achieves sharper focus: 'You say that it is "very likely" that … But what exactly do you mean by this?' But in non-dialogical communication vagueness can be problematic where it causes (1) misunderstanding (as in the IPCC example), and (2) imprecision that is inappropriate for the context in question; 'I cannot respond to this until I know exactly what is meant by …'

Unlike ambiguous sentences, vague statements can form premises and conclusions in arguments where (1) and (2) above do not represent a problem ('I've only got a couple more things to do, therefore I *will* be there in a short while'). Where (1) or (2) is a problem, the issue is similar to the one caused by ambiguity. Vague sentences become, in effect, ones that cannot be determined to be true or false, and therefore cannot function as propositions. When reconstructing arguments, we therefore need to make these meanings more precise; either through an educated guess or through further research. As with the re-wording of ambiguous sentences, the 'principle of charity' should also be applied (see below).

IMPLICIT PREMISES AND CONCLUSIONS

A lot of the time we do not explicitly say everything that is necessary for the complete formulation of the argument being presented. The most implicit an argument can be is when it is presented visually, such as advertisements with minimal written text, or gestures like the two-handed diving motion used to footballers to make the point to the referee that a player took a dive and was not in fact fouled.[5] Partial arguments are most common though; a simple example might be:

> Only extroverts are energised by social situations, so Susan is an extrovert.

The whole argument would run:

> P1: Only extroverts are energised by social situations.
> P2: Susan is energised by social situations.
> C: So Susan is an extrovert.

P2 might typically be missed out in natural language because it is obvious to those listening that this is the implication, or it could already be common knowledge. The Greek word for an argument with a missing premise (or premises) is an **enthymeme**, and when recommending their use, Aristotle notes in *The Art of Rhetoric* that 'obscurity is produced … from length of reasoning, and … it is a waste of time as one is stating the obvious' (1991, p. 195). Being explicit can be unnecessarily wordy and have the effect of being boring, patronising, and in some cases harder to follow.

There is a balance to be struck, however. A couple of years ago, cycling along the same stretch of road where I caused the cattle stampede (see Introduction), a woman driving towards me slowed down her car, lowered the window and shouted: 'They've cut the hedges!' I was very confused as to why she was telling me this. I said: 'Er, yes, it looks great …' She then said something about hawthorns, and the penny dropped – thorny hedge debris would be littering the edge of the road, causing a puncture risk. It was very thoughtful of her, but her initial argument was so condensed that the communication nearly failed.

Reconstructed, her argument was, presumably:

> P1: If the hedges have been cut, there will be hawthorns on the road.
> P2: If there are hawthorns on the road, you risk getting a puncture.

P3: You don't want to risk getting a puncture.

C: You should be careful (or, you should cycle away from the edge of the road).

This illustrates how conclusions as well as premises can be implicit. In this case the inclusion of the conclusion would have been helpful, but in other cases it is unnecessary for the same reasons that it is often unnecessary to include all the relevant premises. For example, towards the end of his speech following the Sandy Hook shooting in 2012, President Obama said, 'We can't tolerate this any more. These tragedies must end. And to end them we must change.' The conclusion is 'therefore we must change', but by this point in the speech, it is clear what he means.

The context of the following letter to a newspaper was the UK Government's response to IS incursions into Iraqi Kurdistan in the summer of 2014. It contains implicit premises and a conclusion that is implied by a sarcastic question: 'Prime Ministers have regularly used war abroad to distract from constitutional matters or problems at home, as history shows. But it couldn't happen today, could it?'[6] A reasonable reconstruction might be:

P1: History shows that prime ministers have regularly used war abroad to distract from constitutional matters or problems at home.

P2: The current government is unpopular.

P3: The current government has involved us in another war abroad.

C1: The current government is using war as a distraction.

C2: Using war as a distraction can still happen today.

Often the reason for making implicit premises explicit is in order to highlight an **assumption** that needs to be questioned. An assumption, in the context of an argument, is a belief that has relevance to the argument, but which has not been defended. Assumptions can be implicit or explicit, and in many cases they do not need to be defended if they are common knowledge or trivially true. Dangerous ones, though, are those that are both implicit and need defending. Making these assumptions explicit is therefore one of the most important functions of reconstructing arguments. For example, should we want to respond to the letter above, it is important to make P2 and C1 explicit.

ARGUMENT STRUCTURE: SUB-CONCLUSIONS
AND THE ORDERING OF PREMISES

More complex arguments can involve what are known as **sub-conclusions** (sometimes referred to as 'intermediate conclusions'). Sub-conclusions indicate that there are one or more smaller arguments that contribute to a larger argument. In our reconstructions it is important to identify and separate these so as to aid clarification and evaluation.

Arguments with sub-conclusions have a structure along these lines:

Premise (1)
Premise (2)
Conclusion (1)
Premise (3)
Conclusion (2)
Premise (4)
Etc.
Overall Conclusion

Arguments containing sub-conclusions are usually what are called chained arguments. In a chained argument each sub-conclusion forms a premise for a further argument, and in these circumstances it is critical that we put the premises in the right order in our reconstruction. Here is an example of a chained argument:

Healthcare is basic to human welfare. Resources basic to human welfare should be free at the point of use, and therefore healthcare should be free at the point of use. Healthcare funded by private insurance is not free at the point of use, so healthcare should not be funded by private insurance.

The correct reconstruction would be:

P1: Resources basic to human welfare should be free at the point of use.
P2: Healthcare is basic to human welfare.
C1: So healthcare should be free at the point of use.
P3: Healthcare funded by private insurance is not free at the point of use.
C2: Therefore healthcare should not be funded by private insurance.

In order to establish C2 (healthcare should not be funded by private insurance), C1 must first be established (healthcare should be free at the point of use). If the two arguments were put the other way around, the overall argument would not make sense:

P1: Healthcare funded by private insurance is not free at the point of use.
C1: Therefore healthcare should not be funded by private insurance.
P2: Resources basic to human welfare should be free at the point of use.
P3: Healthcare is basic to human welfare.
C2: So healthcare should be free at the point of use.

The best approach to deciding whether a conclusion is the main one or a sub-conclusion is to ask what overall point the arguer seems to be making. Then, the coherence or otherwise of your reconstruction will help confirm whether this is right or not.

The passage below is a complex argument found in investigative journalist and author Naomi Klein's article, 'Gulf oil spill: a hole in the world', about the Deepwater Horizon disaster in the Gulf of Mexico in 2010. Quoting from BP's risk assessment prior to the spill she says:

Best of all, should a major spill occur, there is, apparently, 'little risk of contact or impact to the coastline' because of the company's projected speedy response (!) and 'due to the distance [of the rig] to shore' – about 48 miles (77 km). This is the most astonishing claim of all. In a gulf that often sees winds of more than 70 km an hour, not to mention hurricanes, BP had so little respect for the ocean's capacity to ebb and flow, surge and heave, that it did not think oil could make a paltry 77 km trip. None of this sloppiness would have been possible, however, had BP not been making its predictions to a political class eager to believe that nature had indeed been mastered. Some, like Republican Lisa Murkowski, were more eager than others. The Alaskan senator was so awe-struck by the industry's four-dimensional seismic imaging that she proclaimed deep-sea drilling to have reached the very height of controlled artificiality. 'It's better than Disneyland in terms of how you can take technologies and go after a resource that is thousands of years old and do so in an environmentally sound way,' she told the Senate energy committee just seven months ago.[6]

A plausible reconstruction requires a sub–conclusion (as well as an implicit premise):

P1: When presented with the industry's four-dimensional seismic imaging, Republican Lisa Murkowski, the Alaskan Senator, proclaimed deep-sea drilling to have reached the very height of controlled artificiality. She told the Senate energy committee just seven months ago, 'It's better than Disneyland in terms of how you can take technologies and go after a resource that is thousands of years old and do so in an environmentally sound way.'

P2: (implicit) A statement like this is typical of a political class eager to believe that nature had been mastered.

C1: The current political class is eager to believe that nature had been mastered.

P3: BP erroneously claimed that should a major spill occur, there is 'little risk of contact or impact to the coastline'.

P4: (implicit) The sloppiness of BP's 'initial exploration plan' can only be explained by a political class eager to believe that nature had indeed been mastered.

C2: BP were allowed to become sloppy in their planning because it had been making its predictions to a political class eager to believe that nature had indeed been mastered.

Klein is relying on her claim about the eagerness of the current political class to believe that nature had been mastered to support her final conclusion that this is the reason for BP's sloppy risk assessment. Since she is not claiming that BP's sloppiness is the cause of this political attitude, then the two conclusions here must fall in the order presented above.

Arguments that are not chained in this way are known as convergent arguments. With convergent arguments, separate claims serve to reinforce a single conclusion, such that the basic structure is simply:

P1:
P2:
P3:
Etc.
C:

A simple example might be:

> Because it is environmentally friendly, cycling to work is a good thing to do. It also saves money, is good for your health, and helps you feel alert and energised at the start of the day.

Reconstructed:

P1: Cycling to work is environmentally friendly.
P2: Cycling to work saves money.
P3: Cycling to work is good for your health.
P4: Cycling to work helps you feel alert and energised at the start of the day.
C: Therefore cycling to work is a good thing to do.

Convergent arguments can be identified by phrases like 'Another consideration that supports this point is ...'; or 'Also in support of this ...', but these will not always be present. A better test is to see whether the argument retains its coherence no matter what order the premises come in.

THE PRINCIPLE OF CHARITY

It should be clear from the preceding discussions and examples that argument reconstruction cannot always be that accurate. Our efforts will often be provisional; the equivalent of saying in a dialogue 'So is *this* what you mean ...?' But since the person is not present to consult, then the language is more like 'If this is what X means' or 'If I've understood X correctly ..., then this is what the argument looks like.'

This kind of language is recommended. It indicates that you cannot always be sure that you have grasped what the other person is intending to say, and that the true meaning of the argument and its intention rest with them. Such language connotes respect and modesty, and, as discussed in Chapter 2, better serves the aim of a constructive dialogue.

In this vein it is also important to attempt to reconstruct the best (plausible) version of what we are presented with. In the choices that we make concerning: (1) the translation of non-statements into statements; (2) the inclusion of implicit premises; (3) disambiguation; and (4) making precision out of vagueness, we should aim to put the argument in the best light we can. This form of giving the benefit of the doubt has been called the **principle of charity**, and the main reason for employing it is summed up by Johnson and Blair in this way:

> The idea is that since (normally) an author will be *trying* to make logical arguments, it follows that if, in interpreting a passage, we reconstruct the most logical argument we can make it out to contain, then that probably will be the argument the author intended to make.
>
> (2006, p. 15)

Enshrined in this principle is the truth-seeking disposition rather than an attitude to critical thinking that sees it as a means to winning or gaining superiority over others. To return to where we started in this section, being motivated by winning will make us vulnerable to generating straw man arguments. It should be noted, however, that over-eagerness with respect to the principle of charity can lead to the opposite of a straw man – an 'iron man' argument. These are cases where we misrepresent someone else's (or our own) position as being stronger than it is. This could be motivated by a desire to make it easier to defend, but in the context of the principle of charity, it is primarily an error of interpretation.[7]

DISCUSSION QUESTION

The case is made in this chapter for straw man arguments always being fallacious, but is this necessarily the case? Are there circumstances in which it is acceptable to distort someone else's position in order to make it easier to argue against? Two short articles that make a case for this view are by Aikin and Casey (2011, 2016).

EXERCISES

Making use of the techniques explained in this chapter, reconstruct the following arguments:

1. It's okay to lie to children about the existence of Santa Claus until they're older, isn't it? So it's okay not to tell my fiancé that I used to be a man until after we're married.

2. The use of food banks in some parts of the UK has seen a rapid increase since the Tory government came into power and introduced benefit cuts. Some Tories say that food banks are part of the welfare state, but food banks are charities and separate from the welfare state. They are a sign that the welfare state is failing. (Adapted from MP Mhairi Black's maiden speech in the House of Commons (UK), 14 July 2015.)

3. Recently I was knocked off my bicycle by a van coming out of a side road. I was concussed, despite wearing a cycle helmet, which was damaged by the impact of hitting the road. At the hospital, doctors suggested that, without the helmet, I could have died, or at least been in intensive care. And yet there seems to be considerable resistance in some cycling groups to any law requiring the wearing of helmets. Ministers have said it would be impossible to enforce such a law, but couldn't the same argument apply to seatbelts? It is not difficult to see who is wearing a helmet. In Australia, it is illegal to ride a bike or for a child to use a scooter without a helmet. Cyclists have accepted this law. Are Australians more law-abiding than we are? Head injuries cost the NHS a considerable amount of money. I fail to see why helmets are required for motorbikes and not on bicycles, as the head injuries can be much the same. (Letter to the *Daily Telegraph*, 8 April 2011).

FURTHER READING

- For exercises on visual arguments, see Morrow and Weston (2011) *A Workbook for Arguments*; and Lunsford and Ruszkiewicz (2009) *Everything's an Argument*.
- For an instructive article on straw man and iron man arguments, see Aikin and Casey (2016).

NOTES

1 Some good examples are Johnson and Blair (2006); Scriven (1976); Bowell and Kemp (2010), and Morrow and Weston (2011).

2 L. Berk (2010) *Infants, Children, and Adolescents*, 7th edn (Harlow: Pearson International Edition), p. 74.

3 IPCC (2014) *Climate Change 2014: Synthesis Report: Summary for Policy Makers*, p. 5. Available at: www.ipcc.ch/pdf/assessment-report/ar5/syr/AR5_SYR_FINAL_SPM.pdf

4 J. Painter (2013) *Climate Change and the Media* (London: I.B. Tauris).

5 I am wary of using visual arguments for reconstruction and evaluation because the skill required is more one of interpretation than reconstruction, but in the Further Reading you will find some suggestions for good critical thinking books that do go down this path.

6 N. Klein (2010) 'Gulf oil spill: a hole in the world'. Available at: www.theguardian.com/theguardian/2010/jun/19/naomi-klein-gulf-oil-spill.

7 Be aware that the term 'steel manning' has also been coined; not as an alternative to 'iron man' but with the same meaning as the principle of charity.

4

ARGUMENT FORMS
AND FALLACIES

[Fallacies] are like bad habits. They are hard to break.

(John Woods, 2013, p. 5)

In this chapter we will begin to explore the various types of arguments that have been identified by informal logicians and critical thinking scholars, and take an initial look at the types of fallacy (poor arguments) that are associated with them.

There are numerous ways of classifying arguments, and here I will explain two that are important to know about: deductive, inductive and plausible arguments, and argument forms (or 'schemes').

4.1 DEDUCTIVE, INDUCTIVE AND PLAUSIBLE ARGUMENTS

DEDUCTIVE AND INDUCTIVE ARGUMENTS

In books on logic, and some books on critical thinking, you will find discussion of deductive and inductive arguments. My view (and also the view of Scriven (1976) and Johnson and Blair (2006), among others) is that learning about this distinction is of limited value outside of formal logic, but because I do believe they have some value in terms of the effective communication of arguments, and because you will hear these terms being mentioned in some circles, I will pay some attention to them.

A **deductive argument** is one which attempts to provide a line of reasoning in which the conclusion is necessarily deduced from the premises, for example:

P1: Either the Earth has remained in a static state, or it has changed form due to tectonic shifts.
P2: The Earth has not remained in a static state.
C: Therefore it has changed form due to tectonic shifts.

A successfully structured deductive argument is known as a 'valid deductive argument', and valid deductive arguments are what Douglas Walton calls 'airtight' or 'truth preserving' (1989, p. 115). If the premises are true, the conclusion is guaranteed to be true. If a person accepts the premises of a deductive argument, then they must also accept the conclusion because the truth of the conclusion is entirely contained within the truths presented in the premises.

The argument above claims that there are only two options that could be true. If one option is then rejected, the remaining one must be the case.

An **inductive argument**, on the other hand, lacks this airtight quality. An inductive version of the above argument might be:

P1: Either the Earth has remained in a static state, or it has changed form due to tectonic shifts.
P2: As far as the evidence goes, it seems the Earth has not remained in a static state.
C: Therefore it has changed form due to tectonic shifts.

While it is entirely reasonable to reach this conclusion (science is based on this kind of inference), it does not *necessarily* follow from the premises. In other words, it would not be a contradiction to reject the conclusion while accepting the premises.

The reason why I and other critical thinking scholars are not inclined to take this distinction too seriously, however, concerns the ease with which an inductive argument can be turned into a deductive argument, and vice versa. As Michael Scriven says, 'a slight juggling of the premises (by adding some unstated ones) and the conclusions can always convert an inductive argument into a deductive one without any essential loss of the "point of the argument"' (1976, p. 34).

Take this argument:

P1: If the well is poisoned, then Lassie is probably dead.
P2: The well is poisoned.
C: Therefore Lassie is dead.

In this form it is inductive, but if we include the word 'probably' in the conclusion it becomes deductive:

P1: If the well is poisoned, then Lassie is probably dead.
P2: The well is poisoned.
C: Therefore Lassie is probably dead.

Rather than use the first version, we are better off using the second, but in both cases we know that the strength of the argument depends on the truth or falsity of the premises.

If, on the other hand, we are presented with a deductive version along these lines, we are in the same position:

P1: If the well is poisoned, then Lassie is dead.
P2: The well is poisoned.
C: Therefore Lassie is dead.

We can accept that if the premises are true, then the conclusion must also be true, but this is trivial. What matters, again, is the truth or otherwise of the premises, and we will demand (or seek) evidence of this before we accept that Lassie is dead.

We find, then, that most arguments can be presented in deductive or inductive forms without losing 'the point of the argument', so the primary trajectory of critical thinking has been towards more helpful ways to categorise arguments.

PLAUSIBLE ARGUMENTS

In recent decades Douglas Walton (1995, 2006) has provided a characterisation of everyday argumentation in terms of what are called **plausible arguments** (also known as 'presumptive' or 'defeasible' arguments). These are sometimes explained as a third alternative to deductive and inductive arguments, but it is perhaps more helpful to understand them as representing a style of reasoning that functions quite efficiently for certain types of decision-making, particularly in the context of dialogues. Plausible arguments are characterised as:

1. Making claims based on what is reasonably or normally expected in familiar situations.
2. In so doing, shifting the **burden of proof** to any claim that contradicts the one being made.
3. But always recognising that the conclusion drawn is *provisional* in nature; that is, open to being proven wrong should the case in question turn out to be other than what would normally be expected.

Plausible arguments are highly pragmatic. They operate in situations where decisions have to be made fairly quickly, often in the absence of precise information, but in circumstances that are generally familiar. In other words, they operate in many of the situations in which we find ourselves in daily life.

Working with plausible arguments is not the same as **System 1** thinking, but it is significantly vulnerable to biases. Although resulting from a degree of reflection, plausible reasoning is nevertheless a form of generalising that occurs in the thick of life, and it will inevitably rely on heuristics. However, it also embodies an awareness of its own limitations (and thus the provisional nature of its conclusions) and it is this that places it on a different level to System 1 thinking. Plausible reasoning can perhaps be characterised as **System 2** thinking in a hurry.

Clearly enough, plausible arguments are useful in familiar situations and when time is scarce, but we can also view them as the start of a dialogue in which they provide the catalyst for more careful and nuanced reasoning. Thinking slows down as ideas are passed around.

Definitions and classifications become more accurate, and probabilities and alternatives become as well considered and researched as is reasonable under the circumstances.

4.2 ARGUMENT FORMS AND FALLACIES

The value of understanding the nature and prevalence of plausible arguments is that it can sensitise us to the presence of a range of argument forms – and their associated fallacies – that are commonly employed in everyday decision-making. It is to the classification and analysis of such arguments that many books on critical thinking devote themselves, and this will be the focus of the majority of the rest of this book too.

Examples of argument forms (sometimes referred to as 'argument schemes') include 'arguments from authority', 'arguments from analogy', 'causal arguments', 'generalisations', and 'ad hominem arguments'. Argument forms like these will often be recognisable to you, and this is to be expected since critical thinking is about how we think and argue in everyday situations. It provides the tools for assessing different argument forms, and reveals, among other things, how psychology can explain our vulnerability to fallacious versions of them.

The study of argument forms emerged from the study of fallacies. Traditionally in logic, and then in informal logic, space was devoted to a selection of named fallacies, derived initially from Aristotle's 'Sophistical Refutations' (a section of his work on logic, the *Organon*). In terms of practical reasoning, however, it became apparent that it is not always fallacious to argue in these ways; not always irrational or foolish to reach decisions on the basis of arguments from authority, analogy, popular opinion, and so on. Establishing criteria for determining the strength of an argument conforming to a particular type became the focus of many critical thinking scholars' efforts, and these criteria are primarily expressed in terms of what are called **critical questions**. I will say more about these shortly, but will first consider the notion of fallacies in more detail.

A fallacy is defined by Trudy Govier (1988, p. 177) as 'a mistake in reasoning ... which occurs with some frequency in real arguments and which is characteristically deceptive'.

A fallacious argument is one that is not only bad, but bad in a way that:

1. Conforms to a typical type of error that we are prone to make when constructing arguments.
2. Tends to create the (superficial) impression of being a good argument.

Fallacies are, in short, poor arguments of certain types that are used frequently and are liable to be convincing to those not thinking critically. A bad argument that conforms to a certain pattern but that is not particularly deceptive is still a fallacy, but the 'liable to be convincing' clause remains important. One reason is that we often argue fallaciously without realising we are doing so, indicating that, in the moment at least, we think the argument is strong. And if we are deceived, some of our audience are likely to be as well. A second reason is that, since there are many fallacies, any given course or textbook must make choices about what to include and what to prioritise. A sensible criterion for inclusion is a fallacy being 'characteristically deceptive' since these will be the more disabling ones in processes of decision-making.

This book has defined critical thinking in terms of the attempt to avoid reasoning errors, therefore identifying fallacious arguments is clearly central to its purpose. As the previous discussion has indicated, however, fallacies need to be distinguished from argument forms, and this is made harder because, for historical reasons, they tend to share the same names. You will still find books and teachers that refer to arguments from authority, arguments from popular opinion, slippery slope arguments, appeals to emotion, ad hominem arguments, and so on, simply as 'fallacies'. In nearly all cases, however, this is not the right way to understand them, and therefore not the right terminology to apply to them.

The approach of this, and many other, critical thinking textbooks is to analyse argument forms, and (among other things) to determine critical questions that should be applied to them in order to establish how good a particular instance of that argument is. In this context, the word 'fallacy' takes on two, more subtle, meanings:

1. A particularly poor argument conforming to an argument form is often called a 'fallacious ad hominem argument', 'fallacious causal argument', and so on. Alternatively, they can be called 'weak' or 'poor', the terminology does not need to be that precise.

2. There are some argument forms that are always weak or just plain wrong, in which case, the term 'fallacy' can be applied more freely. **Straw man arguments** are potentially one example (see Chapter 3), as are **circular arguments** (see Chapter 8). There are also fallacies that are so common or distinctive that they acquire their own name, despite being an erroneous version of a particular argument form. For example, 'confusing correlation and cause' is a fallacy that can be committed when constructing a causal argument.

4.3 CRITICAL QUESTIONS

'Critical questions' are the questions that are important to ask in order to establish the strength of an argument. There are two kinds: (1) general ones that can be applied to most arguments; and (2) specific ones that are relevant to particular argument forms. Some characteristics of critical questions to be aware of are these:

1. There is no definitive list either of the general or the specific questions, and you will find some variation across different textbooks.

2. Where a list is prescribed, judgement is needed on behalf of the critical thinker to determine which of the questions to apply, and whether some should have priority over others. As always with critical thinking, the context of the argument is a vital guide to how we go about analysing it.

3. Some critical questions will seem to be common sense, others less so. Sometimes, by paying attention to them, we might be doing little more than reminding ourselves of how we can interrogate an argument, but there will also be occasions where we will learn new interrogative techniques and gain new insights into the nature of the argument form under scrutiny.

GENERAL QUESTIONS

Perhaps the best starting place for critical questioning is to ask yourself:

- What kinds of questions would you ask about a claim in deciding whether or not to believe it (and therefore act on it)?

Or

- What kinds of questions would you ask about *this* claim in deciding whether or not to believe it (and therefore act on it)?

These initial or 'meta-questions' are beautiful in their simplicity, and they are the hallmark of a critical thinker. They imply appropriate perspective and a willingness to take responsibility for selecting the tools of one's evaluation. (Before reading on, it is a worthwhile task to apply your mind to the first of these questions and to start generating a list of basic critical questions.)

Ralph H. Johnson and J. Anthony Blair identify three fundamental critical questions, otherwise known as the 'Acceptability, Relevance, Sufficiency' criteria (generating the slightly unfortunate acronym, ARS).[1] **ARS criteria** are briefly explained in Box 4.1.

BOX 4.1   FUNDAMENTAL CRITICAL QUESTIONS

1. Are the premises acceptable, i.e. likely to be true, or likely to be accepted as true or plausible by the people one is attempting to persuade?
2. Are the premises relevant to the conclusion the arguer is seeking to establish?
3. Are the premises sufficient for establishing the conclusion?

These questions are independent of one another. A premise can be acceptable but not relevant, or relevant (if true) but not acceptable, and even if all premises are acceptable and relevant, they might not be sufficient by themselves to persuade us of the truth of the conclusion.

So, for example, it might be claimed that voluntary euthanasia should not be legalised because all killing is wrong. This premise, if true, will be relevant to the conclusion, and because euthanasia is undoubtedly a form of killing, sufficient for establishing the conclusion as well. However, many people will counter that not all killing is wrong, especially not a mercy killing carried out on the basis of someone's valid consent. In this case, they will find the argument unconvincing on the basis of the premise being unacceptable. Someone else might argue that euthanasia is wrong because it contravenes a religiously derived prohibition on suicide. In response to this, it could be argued that religious prohibitions are not relevant in a modern secular society. Or it could be argued that even though mercy killing is permissible, this is a *necessary, but not sufficient*, reason for legalising euthanasia. Possible abuses of the law, and old and terminally ill people feeling that they should die so as not to be a burden on relatives, are potential consequences of legalisation that could outweigh the moral merits of allowing people to choose to end their suffering.

BOX 4.2   NECESSARY AND SUFFICIENT CONDITIONS

In logic, the concepts **necessary** and **sufficient conditions** are important. A necessary condition for something is one that is essential to it – such as having a ball (or ball substitute) being necessary for playing a game of football. Having sufficient conditions means, simply, that everything needed for something being the case has been provided or established. Sometimes some of these conditions are also necessary conditions, but not always. Playing football on a Tuesday night is sufficient to keep me happily occupied for an hour, but many other things could fulfil this role as well.

Box 4.3 shows how each of these fundamental questions can be connected to a range of possible sub-questions (many of which we will look at in detail in subsequent chapters).

BOX 4.3   FUNDAMENTAL CRITICAL QUESTIONS AND SOME EXAMPLES OF SUB-QUESTIONS

1. Are the premises acceptable, i.e. likely to be true, or likely to be accepted as true or plausible by the people the arguer is attempting to persuade?

   - Are the claims being made clear?
   - Is appropriate evidence cited in support of the claims being made in terms of quantity and quality? For example, where experts are cited, are they the right experts? Do they represent a consensus in their field?
   - Is the author biased in a way, or to an extent, that should make us question the objectivity of the evidence presented?
   - Are any of the claims inconsistent with one another?
   - Have opposing positions been accurately represented?

2. Are the premises relevant to the conclusion the arguer is seeking to establish?

   - Has the appropriate kind of evidence been presented? For example, what the general public thinks about who should govern them is relevant to who should govern them, but what they think the effects of a 4 degree global temperature rise will be is not relevant to what these effects will actually be.
   - Where analogies are employed, are they similar enough to the issue being discussed to allow us to reach conclusions based on those analogies?

3. Are the premises sufficient in order to establish the conclusion?

   - If the conclusion is a generalisation, is this one that can be supported on the basis of the evidence provided?
   - Has relevant information or have perspectives been over-looked?
   - What alternative conclusions can be drawn from the evidence?

QUESTIONS SPECIFIC TO PARTICULAR ARGUMENT FORMS

On a British political analysis TV programme in 2015, the possible repeal of the fox hunting ban in Britain was being discussed.[2]

Rock guitarist, astrophysics PhD, and animal welfare activist Brian May wanted to retain the ban, arguing that it is not a sport and that it is cruel. Former Front Bench politician Michael Portillo agreed that it is not a sport but was in favour of repealing the ban because the state should respect certain traditions, even if viewed by others as distasteful or cruel. He is no fan of bullfighting, but said that the argument would extend to allowing this tradition to be maintained as well. At this point, Brian May and the host (experienced journalist Andrew Neil) retorted that the same argument could apply to witch hunts (May) and bear baiting (Neil). Portillo said that it could not; that these were different, and at this point the discussion had to end because they had run out of time.

What we have here is an example of an **argument from analogy**. It is no coincidence that we have come across this type of argument previously in this book because they are extremely common. They are also often quite weak, but even when they are weak, they can be significantly persuasive. Arguments from analogy are, then, important to analyse and will be a central focus of Chapter 7, but for the moment I am going to preview this discussion and use them as an example of specific critical questions.

The basic structure of an argument from analogy is this:

P1: X is similar to Y.
P2: Z is true of Y.
P3: Therefore Z is also true of X.

In the case of Andrew Neil's argument, X, Y and Z can be filled in like this:

P1: Fox hunting as a tradition is similar to bear baiting as a tradition.
P2: Bear baiting was banned.
C1: Therefore fox hunting should also be banned.

Four of the critical questions that can be applied to arguments from analogy are these:

Q1. Is what is said of Y actually true (or plausible)?
Q2. Are there relevant similarities between X and Y?

Q3. Are there dissimilarities between X and Y that undermine the similarities?
Q4. Can convincing counter-analogies be found?

Applied to Neil's argument, the likely answers (i.e. the basis for further research, or what we would put back to him if we were in Portillo's shoes) are these:

1. This is true; bear baiting was a tradition in England until the nineteenth century.
2. There are some relevant similarities; most obviously that both involve harming animals (including the dogs in bear baiting) as a necessary part of a practice from which people derive recreational pleasure.
3. It would appear that there could be sufficient dissimilarities to undermine the similarities. For the sake of this example, it is not appropriate to go into much detail, but factors like the degree of cruelty, the degree of human skill and courage involved, and the victim having a sporting chance, are among several that differentiate the two practices.
4. Portillo mentioned the counter-analogy of bullfighting, but this is not as strong as it might be since there is also a lot of support for banning this. Other possibilities are other traditional forms of hunting (deer, grouse, etc.) that are less controversial.

The first two critical questions tend to be where our basic rationality will take us when encountering arguments from analogy, but I think that the third one is slightly less intuitive (it is also the hardest one to answer since it involves a lot of imaginative work). However, even if all three are relatively obvious, familiarity with a list like this – questions that have been broadly agreed upon by a range of scholars – gives us some confidence that these are the angles we need to pursue in the discussion.

Clearly, this is just the start of a long debate (which is itself just one part of the discussion on fox hunting), but knowing the basic questions to pose once an argument from analogy has been identified is a good start, and one that has the potential to lead the exchange along constructive lines.

Returning to the ARS criteria, note that critical question Q1 for arguments from analogy is a form of the acceptability criterion; Q2 concerns relevance, and Q3 and Q4 question the premises' sufficiency.

CRITICAL QUESTIONS AND IMPLICIT ASSUMPTIONS

When we looked at the process of argument reconstruction, we discussed the importance of making implicit premises explicit. This helps ensure that we do not overlook assumptions the arguer is making that need to be justified. Identifying argument forms in reconstructions is also about making implicit assumptions explicit.

An argument commonly voiced during the 2015 Eurozone crisis (caused by Greece defaulting on a major debt repayment) was that if Greece leaves the single currency, then other countries will follow, leading to the collapse of the Eurozone. This is a version of a **slippery slope argument**, one in which it is claimed that a relatively small and containable happening will inexorably lead to a series of events that ends in disaster (for more on this argument form, see Chapter 6). In the process of identifying something as a slippery slope argument it has become apparent that three assumptions are being made: (1) a specified sequence of cause and effect is likely to happen; (2) if it does, it will be beyond the control of relevant parties to put a stop to; and (3) the final consequences will be significantly negative. (These in turn generate critical questions that examine the likelihood of the sequence of events; whether it really will be unstoppable once it has started, and whether or not the final consequences are in fact disastrous.)

In a similar way, the formal structure of many argument forms contains a premise which makes an often implicit assumption explicit. An **argument from authority**, for example (see Chapter 5), such as:

> Richard Dawkins says that the world would be a better place without organised religion, therefore it is likely that the world would be a better place without organised religion.

Would be fully reconstructed as:

> P1: Richard Dawkins says that the world would be a better place without organised religion.

P2: Richard Dawkins has relevant expertise on the history, politics and ethics of organised religion.

C: Therefore it is likely that the world would be a better place without organised religion.

P2 is the implicit premise that, when made explicit, clearly reveals the argument as an argument from authority. In light of the guidance on reconstructing enthymemes offered in Chapter 3, it might well be unnecessary or inadvisable to fully reconstruct the argument in this way in many situations, but it can certainly be helpful to the process of making clear one's critique of a position that relies on Dawkins' authority on this matter.

THE WIDER ANALYSIS OF ARGUMENT FORMS

The argument forms and associated fallacies that will be discussed in subsequent chapters have been selected because they are particularly prevalent across a wide variety of contexts. Most of them are also what I would call 'interesting' in the sense that an analysis of them can open up deep and wide considerations about the human condition and about oneself. They can, you might say, serve as a portal into the themes underpinning this book: rationality and persuasion, dispositions, and constructive dialogues. From a study of the argument forms we commonly use and the ways in which they can go wrong, we can learn a lot about, not only argument reconstruction and evaluation, but also our character and the way we interact with others. For example, fallacies are, as John Woods puts it, 'like bad habits ... hard to break' (2013, p. 5), and it is their link to biases and heuristics that helps explain, not just why this is case, but why certain argument forms and fallacies are as frequently employed and as 'seductive' as they are.

It is with this in mind that the argument forms and fallacies featuring in Chapters 5–7 will be investigated in terms of the following themes and headings:

- Description and basic structure;
- Critical questions used to guide our evaluation of them;
- Their relationship to heuristics and the psychology of persuasion, or what might be called their 'rhetorical power';

- Dispositions they are liable to foster or to be a sign of, and their significance in terms of our pursuit of constructive dialogues.

EXERCISES

My view is that there is limited value in applying the ARS questions to relatively unfamiliar and de-contextualised arguments, so instead of providing some of these (as I did at the end of the last chapter), my recommendation is that you should select passages that involve arguments from topics and texts you are familiar with and apply the ARS critical questions to them. This could include:

- other disciplines you are studying;
- topical events and debates;
- extended texts such as the ones recommended in this book;
- essays and other assignments that you have written.

FURTHER READING

1. Perhaps the most comprehensive directory of argument forms is Walton, Reed and Macagno's *Argument Schemes* (2008); and a less comprehensive but more discursive book covering the details of a range of important argument forms and fallacies is Christopher Tindale's *Fallacies and Argument Appraisal* (2007).
2. Two sources in which the Acceptability, Relevance, Sufficiency criteria are employed explicitly and with clarity are Johnson and Blair, *Logical Self-Defense* (2006); and Hughes, Lavery and Doran, *Critical Thinking* (2010).
3. If you would like to know more about deductive and inductive arguments, some good sources are Bowell and Kemp (2010) and Ennis (1996a).
4. Ennis (1996a) also has a helpful chapter on the distinctive nature of value-based arguments.

NOTES

1 Originally presented in 1977 in their book, *Logical Self Defense*.
2 *This Week*, 2 July 2015.

5

ARGUMENTS AND SOCIAL POWER

AUTHORITY, THREATS AND OTHER FEATURES OF MESSAGE SOURCE

Facts come wrapped in authority.

(Charles Willard, 1990, p. 13)

God told me to invade Iraq.
(President G.W. Bush, as reported in *The Independent*,
7 October 2005)

Questioning the influence that power and authority have on our beliefs and actions is close to the heart of critical thinking. As we saw in the Introduction, a leading motivation of Western philosophy, as epitomised by the Scientific Revolution and the Enlightenment, is to free ourselves from an uncritical frame of mind. Whether encouraged by social institutions or by our own dispositions, reclining in the comfort of conventional wisdom and its authority figures is typically seen as detrimental, both to individual well-being and to the wider culture.

In the context of argumentation, one of the most effective ways of deflecting requests to justify one's beliefs is to appeal to an authority. By doing so we are saying things like: 'Argue with them, not with me', or 'Do you think you know better than authority X?' In the former case we are failing to take ownership of our belief, perhaps seeing ourselves as part of a larger system with which the responsibility lies. The implication of the second is that there are reasons for thinking that authority X is indeed the right authority to base our beliefs on, and it is this reasoning that turns out to be the most important consideration for critical thinking.

Since we cannot become experts in all of the fields that are relevant to the decisions we make in our personal and professional lives, reliance on authority is unavoidable. There are also plenty of circumstances (and not just in the military) where an unquestioning approach to authority is the best course of action or the best policy. The crucial thing is for us to know why this is the case; why X is the right kind of authority to help inform our beliefs on a particular topic, or why circumstance Y (a battlefield, medical emergency, restaurant kitchen during peak demand, and so on) lends itself to a policy of not questioning orders. Modern analyses of arguments from authority recognise the limitations of individual powers, and the critical questions they generate embody this understanding. In Johnson and Blair's words, 'We are urged to be filters of opinions rather than sponges who soak them up indiscriminately' (2006, p. 167).

These concerns are central to understanding our place in a representative democracy. On the one hand, we need to be appropriately informed on the issues we are voting on (and we need to be willing to exercise critical thinking), and, on the other, we need to choose candidates who are knowledgeable and trustworthy. What constitutes trustworthiness in our elected representatives partly depends on the preferences of the voter in question, but many of us will be looking for someone who shares our values, who is willing and able to be a critical thinker, who has a wide set of critical thinking dispositions (including those, like courage and empathy, that are important for generating constructive dialogues and avoiding **groupthink**), and someone who is in other respects a good person (e.g. honest and reliable).

The authority of the political representative derives from some combination of her legitimacy, her expertise, and her character. Character matters because shared values matter (they are in an important sense 'like us'), and because we must trust them to act appropriately in circumstances that are not entirely predictable in terms of previous experiences. They will, for example, need to vote on matters that their current expertise does not prepare them for, and they will need to conduct themselves in pressured situations that will test their courage, persistence, decency, self-control and humility. To a great extent, this is because failings in these ways will impede their critical thinking, but it can also be because we want them to represent what is best in us and to act as role models.

The flipside of appealing to authority in support of our positions is attempting to discredit the views of those who oppose our beliefs. This can be on the basis of their lack of expertise; their biased view on the subject; inconsistency between what they advocate and what they do, or simply because of their undesirable character (or links to other undesirable characters). All of these forms of argument are known as **ad hominem arguments**.

This chapter is about arguments in which either characteristics of the arguer, or people that the arguer refers to, constitute the main premise. It will stretch its net wider than arguments that appeal to, or discredit expert authority, addressing a number of argument forms that rely on what has been called social power. The concept of social power is a broad one, but generally refers to the ability of one person (or a collection of people) to influence another person (or collection of people). By influence is meant a change in behaviour and/or beliefs and attitudes.

In their widely employed analysis of the subject, social psychologists John French and Bertram Raven (1959) identified five types of social power: (1) legitimate power; (2) expert power; (3) reward power; (4) coercive power; and (5) referent power. A sixth type – information power – was later added by Raven (1965). Other theorists (from a range of disciplines including argumentation, rhetoric and leadership) have suggested further categories and sub-categories, including witness testimony (which I will treat as a sub-type of information power) and ethotic power.[1] These six types and one sub-type are explained in Box 5.1, and it is these categories that will form the bones of this chapter.

BOX 5.1   FRENCH AND RAVEN'S 'BASES OF SOCIAL POWER'

- *Expert power.* The authority of someone who is an expert, and whose expertise is relevant to the issue at hand. We would thus take seriously the view of a well-respected scholar of twentieth-century European social and economic history on the origins of the European Union, but be more cautious about their pronouncements on ancient Egypt.

- *Information power.* There are plenty of situations in which, although a person is not an expert, they do nevertheless possess knowledge that is pertinent and valuable in a certain situation. The black-mailer trades on information power, as does my wife when she hides the channel changer when the cricket is on TV. An important subdivision of information power is **witness testimony**, referring to someone's being present at and observing a one-off event. In court cases the information power of a witness is of course very important in establishing truth.

- *Legitimate power.* The authority conferred upon someone by virtue of the position that they hold (e.g. teacher, judge, parent, checkout worker) or 'some sort of code or standard accepted by the individual, by virtue of which the external agent can assert his power' (French and Raven, 1959, p. 265). Thus, it is important to remember that legitimate authority covers both official positions/jobs AND authority associated moral codes and social norms.

- *Reward power.* Rewards come in many forms, from pay (e.g. the prospect of a bonus at work) to praise (e.g. compliments from a friend on a new hair style). Anyone able to influence the behaviour of others through rewards has 'reward power', which extends this category beyond the positional and normative reach of legitimate power.

- *Coercive power.* The power of someone who is able to punish someone who does not comply with a request or command. It is the opposite of reward power, but similar to it in so far as it can be held by someone without legitimate power.

- *Referent power.* In contrast to the relatively impersonal legitimate and expert power, referent power is held by a group or person with whom you personally connect. They demonstrate values and other qualities that are (or you would like to be) an important part of your identity, and so, without the need for requests, orders, or threats, you desire to conform to group or person's norms, and those norms have power over you.

An additional basis of social power

- *Ethotic power.* The power of a person who is regarded, in a general sense, as a 'good' person (or a virtuous or moral person). It is someone who, without reference to expertise, any position they occupy, or specific codes of conduct they adhere to, is of good character and serves as a role model.

'Power' is quite a general term that is flexible enough to be used in the ways that French and Raven do. 'Authority' is a less general concept that tends to refer to an official or otherwise socially recognised sanctioning of someone's power. The phrase 'by the authority invested in me …' captures this objective quality, and it thus makes sense to talk about 'legitimate authority', 'expert authority' and possibly 'ethotic authority', but less so to use it in relation to the other kinds of power. Other critical thinking textbooks usually concentrate on expert authority under the heading 'arguments from authority', but because the perspective here is wider, both power and authority become relevant (and sometimes interchangeable) terms.

Before moving on to discuss these in detail, I will add a quick comment about the source or location of social power. Put briefly, a person's power does not simply reside in them independently, but is actualised by being recognised or accepted by other people. My mother might be an expert on parenting but her advice will not be heeded by me unless I acknowledge this. This dependency explains the importance of signalling power via, for example, uniforms and badges.

To sum up this introduction, we will consider whether and when it is justified to act, or to form beliefs, in accordance with sources of power with reference to two broad types of argument:

1. *Positive arguments* that claim that because a particular person believes or commands X, we should consider believing or doing X. These include appeals to expert, legitimate and ethotic authority;

arguments based on **information power** (including **witness testimony**) arguments based on **referent power** (a species of which is known as the *ad populum* **argument**), and arguments that are based on coercion (known as *ad baculum* **arguments**). Arguments from authority and power can either be referring to the authority/power of the person who is presenting the argument (the explicit or implicit message that you should take them seriously because of who they are), or they can be referring to a third person.

2. *Negative arguments* – otherwise known as **ad hominem arguments** – which claim the opposite; that because certain beliefs or actions are those of, or those associated with, a particular person, this counts as a reason for *not* believing or doing these things. These are sometimes called 'poisoned well' arguments; the metaphor referring to the source of the view being infected (by lack of expertise, biased views, poor character, and so on) such that anything that springs from it is also infected.

5.1 ARGUMENTS FROM EXPERT AUTHORITY

A vast amount of the information we rely upon to make decisions comes from other people. Since it is not possible to find out everything for ourselves in a direct manner, we have no choice but to include second-hand information in many of our rational deliberations. The question of *which* information to trust becomes the question of *who* to trust.

In the context of public decision-making, Charles Willard (1990, p. 20) makes this sobering observation:

> Action needs facts; decision-makers are dependent on the custodians of facts, the [academic] disciplines. As it is impossible for public actors to acquire expertise in the range of subject matters that confront them, we need to rethink the very ideas of public knowledge and competence.

Part of this re-think concerns the ways in which group decision-making is approached, but of more direct relevance to this chapter is the need for competence in our assessment, not so much in the ideas experts put forward, but in the trustworthiness of the experts in question. By 'expert' we typically mean someone who has undergone substantial education or training. They have significant experience of working in the field of their expertise, and the level of their knowledge is often verified by qualifications, influence, and peer approval.

The basic structure for any argument that offers proof or evidence for a position by appealing to the expertise of the person or people supporting that position is this:

P1: X is an expert in the domain of Y.
P2: X believes that Z in relation to Y is true.
C: Therefore Z is true (or Z is plausible).

Other argumentation and critical thinking textbooks vary in the number of critical questions they list,[2] but I will organise the essential criteria for assessing this type of argument into four main questions:

Q1: Is the authority cited an expert in their field? [Acceptability]
Q2: If so, is this field relevant to the issue under discussion? [Relevance]
Q3: If so, is the authority cited to be trusted? [Acceptability]
Q4: If so, is the strength of the conclusion reached appropriate? [Sufficiency]

Each of these, though, is associated with a number of important sub-questions, and some of these will be discussed below.

THE NATURE OF THE EXPERTISE

Is the authority cited an expert in their field, and is this field relevant to the issue under discussion? If someone is a medical doctor, and they are giving their opinion on a common bodily ailment, then we can say yes to Q1 and Q2. If they are making a claim about a psychological condition, then we need to be more cautious. This much is obvious, but if we're not concentrating we can easily be fooled. Not every historian is an expert on Scottish history, and not every Scottish historian is an expert on the Jacobite Risings, but if someone commenting on the Battle of Culloden is only introduced as a 'historian' or even 'Scottish historian', then we do not yet know if we are in safe hands.

Expert knowledge tends to be highly specialised, and this is why Q1 and Q2 are so important. However, we also need to recognise that generalist and interdisciplinary writing and research have a couple of vitally important functions:

- Most of the big issues affecting us (such as climate change, global inequality, terrorism) require multiple disciplinary perspectives to make sense of and formulate responses to them.
- Generalist writers (such as journalists) are often better at communicating these issues to wider publics than are specialists.

There is, then, an unavoidable pay-off between specialist expertise and a broader perspective, and we need to keep this in mind when assessing the value of blogs, columns, books and documentaries which tackle big questions for non-specialist consumption (including any influence they might have on policy-makers). The books of journalist and political activist Naomi Klein are good examples. Her 2015 work *This Changes Everything* combines climate science with ethics, politics and economics. Few people, including academics, are experts in all of these areas, but it is entirely reasonable to argue that someone needed to write this book, and that that someone needed to be able to reach a large and broad audience. Klein's lack of formal expertise in climate science inevitably affects the book's credibility, but three factors help to limit its negative impact: (1) she is very open about the efforts she has made in the years researching the book to properly understand climate science and its implications; (2) she makes continual reference to multiple sources to support her arguments, and includes a large number of endnotes detailing their origin; and (3) in her many years as a journalist and writer, she has gained a reputation for scholarly research and professional and personal integrity.

So, when asking questions about expertise we need to be sensitive to the limitations of specialist knowledge. We also need people willing to investigate more than one discipline and synthesise the findings of a range of experts in pursuit of solutions to urgent but complex problems. Our evaluation of such efforts needs to be differently oriented: to be more generous and tolerant, and to recognise that they belong to an applied agenda rather than the pursuit of knowledge for its own sake.

THE TRUSTWORTHINESS OF THE EXPERT

Trustworthiness refers to our confidence that the individual's expertise will be appropriately applied to the current situation. Indicators of trustworthiness include the extent to which the expert's views on the issue are shared by her peers (consensus), the ways in which she appears to be applying her knowledge to the problem (judgement), and whether some form of bias might be compromising her objectivity. The question of bias will be considered under circumstantial ad hominem arguments (below), and in this section I will make some observations about consensus and judgement.

Consensus

In a radio programme[3] interviewing the world-famous entomologist and founder of sociobiology, E.O. Wilson, Wilson defended his theory of group selection over the selfish gene theory of cooperative behaviour.[4] In this peak hour broadcast, it was instructive to see how this complex debate was defended by both Wilson and his rival Richard Dawkins (who had also been interviewed on the subject). Most of the audience would lack the expertise to be convinced one way or the other by the scientific arguments, so both relied significantly on arguments from authority. Wilson made the point that mathematical modelling disproved the selfish gene theory. He had little option but to spare us the maths, but did stress that his co-researchers were two well-respected Harvard mathematicians: Martin Nowak and the 'genius' Corina Tarnita.

Beyond this, it should be added, Wilson went some distance to explain and defend his theory without reference to authority, but Dawkins was quite explicit about needing to use an argument from authority (something he said he generally dislikes doing) and simply pointed out that a reply to Wilson's paper elicited a damning response in the form of a letter to the journal *Nature* (the journal that published Wilson's article) from 140 eminent evolutionary biologists. His argument came down to numbers: yes, Wilson is a leading authority in evolutionary biology, but on this issue he is vastly out-numbered by other authorities. Who are you going to trust? The first part of Wilson's response to this was to draw an analogy with a 1921 paper entitled 'One-hundred physicists against Einstein', which erro-neously argued against the general theory of relativity.

It is also noteworthy that the rationale for the letter sent to *Nature* referred to above was to 'keep non-specialists from wasting time' on the theory, and that wasted time was a genuine concern because of 'Nowak's fame and *Nature*'s prestige'.[5] The non-specialists referred to would presumably include academics from other disci-plines (such as psychology) and journalists, again underlining the risks associated with generalist and interdisciplinary writing and research. In the Klein case, discussed above, there appears to be enough of a consensus among relevant scientists about enough of the points she makes to maintain the thrust of her economic and political argument. But in the case of Wilson's theory the non-expert would have to tread very carefully indeed, and the letter to *Nature* was intended as a warning to this effect; one that was perhaps seen as necessary because of various heuristics triggered by the big names involved.

Expertise and judgement

A different angle on the trustworthiness of experts concerns the intellectual activity that contributes to their decision-making. For example, I may have every reason to have confidence in the expertise of my dentist, but if he recommends a certain (significant or drastic) treatment on a day in which he appears to be particularly harried or distracted it might well be sensible not to act on this until I see him again, or until I seek a second opinion. This highlights how expertise is not just about years of learning and practice, it is also about the judgements made which apply this experience to the matter at hand. Put another way, as a critical thinker, our judgement on the expert authority of someone includes our consideration of them as a critical thinker. What to look out for in this respect is broadly covered by the critical thinking dispositions (see Chapter 2), and the relevant critical question supplementing the broad reliability question is:

Is the authority in question behaving in accordance with relevant critical thinking dispositions? (For example, are they attending carefully to the precise facts of the matter; or being open-minded rather than dogmatic when considering options?)

In some situations an additional relevant question(Goodwin, 2011) might be:

What do they have to lose if they turn out to be wrong?

Of course, a learned practitioner might have developed some habitual weaknesses in this respect, in which case the direct (or abusive) ad hominem argument can legitimately be employed against him. This will be discussed further under 'Arguments appealing to character'.[6]

THE STRENGTH OF THE CONCLUSION

The appropriate degree of confidence in an argument appealing to expert authority hinges importantly on whether the conclusion concerns a course of action, or whether it concerns what to believe. In the latter case, an element of caution is often appropriate, but in cases where there is total consensus among experts, the better approach is perhaps one of acknowledging one's distance; not 'X is true', but 'I have every reason to believe that X is true.'

We should now be applying this kind of language to our belief in anthropogenic climate change, but even if the IPCC were less sure than they are (for example, if it was 87 per cent of scientists rather than 97 per cent), the argument for *acting* as if it were true has a firmer conclusion:

P1: A clear majority of scientists believe that human activity is a significant cause of global warming, and that the consequences of global warming will be very serious indeed.

P2: A clear majority of scientists believe that immediate reductions in carbon emissions will slow down global warming, leading to less severe consequences.

C: Therefore we need to act now to reduce carbon emissions.

This example also highlights the value of an extra critical question introduced by Christopher Tindale (2007, p. 142): 'What are the consequences of accepting what the authority says, or ignoring what is said?' With climate change, if the experts are right, then the consequences will be severe, so we ignore them at our peril. For most of us at least, the same cannot be said for authoritative views on the surface temperature of Venus, or the history of cricket.

EXPERT AUTHORITY: PSYCHOLOGY AND RHETORIC

It is unsurprising that psychologists have identified an 'expertise heuristic' which prompts us to jump to conclusions when expertise – or the appearance of expertise – is associated with an idea or product (Smith *et al.*, 2014, pp. 248–9). In order to exploit these heuristics, a professional persuader will need to know who the trusted experts are for a particular audience, and they will need to know what the potent signifiers of expertise (or competence) are.

Once experts are known, persuaders can play on our tendency to erroneously generalise expertise (interrogated by Q1). For example, Carol Vorderman, an engineering graduate and TV presenter (initially doing the maths on the game show *Countdown*) is employed to lend scientific credibility to fish oil and other health products. Generalisation of this sort can be partly explained by the **halo effect**, i.e. assuming, without evidence, further positive qualities in a person on the basis of a few known positive qualities. (This is discussed in more detail below, under ethotic arguments.)

Rapid message delivery, steady eye contact, and even face shape (Smith *et al.*, 2014) are among the many non-verbal and paralinguistic signs of expertise and trustworthiness. Owen Hargie and David Dickson (2004, p. 344) identify the 'Three Ts of expert power': (1) titles (Professor, Doctor); (2) threads (clothes, uniforms); and (3) trappings (other signs, such as framed degree certificates, shelves of technical books and journals, or specialist equipment). During the UK Labour Party leadership election in the summer of 2015, a letter was published in *The Guardian* in support of one of the candidates. It was signed in this way:

Richard Wilkinson *Emeritus Professor, University of Nottingham*, Kate Pickett *Professor, University of York*, Steve Keen, *Professor, Kingston University*, Elizabeth Dore, *Emeritus Professor, University of Southampton* and 23 others.[7]

The full list is online and the nearly everyone there is a professor. Very few though are professors of politics, so presumably their titles are meant to add to the persuasiveness of the argument presented in the letter by virtue of the expertise heuristic.

EXPERT AUTHORITY, DISPOSITIONS AND CONSTRUCTIVE DIALOGUES

Kant pointed to 'laziness and cowardice' as

> the reasons why so great a proportion of men ... gladly remain in lifelong tutelage, and why it is so easy for others to establish themselves as their guardians. It is so easy to be immature. If I have a book to serve as my understanding, a pastor to serve as my conscience, a physician to determine my diet for me, and so on, I need not exert myself at all. I need not think, if only I can pay: others will readily undertake the irksome work for me.

> ([1784] 1963, p. 35)

If 'laziness and cowardice' can make us too keen on authority-based arguments, then an absence of modesty can have the reverse effect. The person lacking respect for authority is typically as closed-minded at the person with too much. In both cases, the fault lies with over-reliance on limited sources – on oneself in the case of the immodest person, and on too few others in the case of the dogmatic tradition-alist. In the latter case, open-mindedness would usually reveal that there are multiple authoritative points of view, and this knowledge alone should mitigate any tendency to confuse authority with truth. A balance is needed between excesses of independence and dependency, mediated by dispositions like courage, open-mindedness and modesty.

In terms of its effect on dialogues, it has been claimed, reasonably, that 'to invoke authority is to abort debate' (Willard, 1990, p. 18).

The effect of an appeal to authority that is accepted by the other person is that it shifts the **burden of proof**. A matter is disputed; neither party is able to convince the other through other forms of argument; but discussant 1 says that he has it on good authority that what he is saying is the case. If enough of the criteria for a strong appeal to authority appear to be met, then the ball is now in discussant 2's court. Discussant 1 is not only unconvinced by Discussant 2's argument, he has an authority to support his view, and so at this stage there is little more Discussant 2 can do but to research the views and relevant attributes of the authority in detail and/or find her own authorities in support of her view.

None of this is unconstructive so long as: (1) the argumentation process really has gone as far as it can under the circumstances; and (2) all participants understand the reasons why this is the case. In this way, frustration is avoided and the door is open for the dialogue to recommence. In an important sense, responsibility is shifted to authorities, but these critical thinkers retain control over the situation in a number of respects: they are responsible for finding the relevant authorities; for understanding them as far as they can, and, importantly, for recognising that an appeal to authority is the right way to proceed if any agreement is to be reached.

It should also be said that this information-seeking part of the discussion process need not be combative in the way implied here. There is no reason why all parties cannot jointly research the subject in order to make progress. Indeed, a willingness to do this suggests suitable open-mindedness and the collaborative process (so long as groupthink is avoided) could itself lead to a softening of biases.

5.2 ARGUMENTS FROM POSITION TO KNOW (INFORMATION POWER)

The significance of information power is concisely expressed by Alan Brinton in this way:

> Sometimes another person has access to information or evidence which we do not have, either because it is inaccessible to us or because the demands of the situation make it impracticable for us to get it.
>
> (1986, p. 255)

A corollary of information power in argumentation is arguments from 'position to know' (Walton *et al.*, 2008). Being in a position to know is to have 'access to facts', whereas expertise refers to deep and broad knowledge of the field in which those facts are located. Examples of position to know range from our local geographical and cultural knowledge (where the local library is; where the best place to look for job ads is; how much, if at all, should we tip bar or restaurant staff) and basic procedures and norms of the workplace (who to send expenses forms to; how to address senior staff in an email), through to the boss who withholds or distorts information gathered at high-level committee meetings in order to maintain control over subordinates,[8] and altogether juicier revelations found in autobiographies or information given to us in confidence (or obtained through snooping or computer hacking) on things like love affairs and criminal behaviour.

Examples of position to know arguments are endless, and take us directly to some deep issues in ethical and political philosophy. Information power is employed by governments in undemocratic acts of propaganda; by civil servants who keep government ministers in the dark, and it exists in the unavoidable agenda-setting that goes on in news media. Information power can also be used benignly, and on occasion – like those who wish not to know the full details and extent of their terminal medical conditions – we can justifiably choose to remain ignorant.

An important consideration for the position to know argument is the contrast between expertise and experience. Consider, for example, the difference between knowing all about cancer from a scientific perspective and living through cancer; or between knowing about heartbreak from a literary and psychological point of view and having your heart broken. One way of appreciating the significance of this difference is in terms of the knowledge that qualitative research often seeks out. In its quest for expert knowledge, it finds out about the first-hand accounts of people who have had certain experiences. Alternatively think of how news reporting typically combines the experiences of people at the sharp end of, say, welfare cuts or health service reforms, with expert economic or political analysis. It is important not to view accounts of experiences as provisional or otherwise inferior to theoretical understanding. For a number of reasons – including contextual and 'felt' qualities – it offers a qualitatively distinct perspective on an issue, rather than one that is simply waiting to be reduced to and replaced by a theoretical account.

The basic structure of position to know arguments is:

P1: X has access to knowledge about Y.
P2: X believes that Z in relation to Y is true.
C: Therefore Z is true (or Z is plausible).

The critical questions are similar to those of arguments from expert authority:

Q1: Is appealing to position to know appropriate in these circumstances? [Relevance]
Q2: If so, is X really in a position to know? [Acceptability]
Q3: If so, is X trustworthy? [Acceptability]
Q4: If so, is the strength of the conclusion reached appropriate? [Sufficiency]

Q1 is worthy of some elaboration, mostly in the form of sub-questions. First, we should ask whether this is information we are able to find out for ourselves, and, if so, question our motives for relying on others (which might of course be entirely reasonable). Second, though, if someone or something is stopping us from finding out, does this prohibition have legal, moral or normative (such as position-based, as in the case of a parent) legitimacy? If not, can we exercise legitimate powers in order to obtain the information (such as the Freedom of Information Act, or a moral appeal)? But if so, is it worth the effort? (Or is it, for example, better to remain ignorant, or pay someone to inform us?)

WITNESS TESTIMONY

For certain kinds of news stories (such as extreme weather events, or terrorist attacks) news media rely heavily on **witness testimony**. Witness testimony differs from position to know in that it refers to situations where people experience an unusual event first-hand, and thus become valuable for establishing the truth about it. Position to know as a corollary of information power implies a degree of stability in the information's availability so that it is there for anyone who happens to be in a 'position to know'. The eye witness, in contrast, happens upon something through luck (or ill luck) rather than anything about them or their station in life. And that thing is in important senses a one-off, rather than something we can (or would want to) recreate.

As well as news reporting, eye-witness testimony can of course be important in court cases (it plays a pivotal role in *Twelve Angry Men*), the school playground ('Who saw what happened to Brian's lunch box?'), and many other circumstances. It is, however, notoriously unreliable in two interrelated respects:

- *Mistaken beliefs*: cognitive psychology has demonstrated that there tends to be a substantial gap between what we confidently believe we have seen and what actually happened.
- *Lying*: in circumstances where a person stands to gain from an event to which they are the only witness, the temptation will be there to distort or fabricate the truth. This can of course work at a subconscious level as well (see **rationalisation** and **cognitive dissonance**, in Chapter 1), with the outcome of creating distinctly convenient mistaken beliefs ('The cat was already dead when I ran over it'; 'the person I saw with that good-looking stranger in a dimly-lit restaurant looked too young to be my wife').

In David Hume's famous essay 'On Miracles', motivations like this are among the reasons he gives for why a sole witness to a supposed miracle should never be believed. In short, it will always be more likely that the person is mistaken or lying than that a law of nature has been contravened.

Miracles aside, and despite these problems, witness testimony remains important because it is sometimes all we have to go on. In order for us to have greater confidence in witness accounts, the following critical questions can be posed (based on Walton *et al.*, 2008, p. 91):

Q1: Is what the witness says internally consistent? [Acceptability]
Q2: Is what they say consistent with what is otherwise known about the event, including what others have said? [Acceptability]

Q3: Is the witness liable to be biased? (In *Twelve Angry Men*, for exam-
ple, it is suggested that one of the witnesses was motivated by the
chance to testify in court and feel important, rather than his genu-
ine knowledge of events surrounding the murder.) [Relevance]
Q4: Is what they have said plausible? (In the case of miracles and
UFOs, it is presumably not.) [Acceptability]
Q5: If so, is the strength of the conclusion reached appropriate?
[Sufficiency]

CIRCUMSTANTIAL AD HOMINEM ARGUMENTS

Arguments imputing bias in those who otherwise have expert or
information power are known as **circumstantial ad hominem
arguments**. Their basic structure is:

P1: X believes/advocates Y.
P2: X is biased in a way that could prejudice his beliefs/advocacy of Y.
P3: We should disregard/be cautious about the views of someone who
could be biased in this way.
C: Therefore we should disregard/be cautious about X's views on Y.

In a recent example, it was proving so difficult to find someone
not linked to possible suspects to chair a UK inquiry into child
sex abuse – one that includes government-level suspects like former Prime Minister Ted Heath and stretches back at least until the
1970s – it was necessary to bring in a judge from New Zealand
(Lowell Goddard). In this instance a series of strong circumstantial
ad hominem arguments righty delayed the process by over a year.[9]

Rather less convincing was the foundational accusation of the documentary *The Great Global Warming Swindle* (Martin Durkin, 2007)
that the scientists who have found evidence for anthropogenic global
warming have, in fact, known for a long time that their views have
been disproved. They maintain their defence of this view, though,
in order to keep their lucrative positions on the Intergovernmental
Panel on Climate Change. (Their view has, of course, not been
disproved, and their position on the IPCC is voluntary and unpaid.)

The critical questions that can be applied to all types of ad hominem argument are these:[10]

Q1: It what is claimed about the person's ability, character or circumstances true? [Acceptability]

Q2: Is this attack relevant to the claim that the argument makes? [Relevance]

Q3: Where it is relevant, is the right kind of conclusion drawn from it? (For example, quite often someone's position is rejected outright on the basis of an ad hominem attack whereas at most it should be called into doubt.) [Sufficiency]

Towards the end of Martin Luther King's *Letter from Birmingham Jail* is a circumstantial ad hominem attack that is harder to judge than the previous two examples. Here he pricks the conscience of America's white moderates by offering a theory for their lack of support for his methods. After explaining his reasons for the necessity of non-violent direct action he says:

> I had hoped that the white moderate would see this. Maybe I was too optimistic. Maybe I expected too much. I guess I should have realized that few members of a race that has oppressed another race can understand or appreciate the deep groans and passionate yearnings of those that have been oppressed, and still fewer have the vision to see that injustice must be rooted out by strong, persistent, and determined action.
>
> (King, 1963)

The ad hominem argument in this passage, reconstructed in a summarised form, seems to be this:

P1: Most white moderates do not support our methods.

P2: Members of the oppressing race will typically not appreciate the psychological condition of the oppressed.

P3: White moderates are members of an oppressing race.

C1: White moderates will typically not appreciate the psychological condition of the oppressed.

C2: The white moderates are wrong not to support our methods.

Here the reasoning is that white moderates, unlike the oppressed blacks, are not in a position to know. Their experience is such that they are unable or unwilling to put themselves in the shoes of the people that King is leading, and, as a result, the right kind of belief or response is not to be expected.

If we apply the critical questions, Q2 can be answered in the affirmative since not being in a position to know (in the form of life experience), if true, is relevant to King's conclusion. Whether it is true though (Q1) is another matter; quite possibly it is, but this is not something that can be answered easily from a lay-person's point of view. Since much of the rest of the speech is dealing with the white moderates' arguments, then this ad hominem attack cannot be rejected as simply crude or dismissive, and nor can the conclusion he draws from it. If the entire message had been based on an ad hominem argument of this type, then it would be fair to regard his, quite firm, conclusion as inappropriate (Q3).

INFORMATION POWER: PSYCHOLOGY AND RHETORIC

We tend to be impressed by first-hand accounts and to overlook the errors that actors and observers are prone to. Acting on them can be the result of the **availability heuristic** (see Chapter 1), and one reason for this – especially in the case of witness testimony – is that they have a narrative quality to them that is absent from statistics and other more abstract data. Reasons why stories can be so persuasive include their being concrete, personal and moving, and thus more memorable. We find the details of particular human experiences engaging in a way that abstract reasoning tends not to be, which is why documentaries and books with serious messages trying to reach wide audiences are either told via stories, or mix personal experience with more technical arguments. (The climate change films, *An Inconvenient Truth* (2006) and *The Age of Stupid* (2009) are quite typical in this respect.)

INFORMATION POWER, DISPOSITIONS AND CONSTRUCTIVE DIALOGUES

Critical thinking will teach us to be on our guard against the tendency to rely on our own experiences and immediate responses to situations. Not only are these prone to error, but they are subject to the debilitating meta-error of over-confidence. However, like most dispositions, there is a balance to be sought, and due regard for power and authority, in all of the forms we have encountered them here, does not rule out the possibility of rejecting them in favour of what we 'know' or even 'feel' to be right.

At the start of *Twelve Angry Men*, Juror 8 struggles to articulate why he feels that the guilty verdict is wrong, but he rightly allows this intuition to motivate further thinking about the case, even in the face of severe and (especially if we include the lawyers and expert witnesses) authoritative opposition. In other situations, we might experience or witness, or otherwise believe something that is so extraordinary that we should not expect others (who have not experienced the same thing) to believe us. The critical thinker would know this limitation, but not necessarily reject their belief. Miracles and religious experiences serve as an example, and even Hume was not saying that the person themselves should not believe what they have seen.

A further type of situation where personal conviction can be justified is one in which there is something inherently personal about a particular belief. It could be an aesthetic conviction, a love for someone, or a form of life that most or all others do not share or understand, but which is not incompatible with critical thinking on the grounds that the person has good reasons for why this is an area which is not (or should not be) amenable to reasoned justification. 'The universalizable does not,' says virtue ethicist Martha Nussbaum, 'determine every dimension of choice; ... there are silences of the heart within which its demands cannot, and should not, be heard' (1990, pp. 39–40).

Beware though, because this is an area where 'HANDLE WITH CARE' is stamped in large letters. The line between admirable integrity and a dogmatic refusal to subject one's beliefs to scrutiny is thin, and the latter too often hides behind the justification of the former. As with other examples of this apparent rejection of critical questions that we will come across in this book, there are subtle forms of justification which help establish the credibility of lonely decisions like these. Ethotic authority is one, and another is simply the person's willingness to acknowledge how their situation can seem peculiar to others; that by normal standards (i.e. standards that they otherwise respect), what they are choosing would be regarded as wrong or foolish.

5.3 LEGITIMATE, REWARD AND COERCIVE POWER

THE MILGRAM EXPERIMENTS

Stanley Milgram's experiments in the 1960s measuring and analysing obedience to authority remain influential and important. They are quite well known these days (beyond those studying psychology), not only because the results are highly surprising and sobering, but because the experiments themselves are dramatic and involve electric shocks. Here I want to pay attention to the processes of power and authority that explain the results. These are discussed at length in Milgram's book *Obedience to Authority* ([1974] 2005), and they serve both as an excellent example of arguments from various forms of authority and power – including legitimate, reward and coercive – and as an insight into the psychology of persuasion that is associated with appeals to authority.

Motivated by the high obedience levels among soldiers and Nazi officials in the World War II death camps, and by the trial of Adolf Eichmann in 1961,[11] Milgram wanted to examine obedience behaviour in the laboratory. Members of the public were asked to volunteer for a memory experiment at Yale University. If selected, they would turn up at the lab, have the procedure explained to them, and meet their partner, another (apparent) volunteer called Mr Wallace.

As one of these participants you would be (seemingly randomly) assigned the role of 'teacher', with Mr Wallace as the 'learner'. You would read out a list of pairs of words to Mr Wallace, and then test his learning by reading out the first word from each pair, followed by four options from which the he would try to choose the correct pairing. The twist in this procedure is that every time Mr Wallace gets one of these wrong, you are required to deliver an electric shock (the supposed purpose of the experiment being to test the effects of pain in motivating memory). A screen separates you and poor Mr Wallace, but prior to the experiment starting you see him being hooked up to the shock machine and strapped into a chair. In front of you is a row of switches delivering shocks in 15V increments from 15V to 450V. You are instructed to increase the level of shock every time the subject gets a question wrong (15V, 30V, 45V, 60V, etc.).

Pretty quickly Mr Wallace (who is, by the way, a stooge and is not actually receiving shocks) starts to make mistakes and the shock level duly increases. As the shocks become more severe, at various stages he starts, for example, groaning (135V), demanding to be allowed to leave (150–65V) (the cry of 'Get me out of here!' becomes continuous amidst other responses), screaming in pain (270V), refusing to answer questions (300V), violently screaming (315V) and then (if you are still participating by this point) after around 330V Mr Wallace falls silent.

As this develops, if you are a typical teacher, you would plead with the experimenter and question the wisdom of continuing. In response to this predictable reluctance, the experimenter has a series of carefully scripted prods to help you continue ('Please continue'; 'The experiment requires that you continue'; 'It is absolutely essential that you continue'; and finally 'You have no other choice – you must go on').

The question is; at what point do you refuse to continue administering shocks? The surprising result of this basic experimental set-up was that 100 per cent of subjects went as far as 300V, and 65 per cent went to 450V. Variations of the experiment carried out by Milgram and by other psychologists in a wide variety of countries and cultures across several decades show similar results. The implication is that many of us, under these conditions, would be unwilling or unable to disobey commands to administer potentially lethal electric shocks to a stranger under circumstance in which the punishment for disobedience is no more than the experimenter's disapproval. Milgram concluded:

[I]f a system of death camps were set up in the United States of the sort we had seen in Nazi Germany, one would be able to find sufficient personnel for those camps in any medium-sized American town.

(Cited in Blass, 2000, p. 35)

Explaining Milgram's findings

So what's behind this? Milgram offers a complex, multi-layered explanation that includes an evolved disposition towards obedience (because of the survival advantage of individuals who are able to operate in hierarchies), social learning (hierarchical structures of rewards and punishments in families, schools and the workplace), and a series of social norms that bind subjects to the experimental situation once they have entered it. These 'binding factors' include: (1) their voluntary agreement to participate (**commitment and consistency**); (2) receiving payment for participating (**reciprocation**); and (3) the forms of **expert** and **legitimate authority** represented by science and its methods, Yale University, the laboratory environment, and the experimenter's lab coat and calm, confident demeanour.

The power of these social norms and their antecedents may seem trivial compared to the pain inflicted, but these experiments show that they are not. They all contribute to a 'barrier' of anxiety (Milgram, 2005, p. 154) that the majority of subjects were unable to surmount, leading Milgram to conclude:

> The conflict between conscience and authority is not a wholly philosophical or moral issue. Many of the subjects felt, at the philosophical level of values, that they ought not to go on, but they were unable to translate this conviction into action.
>
> (Milgram, cited in Blass, 2000, p. 35)

The view of Milgram and other researchers (e.g. Blass, 2000) is that it is the combination of legitimate and expert power that makes disobedience so difficult. Legitimate power can be fairly easily understood and identified in terms of positions held and principles stood for, but its reality is quite fuzzy. It often encompasses information or expert power (the person has their position because of what they know), and it invariably comes with forms of reward and coercive power.

Numerous factors in the experiment ensure the experimenter's legitimacy: his management of the procedure; his control of the space (the lab); his relationship to the place (the university) in which the experiment takes place; and the epistemic and moral authority of science (which is signified by all of the above), plus his demeanour and dress. The wording of his 'prods' makes no direct reference to any punishments for not continuing, and in fact do not make a great deal of sense as arguments. If you still have your wits about you that is. 'You have no other choice – you must go on' is easily countered, as demonstrated by one subject:

I do have a choice. [Incredulous and indignant:] Why don't I have a choice? I came here on my own free will. I thought I was on a research project. But if I have to hurt somebody to do that, or if I was in his place, too I wouldn't stay there. I can't continue.

(Ibid., p. 52)

The implication is that this is not what the subject signed up for; that the experimenter no longer has legitimate power over him. If the subject refuses to continue, all the experimenter can say is that the experiment must come to an end, highlighting the limits of his power. Nevertheless, prior to this the barrier of anxiety that so many subjects were unable to overcome was the result of fear of the experimenter's disapproval, which itself – Milgram plausibly speculates – is in large part caused by a generalising of an internalised association between authority, rewards and punishment which begins in childhood.

LEGITIMATE AUTHORITY: STRUCTURE AND CRITICAL QUESTIONS

The general structure of an argument from legitimate authority is this:

P1: X has legitimate authority in the domain of Y.
P2: X believes that action Z in relation to Y must be performed.
C: Therefore Z must be performed.

The main critical questions applying to arguments from legitimate authority are:

Q1: Is the power in question legitimate? [Acceptability]
Q2: Is this person currently in a position to exercise this power? [Relevance] (This refers to circumstances in which someone tries to impose their otherwise legitimate authority in the wrong domain, such as Robert De Niro's ex-CIA operant and possessive father's inappropriate spying on his daughter's fiancé in the film, *Meet the Parents* (Jay Roach, 2000).)
Q3: Are there other considerations that might override the person's legitimacy (for example, the legitimacy of a competing authority)? [Sufficiency]

The Milgram procedure is primarily vulnerable to Q3 – the experimenter's otherwise legitimate and relevant authority is challenged by the authority of established moral standards concerning compassion and people's rights.

COERCIVE POWER AND *AD BACULUM* ARGUMENTS

In argumentation, coercive power is usually analysed in terms of what are called **ad baculum arguments**. *Ad baculum* means in Latin 'to the stick', and refers to arguments that threaten someone with harm of some kind (inflicted by the arguer) if they do not do a certain thing. They are sometimes referred to as 'appeals to force'; their basic form being:

P1: If you do not bring about X, then I will commit myself to seeing to it that consequence Y will occur.
P2: Consequence Y is not in your interests.
C: You should bring about X.

An immediate distinction to make is that between threats and warnings. In general linguistic usage, these terms are fairly interchangeable, but one important difference is relevant to our discussion. The manner in which we relate to someone who potentially holds the power of punishment over us is quite different if that power is legitimate. A warning might more typically be seen as the expression of legitimate power (coming from the law courts, one's teacher, spouse, and so on), whereas a threat implies someone 'taking the law into their own hands'. That said, the IRA issued plenty of bomb warnings, and the Mafia will also 'warn' people, but arguably these organisations use this language precisely in order to create or sustain an air of legitimacy. 'Threat' sounds thuggish, 'warning' sounds principled.

Important for us though is that we recognise this distinction between legitimate and non-legitimate appeals to force. In the fields of applied ethics and politics this is foundational for discussions on whether and under what circumstances direct action (for example, blockading, occupying, boycotting), war and terrorism are acceptable. These are profoundly important questions for those who regard the physical punishment of others as extreme and uncivilised, and very much a last resort.

Legitimacy, then, determines one of the critical questions, and the others address more practical considerations. The complete list is:

Q1: Is the person making the threat a legitimate authority acting within the context of her power? [Relevance]
Q2: Where not legitimate, is the person making the threat able to use the force they have threatened? [Acceptability]
Q3: Is the person being threatened *able* to comply? [Acceptability]
Q4: Is the person *willing* to comply (is it worth it for them)? [Sufficiency]

Consider the difference between these *ad baculum* arguments:

Argument 1

P1: If you do not attempt to adhere to professionally accepted standards, then we will make you redundant.
P2: You want to avoid being made redundant.
C: You should try harder to adhere to professionally accepted standards.

Argument 2

P1: If you complain again about unpaid overtime, then I will see to it that you are fired.
P2: You want to avoid being fired.
C: You should stop complaining about unpaid overtime.

It is easy to imagine a situation in which *Argument 1* meets the criteria implied by all four critical questions; the targets referred to have been agreed upon and are generally recognised as achievable, the person being threatened has a strong desire to keep their job, and the person presenting the argument is a legitimate authority (rather than, say, the person's subordinate). It is also easy to imagine a situation in which any combination of them is not met, despite the broad context being one of a target-led environment, for example: it has not been agreed that performance in terms of unmet targets is grounds for dismissal, it is only these grounds that could be the basis of dismissal in this case, the targets are not reasonably achievable by anyone, and the person has other jobs they can happily go to.

It is harder to imagine a circumstance in which *Argument 2* satisfactorily answers Q1 (but it is certainly not impossible). This is a situation in which the legitimacy of the threat is in question, and quite possibly it is a case of bullying. Significantly, though, we can still see how it could be a strong argument even in the absence of legitimacy. If the arguer is in fact able to have the person fired (perhaps through manufacturing legitimate grounds), the person is able to stop complaining (which is entirely possible), and they want the job badly enough (maybe it is with a prestigious organisation), then this could be enough to accept the conclusion. At this point though, this form of argument analysis seems to let us down. There clearly *is* something wrong here, and just what that is will be discussed shortly under 'Constructive Dialogues'.

Beforehand, I will briefly say something about what can be meant by 'harm'. *Ad baculum* arguments primarily refer to physical threats, but they can apply to psychological threats as well; 'If you don't accept my point of view, I will disrespect or dislike you.' Sometimes this implied threat is unavoidable (in trying to convert a racist, for example), and is perhaps implied in quite a number of discussions. Open-mindedness is limited by what is clearly false, implausible and morally unacceptable, and so argumentation has the power to begin or end relationships. Also, however, a consequence of argumentation is that we find out who we do and do not agree with, and sharing views is a determinant of liking and respect.

AD BACULUM ARGUMENTS: PSYCHOLOGY AND RHETORIC

Ad baculum arguments are a subcategory of what are known as appeals to fear. An appeal to fear is any argument that uses the possibility of a fearful consequence as a premise for accepting a certain conclusion. As well as appeals to force, these encompass events that are not subject to official decree – disease, death, climate change – where it makes no sense to question legitimacy; 'If you continue to do this, this is liable to happen', rather than 'If you continue to do this, I will make this happen.'

In both cases, it is fear of a certain consequence that leads us to accept the conclusion, and, as we saw in Chapter 1, emotions tend to cloud and bias our thinking. Once the fearful possibility is raised, critical questions can be overlooked or our capacity to investigate them accurately is to some degree impaired. An extreme case is terrorism, the potency of which relies on 'an irrational tendency in human nature ... to magnify unexpected and "mysterious" evils out of their true proportion' (Narveson, 1993, p. 154). The antidote, Narveson says, is: 'Rationality, plus a modicum of courage. The life expectancy of the average citizen is very little reduced by terrorism, whereas the expected evil if we accede to the terrorist's demands is great' (1993, p. 154).

The critical questions to apply to the fear element of *ad baculum* arguments (i.e. the general questions applicable to all appeals to emotion) can be found in Chapter 1.

AD BACULUM ARGUMENTS, DISPOSITIONS AND CONSTRUCTIVE DIALOGUES

Ad baculum arguments can be strong arguments in so far as the premises can be true, and if we accept these premises, then we must also accept the conclusion. The main problem with them is the effect they have on a dialogue, which is typically to end it.

In the case of threats or warnings issued legitimately, further discussion can ensue around the nature of this legitimacy, but if it is simply someone forcing you to do or believe something or else suffer the consequences, then they are effectively declaring the discussion over. This is what happens when peace talks collapse, and typically this is what war is – an unwillingness or inability to live with a disagreement that has proved unsolvable through dialogue.

Implicit *ad baculums* can occur via the disapproval we often signal through non-verbal cues such as facial expressions and by paralinguistic cues such as tone of voice. Even if what is being communicated verbally is not aggressive, the asymmetric raised lip of contempt or inappropriate sigh can let other discussants know that they risk losing your respect if they do not agree with your position. (This is very common in dialogues, and there are endless examples of it in *Twelve Angry Men*.) This might be a calculated act of intimidation, but it might also be unconscious and unintended; you might feel this way at some level, but do not want to license this feeling, or communicate it, precisely because it will prematurely close down the dialogue. In cases like this, the dispositions of **meta-cognition** and self-control become valuable for maintaining a constructive dialogue.

A final point worth considering is that there is one type of dialogue in which threats are accepted as legitimate – the negotiation.[12] The structure of a negotiation is for each side to make demands, which, if not met, will result in various sanctions (such as strike action, lay-offs, no longer allowing your van to be used for transporting the band's gear). Opposing parties are effectively trading *ad baculum* arguments, but in a way that is legitimised by a mutual, if often unstated, under-standing of the 'rules of the game': a recognition that the purpose is to reach a compromised agreement, and an expectation that reasons will be given to explain each side's demands.[13]

MILGRAM AND DISPOSITIONS

In his discussion of individual responses to the experimental condi-tions, Milgram distinguishes between a 'Professor of Old Testament' (2005, pp. 49–50) who disobeyed orders on the basis of a differ-ent ('good') authority (God); and a woman (referred to as Gretchen Brandt), whom he sees as having firmly integrated ethical values which are able to empower her refusal (ibid., pp. 87–8). There is an independence exhibited in Brandt's behaviour that makes her a good example of a critical thinker, and Milgram is clearly impressed by what he sees as her 'total control of her own action' which 'seems to make disobedience a simple and rational deed' (ibid., p. 88).

Also, in most cases of disobedience, a significant amount of courage – similar to that needed to prevent **groupthink** – is required. Not only is it a matter of disobeying orders from an authority whose position is still upheld by a situation or by the perceptions of the majority as legitimate, but of transgressing broad social hierarchies. Among other things, to disobey is to disrespect and to discredit, and it is therefore to embarrass the other person (which will also embar-rass us). Milgram makes the point by suggesting that readers think of someone they have respect for:

> preferably someone older that yourself at least by a generation, and who
> represents an authority in an important life domain [teacher, priest, possibly

a parent] ... a person you would refer to with some title [Professor, Dr, Father, etc.] ... a person who represents to you the distance and solemnity of a genuine authority. To understand what it means to breach the etiquette of relations with authority, you need merely present yourself to the person, and in place of using his title ... address him using his first name, or perhaps even an appropriate nickname.

(Ibid., p. 152)

Chances are we will not be able to do it, and even if we could, we would experience profound anxiety beforehand. Milgram's point is that hierarchical etiquette of this kind is so deeply embedded in our relations with others that it will significantly contribute to our inability to disobey what are clearly inappropriate and unethical commands.

Not only do we need courage to stand up to de-legitimise a powerful authority but, as we saw in Chapter 1, the anxiety that such situations provoke can severely disable our ability to think critically. In a state of anxiety, we are more likely to let ourselves be led by those (in this case the experimenter) who display confidence, and we are more likely to spontaneously generate rationalisations for our continued obedient behaviour, such as seeing the experimenter as responsible for the harm rather than ourselves, or viewing the learner as deserving of their discomfort because they are stupid or stubborn (ibid., pp. 47–8).

Milgram, legitimacy and framing

Framing was discussed in some detail in Chapter 1. Milgram uses it to explain how someone perceived as having legitimate power is in a position to define the meaning of a situation, and in that way have greater control over people's subsequent beliefs and behaviour (ibid., pp. 146–7). Drawing a comparison with propaganda, the trick with obedience is to put people in a position in which they willingly go along with commands because these commands are consistent with an already accepted definition of the meaning or purpose of a situation. In this case the experiment is saturated from the beginning with the ideology of science so that subsequent requests and commands are liable to be interpreted through the lens of scientific legitimacy and expertise. For the subject, what is going on *could* be seen as wrong, but the behaviour of those who continue to represent this frame of reference suggests otherwise. In most instances, this contributes to obedience, and only in a minority of cases is the competing frame of independent ethical thinking able to gain enough of a foothold to help leverage disobedience.

As we have noted on a few occasions, of enormous importance for effective critical thinking is the willingness and ability to think beyond a situation or problem as it is immediately understood, or as it is presented to us by others. As critical thinkers we must be prepared to ask ourselves 'Is there another way of looking at this?' And usually there is.

REWARD POWER

Like punishments, rewards are a fundamental aspect of life, and come in many forms (from pay to praise). Anyone able to influence the behaviour of others through rewards has 'reward power'. Often rewards are traded as we negotiate with others (longer holidays for a pay cut; school children working hard for praise, and so on). And we can control our own behaviour through self-rewards such as giving ourselves 'treats' – a session on *Angry Birds*, an episode of *The Walking Dead*, a biscuit even – for accomplishing unpleasant or difficult tasks. The structure of this kind of argument and the critical questions are similar to those of *ad baculum* arguments:

P1: If you bring about X, then you will receive Y.
P2: Y is something that you want.
C: You should bring about X.

Critical questions:

Q1: Can the person genuinely provide the reward in question, and are they likely to? [Acceptability]
Q2: Are you *able* to do what is required to receive the reward offered? [Acceptability]
Q3: Are you (or *should* you be) *willing* to pay the necessary price? [Sufficiency]

The relevance of these questions for Milgram's subjects is clear enough. Perhaps most crucial is Q1 if Milgram is right to suggest that the approval we seek from the experimenter is conditioned by a lifetime of associating approval with obedience. System 1 thinking will happily, but erroneously, generalise early family and school experiences to our relationship with the source of authority in this situation.

5.4 ARGUMENTS APPEALING TO CHARACTER

The structure of ethotic arguments is set out by Walton, Reed and Macagno (2008, p. 336) in this way:

P1: If X is a person of good (bad) moral character, then what X says should be accepted as more plausible (rejected as less plausible).
P2: X is a person of good (bad) moral character.
C: Therefore what X says should be accepted as more plausible (rejected as less plausible).

In the broadest sense then, ethotic arguments employ the moral character of the person upholding a position to help establish the plausibility of that position. As you can see from the scheme above, this can refer to good or bad aspects of that character, depending on whether the arguer's aim is to support or reject a particular conclusion.

In this section I am going to use 'ethotic authority' to refer to arguments appealing in a positive way to moral character, and 'abusive ad hominem' for arguments that appeal to it in a negative way.

ETHOTIC AUTHORITY

Direct (or abusive) ad hominem arguments are discussed in most textbooks that deal with argument forms and fallacies, but ethotic authority is often overlooked. On the face of it, this is surprising, but on closer inspection it begins to make sense. Perhaps the main problem with offering an argument from moral character is that it will often collapse into one of the other categories of authority – typically expert or legitimate.

For example, if we are swayed by the empathetic nature of a friend who argues for campaigning against further cuts to low income benefits, any argument to this effect would likely identify a form of moral *expertise* as the basis of believing its plausibility. Or if we are impressed by the views of a modest colleague on the contribution of another colleague to a project we are working on, this would be down to the modest person's relatively unbiased insight into these types of situation. In another kind of example, if a person's good character is typical of Christian ethics, then the appeal is less to them as a person and more to them as someone who instantiates the legitimate authority (for many) of Christianity.

We are, however, sometimes influenced by a more holistic impression of someone we regard as a 'good person'. Juror 8 in *Twelve Angry Men* and Mikael Blomkvist in Stieg Larsson's novel *The Girl with the Dragon Tattoo* might be examples, as are many other fictional heroes and heroines. In real life, Oprah Winfrey seems to be this for many Americans, Sir David Attenborough for many British people, and Nelson Mandela globally. In cases where these people are cited in support of a claim, or as making that claim themselves, we will, as a matter of fact, be more likely to agree with them. But the circumstances in which this can form the basis of a strong argument and where the person's being good is not reducible to a form of moral expertise as previously discussed, will be quite select.

We can conclude though that positive ethotic arguments are most clearly defined by situations in which, with no further expertise implied, a culturally conditioned notion of a good person is used as a heuristic for the right thing to do or believe.

Most typically it will be cases in which we have very little to go on, and where our acceptance of plausibility will be highly provisional. A good example is near the start of *Twelve Angry Men* when Juror 8 is attempting to persuade the others that they should spend time discussing the case even though they are all convinced of the defendant's guilt. Juror 9 is quite explicit when he argues that he is willing to accept the request because he is impressed by certain characteristics of Juror 8 – such as his willingness to stand up to the majority – which are not relevant to the case itself.

In his unusual and very readable social psychology text book, Roger Brown (1986) endorses the practical necessity of this type of reasoning under circumstances of unavoidable ignorance. He describes the hypothetical situation of being a member of a committee that has to make some technical decisions on an issue where he is clueless (concerning bringing cable TV to Cambridge, Massachusetts, in 1983). Ideally he should absent himself, but not wanting to admit his ignorance, his next best bet is to base his decision on the choices made by those people on the committee he most admires in ethotic terms:

> In a good expressive discussion ... information is transmitted that is not part of any relevant argument. Each participant in some degree expresses his ... assertiveness, intelligence, education, fair-mindedness, compassion, prejudice, cowardice, and so on.
>
> (Ibid., p. 234)

The critical questions relating to ethotic arguments are these:

Q1. Is the person someone who can reasonably be regarded as having good character? [Acceptability]

Q2. Is the good character of the person of the right kind to be relevant to the situation in question? (Counteracting the '**halo effect**' (see below).) [Relevance]

Q3. Is the weight placed on their character proportionate for the situation in question? [Sufficiency]

Q1 is dependent on the prior question of what constitutes good moral character. Invariably it will involve a collection of virtues that are, to a degree, culturally specific or practice-specific, but the preceding discussion indicates that in many cases it will encompass someone who exhibits some of the core critical thinking dispositions.

Q2 highlights the situation-specific nature of good character; Juror 8 is the right beacon in a jury room, but not necessarily on the battlefield.

Q3 serves as a reminder that placing significant emphasis on ethotic arguments is often most appropriate in situations of uncertainty. As is explained in relation to direct ad hominem arguments (below), appealing to this kind of authority (in the form of role models or charismatic leaders) can be motivated by a desire to not take responsibility for our actions in situations where we should be.

ETHOTIC AUTHORITY: PSYCHOLOGY AND RHETORIC

Someone possessing ethotic power will tend to function as a role model. A role model is someone we imitate, and this notion is helpful for understanding a difference between adherence to rules (a type of legitimate authority) and ethotic power. The focus of the latter is the individual rather than the abstract rule; a good recent example being the fashion among young Christians for wristbands with the slogan 'What would Jesus do?'

Ethotic authority has persuasive potency because role models provide a vivid and memorable means for beginning our deliberations on how to respond to a range of situations. Making reference to the Roman philosopher Seneca, Alan Brinton says: 'It is easier to recognise a virtuous person when we see one than it is to give or understand and evaluate (or be moved by) abstract accounts of the nature of virtue' (1986, p. 253).

Like Jesus for Christians, the virtues these people embody are widely relevant and we are capable of imaginatively applying them by putting ourselves in the shoes of our ethotic heroine or hero: 'What would Juror 8 do?'; 'What would Oprah do?'; 'What would Blomkvist do?'; 'What would Ripley (from the *Alien* films) do?'; 'What would Grandma do?'

A common approach in marketing is to employ the ethotic qualities of celebrities to enhance the appeal of products. The idea is that the intelligence, sincerity, or good taste of people like George Clooney or Stephen Fry rub off on the product. The consumer makes an implicit association between the celebrity's assumed qualities and the brand, and thus to the extent the celebrity acts as a role model for the consumer, the brand becomes more appealing. (This process of persuasion is the opposite of certain forms of **guilt by association**, discussed below.)

A risk with ethotic authority, underlining the importance of the second critical question, is what is known to social psychologists as the '**halo effect**'. The name – credited to early twentieth-century psychologist Edward Thorndike – refers to our tendency to generalise from a person's known positive qualities to an assumption that they possess other positive qualities. An intelligent person is more likely (without any evidence to support this) to be judged a morally good person than a less intelligent person; someone attractive is assumed to be above average in intelligence, and so on. This effect is explained by Daniel Kahneman, who calls it 'exaggerated emotional coherence', as a best guess made on the basis of our feeling about someone. We meet Joan at a party (to use his example) and find her 'personable and easy to talk to'. In a later conversation the question is raised as to whether she is likely to contribute to charity.

> What do you know about Joan's generosity? The correct answer is that you know virtually nothing because there is little reason to believe that people who are agreeable in social situations are also generous contributors to charities. But you like Joan and you will retrieve the feeling of liking when you think of her. You also like generosity and generous people. By association, you are now disposed to believe that Joan is generous ... Real evidence of generosity is missing in the story of Joan, and the gap is filled by a guess that fits one's emotional response to her.
>
> (2012, p. 82)

It is easy to see how the halo effect makes us vulnerable to making and accepting weak ethotic arguments. Its reverse – sometimes known as the **horn effect** – is also recognised, and is relevant to the psychology behind the persuasiveness of ad hominem arguments.

DIRECT AD HOMINEM ARGUMENTS

In the **direct ad hominem argument** it is aspects of the general character of the person that are attacked in order to cast doubt on their view. It is a 'direct' attack because, unlike the other types of ad hominem argument, it is aimed squarely at personal characteristics rather than more behavioural features (what the person has done or said). However, it is also, confusingly, indirect because the causal relationship between the characteristic and what the person believes or states is more oblique.

The target of direct ad hominems can be failings in terms of critical thinking dispositions. In certain circumstances, a person's views can rightfully be taken less seriously if they are dishonest, dogmatic, arrogant, inflexible, cowardly, disrespectful, and so on. The implication is that possession of such flaws will compromise their knowledge or judgement, or their willingness or ability to communicate the truth.

In other situations a wider range of dispositions can be relevant to our decisions about what to do. For instance, the capacity for compassion is unlikely to figure in how we assess someone's views on astronomy, but it probably will figure in our decision on who to vote for as the leader of our country. Quite often though, direct ad hominem attacks are abusive and have a whiff of desperation about them. They are moves that we tend to resort to automatically when under pressure and when emotions are strong.

ETHOTIC ARGUMENTS, DISPOSITIONS AND CONSTRUCTIVE DIALOGUES

One form of direct ad hominem concerns the questioning of some-one's motivations for appealing to authority in their arguments. This is worth paying some attention to here because it focuses on the important critical thinking dispositions of a willingness to think independently, and to take responsibility for one's commitments. As mentioned, appeals to authority can indicate due modesty and recognition of the quite enormous limitations on what we can know first-hand, but they can also indicate a lack of persistence in securing first-hand understanding, or they can be used to shield us from the consequences of our actions. In dialogical terms the individual opts out and directs the questioner elsewhere.

In this chapter's epigraph we find the claim that George W. Bush placed responsibility for the invasion of Iraq in God's hands; the Yorkshire Ripper did the same with respect to his murders; more recently boxer Tyson Fury refers us to the Bible when asked to defend his offensive remarks on homosexuality, and of course the 'following orders' defence was used by Eichmann and other war criminals. In his experiments on obedience to authority, Milgram found that there as a 'reduction in strain' in subjects when it was acknowledged that the experimenter would take responsibility for the consequences of the procedure (2005, pp. 161–2).

A more comprehensive and quite vivid example of abrogation of responsibility is that of the cult member and other situations in which a particular expert or leader has, for some, an aura of untouchability. This is studied under 'charismatic leadership'. Charisma is a form of ethotic power that is notoriously hard to define but is associated with 'special gifts' and 'hypnotic' or 'magical' qualities to someone's personality that inspires love and makes people want to follow them (see Weber, 1978, pp. 242–3; Burns, 1978, Chapter 9).[14]

In all of these cases there is a comforting sense of security and certainty that comes with handing over responsibility to someone else. In some situations (such as small child to parent) there is nothing wrong with this, but in many others it can be a dangerous illusion. With people in positions of power considered as charismatic, there can often be a willingness to assume this responsibility, and history attests that the two motivations combined can have tragic consequences.

Determining when an appeal to authority is wrongly motivated is significantly context dependent, but the questions we need to ask are clear enough. First:

> Is this a situation in which the person should take direct responsibility for their belief (or action), or is it one in which it is reasonable for them to refer us to a particular authority?

If the answer is that responsibility should be taken, then the space is created for a further question along the lines of:

> What does the person stand to gain from shifting responsibility for a decision to an authority?

If there is a plausible case for there being a questionable motive for the appeal to authority, then we have the basis for a motivation-based direct ad hominem argument.

Direct ad hominem arguments and prejudice

However, direct ad hominem arguments also come with an increasingly familiar warning. Because they are in an important sense indirect, then they can carry all manner of prejudiced assumptions relating to people's credibility.[15] Racial and other stereotypes are fallacious direct ad hominem arguments. When hearing or making direct ad hominem arguments, we should pause to consider the critical question:

What is motivating this attack?

And this could of course be the start of a further direct ad hominem argument, generated by us (and potentially aimed at ourselves). To mitigate prejudice, dispositions associated with listening and respect are fundamental. Also important is a certain form of **meta-cognition** that is attuned to forms of bias that research in social cognition has revealed to be both far more prevalent than we would imagine, and often under our conscious radar (see Fiske, 2005 for a review).

TU QUOQUE ARGUMENTS

Wife: I really wish you'd be nicer to my family ...
Husband: Oh, and I suppose you're a model of tolerance towards mine all the time, are you?

This kind of interchange is remarkably common; instead of respond-ing directly to a criticism, we hit back with a version of the same criticism (*tu quoque* translates from Latin as 'you too'). **Tu quoque** is a peculiar piece of argumentation because, on the one hand, it's typi-cally highly reactive and defensive (and thus damaging to the progress of the dialogue), but on the other there is often something in it. That something is along the lines of 'don't judge me by standards you don't yourself uphold', or 'you are being a hypocrite'. You are saying that the person is not in a position to judge, and therefore providing a reason for why you should not have to respond to their accusation.

The strength of this type of argument is heavily dependent on a range of contextual factors concerning the relationship between the people involved, the type of behaviour under discussion, and the motivation of the person who uses it. For example, the parent who smokes twenty-a-day and who warns their teenage child against smoking arguably *is* in a position to judge. They wish they had not started as a teenager and now they cannot stop, and that is one of the reasons they are passing on the benefits of their experience to their child. If the teenager's response is along the lines of 'Who are you to talk?', the parent can punctuate a highly convincing answer with a hacking cough.

More considered *tu quoque* attacks are personal in quite a serious way because inconsistency, or hypocrisy, is seen as a significant character flaw. A strong *tu quoque* argument will not only damage the other arguer's position, it can have a broader impact on subsequent arguments they present by making them seem less trustworthy.

Evaluations of *tu quoque* arguments will place a lot of emphasis on the second critical question for ad hominem arguments:

Q2. Is this attack relevant to the claim that the argument makes?

Al Gore received criticism for flying the world to promote his eco film *An Inconvenient Truth* (2006), but this is not relevant to the conclusion that he is hypocritical or otherwise lacks credibility. Al Gore's choosing not to fly might have sent some kind of message, but not if his film is not making an impact on publics and policy-makers in the first place. Arguably it was his presence in these places (plus the commitment to the cause that his touring demonstrated) that made people pay attention.[16]

On the other hand, the Church of England criticising payday loan companies, while at the same time investing in one of them (Wonga) looks like a stronger *tu quoque* argument.[17] As does a recent attack of the Speaker of the House of Commons John Bercow for (among other things) spending £367 'taking a car to Luton [about 35 miles from central London] to deliver a speech on how MPs were restoring their reputation after the expenses scandal'.[18]

In the wife and husband dialogue in the epigraph, things are more complicated. It is possible that the husband's response is entirely defensive and that his counter-accusation is simply a means of deflecting the discussion away from the fact that he does indeed need to be nicer to his in-laws. It is also possible that, even if true of the husband, the wife's accusation is indeed mirrored by her own behaviour. Under these circumstances cool heads are needed (the very cool heads that ad hominem arguments tend not to encourage). Other things being equal, both parties should, ideally, reflect on their own behaviour and reach a joint conclusion that: (1) both need to improve in this way; and, importantly, (2) that one cannot reasonably expect the other to do this unless they do it themselves.

Underpinning this is the need for reciprocity in so many social encounters (see Chapter 1). Since we cannot expect perfection in our moral and social behaviour, our standards must, to a great extent, be relative to the norms that surround us. In other words, if our peers demand things of us we expect them to demand the same of themselves.

It is, however, this same rule of reciprocity that can cause a group (or couple) conspiracy of silence. In order not the provoke the rows and fallings-out that criticisms tend to generate, and in order to avoid the critical spotlight being turned in our direction, we can find ourselves not criticising others when we should be. In terms of personal development and group deliberations, *tu quoque* responses could have a detrimental long-term impact because people become unwilling to offer constructive feedback that would otherwise serve us, or the group, well. It is easy to imagine the role that this kind of response could play in groupthink; if a critical suggestion is met with the messenger being shot, fewer messengers will be turning up, a greater number of poor premises or arguments will go unchallenged, and the 'illusion of unanimity' will be strengthened.

GUILT BY ASSOCIATION

Guilt by association is a variation of ad hominem arguments in which an arguer's association with a person or organisation considered disreputable is transferred onto them. These arguments can be strong if the association in question has an actual and relevant bearing on the credibility of a person's position. This might be circumstantial (for example a football official who is on friendly terms with a number of club owners); direct (such as a male politician's membership of a club known to be misogynistic), or *tu quoque* guilt by association (a rebellious rocker who frequents royal garden parties and has friends in the Establishment).

An example of a fallacious guilt by association argument was the *Daily Mail*'s smear campaign against Ed Miliband (then leader of the UK Labour Party) based on his father's Marxism. Journalist Tim Stanley pointed out the absurdity of this, saying: 'The *Daily Mail* published a silly thesis (Ralph Miliband was a commie, so maybe Ed is too) under a daft headline ('The Man Who Hated Britain').[19]

More recently I've seen a placard in a demonstration against 'Obamacare' which read:

FIDEL CASTRO SAYS HE LIKES OBAMACARE. THE RIGHT DIRECTION FOR AMERICA?

The argument is flimsy and vague, but the negative association will be powerful for many Americans. In the 2015 UK General Election, Nigel Farage – leader of the right-wing UK Independence Party – was constantly being let down by his racially insensitive party members and supporters. The lowest point for Farage was when UKIP turned out to be the party of choice for one of the country's most hated individuals – child serial killer, Ian Brady.

During his election campaign in 2015, the candidate for the Labour leadership Jeremy Corbyn was accused of 'sharing a platform' with two Arab leaders who are anti-Semitic.[20] It is clear that Corbyn is not a racist, but whatever the intentions of this attack, what could stick to someone perceived by many as being quite far to the left like Corbyn is an aura of the more dangerous or unpleasant aspects of radical politics.

5.5 APPEALS TO REFERENT POWER, AND *AD POPULUM* ARGUMENTS

The influence on our beliefs or actions originating from the commitments and behaviour of people who we see as being 'like us' is called **referent power**. Peer pressure is an example, but so is any attempt to persuade us that involves reference to a group of people we identify with. It relies on what is termed our 'social identity', the aspects of who we take ourselves to be (including what gives us esteem) that derive from the groups that we belong to (Tajfel and Turner, 1986).

In argumentation, referent power falls under the broader heading of *ad populum* arguments, which are defined as arguments that appeal to the fact that a position is generally held to be true as a reason for accepting that it is true. In its simplest form it has this structure:

P1: Everyone (or a large majority of people) believes X.

P2: Whenever something is generally accepted as true there's a strong likelihood that it is true.

C: Therefore X is true (or X is plausible).

A variation that appeals to referent power is:

P1: Everyone (or a large majority of people) belonging to my referent group Y believes X about subject Z.

P2: Whenever something is generally accepted by my referent group Y about subject Z as true, there's a strong likelihood that it is true.

C: Therefore X is true (or X is plausible).

On the face of it, *ad populum* arguments are the antithesis of critical thinking; basing one's beliefs on second-hand evidence from a group of non-experts. However, they are not always poor arguments, as an analysis of the relevant critical questions will demonstrate. These critical questions are:

Q1: Is X, in fact, generally believed to be the case? [Acceptability]

Q2: If so, is X a domain of knowledge where popular belief is relevant to its truth? [Relevance]

Q3: If so, is the population whose beliefs are referred to the one with the appropriate knowledge of X? [Acceptability]

Q4: If so, is this group of people reliable? (For example, are there signs that the views of the group in question have been corrupted by processes like groupthink, or that they have reasons not to be truthful?) [Acceptability]

Q5: If so, is the conclusion reached on the basis of general belief appropriate (e.g. suitably cautious). [Sufficiency]

Q1 guards against a mistaken belief about what is common knowledge. It is the kind of error that can result from someone's confident (and potentially intimidating) claim that 'everybody knows that!' being accepted too readily. Asking a selection of one's friends and peers, checking with opinion polls, or simply pausing for reflection are ways to attain answers to this question.

Sometimes Q2 can generate a clear 'yes'; typically concerning aspects of life that most people who have been around for a while are in a position to know. One example is local knowledge: that Old Gregor at number 34 is a bit weird but essentially harmless; that the dog at the building supplies outlet's bark is indeed worse than its bite; that Morton's fish and chips are the best in town. Another is practice-based knowledge: gardeners knowing that grass benefits from being cut whereas weeds do not; comedians knowing that jokes about sex will go down well with most audiences, or football managers knowing that making a substitution as you are about to defend a corner kick is risky.

More often a carefully worded *ad populum* will give rise to a conclusion that is plausible, or at least indicates that a position is worthy of a closer look. Some will be variations of **position to know** arguments where we are told that something is true because everyone who has had certain experiences (relating to their job or other life experience) gets it. This can be the basis of an important argument when those who are not in that position tend not to agree.

Or we might just answer 'no' to Q2. Religious belief is an outstanding example; it could be true, but millions believing that it is does not count as a reason for a neutral to believe that it is. Also, in science there are numerous cases where what the public believes and what experts believe are clearly at odds. Climate change denial among the America Christian right is a specific and serious example, and the exposing of commonly held beliefs as myths is common in popular science forums.[21]

Overall we need to be aware that potentially momentous changes can occur in scientific or moral knowledge which contradict but fail to dislodge traditional beliefs. This inertia could be a simple matter of ignorance and the time it takes for knowledge to seep into a culture, but some beliefs remain common because they are comforting or otherwise useful.

Q3 is covered by previous analyses of position to know arguments. Q4 is directed at ideas like groupthink, but also covers dogmatic, lazy, fearful, antagonistic, or competitive group mind-sets that create dangerous biases and unreliable communication. The self-fulfilling deliberations that impede critical thinking in *Twelve Angry Men* serve as an example. We also need to be careful not to conflate witness testimony type cases with straightforward examples of *ad populum* position to know arguments, since immersion in situations can come with its own biases. We can have some sympathy for 'You weren't there, man!' or 'You can't handle the truth!' defences of dubious military practices, but they are not going to be the last word on the matter.

Twelve Angry Men is also helpful for illustrating the important difference between *ad populum* arguments that refer to actions and those that refer to beliefs. As discussed in Chapter 1, a bargaining tool to persuade the other jury members to talk about the case, Juror 8 proposes that if he cannot change their opinion after an hour of discussion, then he would change his vote to guilty. He is not suggesting that he will have changed his mind about the case, but is offering, rather, a practical solution. This is of course quite common; it is basic to democracies and, in general, to situations where going along with the majority – despite not agreeing with them – can be the best or right thing to do. Needless to say, these kinds of deliberation come with their own critical questions (for example, even in a democracy a case can be made for it not always being right to go along with majority decisions), but the main point here is that basing one's action on the popular view is very different from basing one's belief on it.

Some recent cases of social media-based 'mob pressure' or 'witch hunts' do, however, raise some intriguing questions concerning the power of *ad populums*. One high profile example is footballer and (at the time) convicted rapist Ched Evans, in whom several clubs were interested on his release from prison in 2014, but in each case the vigorous petitioning of fans led to the clubs deciding against this. Evans has always denied the charges, and at the time of writing he is yet to resume his professional career.

Another is the forced resignation of Nobel Laureate Sir Tim Hunt from his academic post at University College London, after making sexist comments (in the form of a joke) at a conference. UCL's decision is regarded as controversial, and some, including high profile astrophysicist and TV presenter Brian Cox, blame a 'trial by social media' for forcing their hand. Commenting on the story, an editorial in *The Guardian* concludes that:

> Twitter is loud, shouty and mainly male. It is rubbish at nuance, detail or ambivalence but it is perfect for rushing noisily to judgment, sometimes ...

in a downright threatening way. The experience of UCL is another warning that a Twitterstorm is a digital riot, and that is how it should be treated.[22]

The influence of social media in the Ched Evans case is clearer cut than with UCL and Tim Hunt, but if we assume that this medium is able to amplify what *appears to be* popular moral views in a way that has, or can have, this kind of impact, then the helpfulness of the critical questions in guiding our analysis of such situations is plain. The answer to each of them is not obvious and requires not only an investigation of the details of the case, but philosophical questioning about the appropriate role of popular opinion in the making of moral and political judgements.

REFERENT POWER: PSYCHOLOGY AND RHETORIC

As the discussion of **social proof** in Chapter 1 shows, appeals to popular beliefs and behaviours are known to be extremely persuasive; having an immediate and powerful effect across a wide range of situations. Schultz *et al.* (2007) measured the effects of social proof – and in particular referent power – on energy consumption by adding to the electricity bills of the residents of a particular street information which demonstrated their household consumption in comparison with their neighbours. This had an effect on electricity usage referred to as a 'rush to the middle'; those with higher than average bill consumed less, and those with lower consumed more.

This is further evidence for the power of social proof, but the aim of the study was to find a way to persuade people to use less energy, not bring everyone closer to the average. The solution was to add to this purely descriptive norm a moral norm, originally in the form of a smiley face for lower than average consumption and a sad face for above average. The effectiveness of the moral norm can seemingly be attributed to the broad legitimacy of environmental values (or at least of not being wasteful), but the adoption of this practice by a progressive company called Opower serves as an example of referent power. The moral (or 'injunctive') norm method works, but not always for customers with a non–progressive political leaning (Republican voters), some of whom *increased* their consumption. Unlike liberal customers, they will not identify with the overtly progressive approach of Opower and the kind of people who might aim to reduce consumption. But rather than this simply not affecting how much electricity they use, it could lead to a slight increase as an act of defiance.[23]

The general understanding among social psychologists is that we tend to rely on referent power in particular when we are unsure how to behave in a particular situation (see Chapter 1). A variation of the Milgram experiments involved three teachers (two stooges plus the subject). At different stages the stooges rebel, resulting in the obedience rates for the remaining (real) subject dropping dramatically (2005, pp. 117–22). Exactly what constitutes an acceptable level of energy to consume is a difficult question, and it makes sense that it falls under the kind of situation in which we turn to those who are 'like us' for a benchmark.

REFERENT POWER, DISPOSITIONS AND CONSTRUCTIVE DIALOGUES

The way we handle arguments from popular opinion or that carry referent power is, in part, a function of our courage and of our willingness to take responsibility for our commitments. Zachary Seech rightly emphasises the pressure that can come from *ad populum* arguments, not so much towards changing our minds, but to silencing us through fear of appearing stupid or out of touch:

> When someone says, 'Everyone knows that!' an implication seems to be that any person who doesn't possess this common information must be especially dense or poorly informed. In the company of peers or ... superiors, many people will relinquish [i.e. not defend rather than necessarily stop believing] even the most secure positions ... Other familiar phrases are ... 'No one seriously doubts that' or 'No one in his right mind could doubt that' or 'No educated person would doubt that'. The latter two are especially intimidating.
>
> (1993, p. 134)

Referent power implies the threat of some level of rejection by the group, and this can be more fearful than the consequences referred to in *ad baculum* arguments. One of Christopher Tindale's *ad populum* critical questions (that seems to combine Q1 and Q2, above) is:

'Is the ... belief or practice so widely known to be correct that the burden of proof would lie with anyone who questioned it?' (2007, p. 107). This underlines the dialogical implications of going against the grain. Like Juror 8, you are faced with a group of people (or a representative of that group) with nothing to prove, and who are more than likely annoyed that you *do* have something to prove. Like Socrates, you are regarded as an irritant.

On the other side of this, however, our critical thinking dispositions are also important for handling *ad populum* arguments that are personal in nature. There are ways in which other people can know us better than we know ourselves, and if we are to gain insight and improve ourselves, then it is important to be receptive to the, often painful, feedback that they can provide. While it can sometimes be right to be sceptical of isolated comments about our character or behaviour, to remain dismissive of the possibility that we are indeed arrogant, self-centred, fickle, smelly (or whatever the criticism might be) in the face of unanimous agreement among disparate friends, relatives, colleagues, and so on tends to indicate a failing of dispositions such as courage, modesty or open-mindedness.

FURTHER READING

As with other chapters, use the in-text references as a guide to further reading on specific aspects of this chapter. A couple of further recommendations are Douglas Walton's book *Ad Hominem Arguments* (2009), and for a concise and illuminating discussion of *ad baculum* arguments, see J. Woods (1995) 'Appeal to force'.

EXERCISES

1. Assess the following *tu quoque* argument (from Roger Scruton, *On Hunting* (1999), pp. 139–40) by applying the *ad hominem* critical questions to it.

   It puzzles me that [those who oppose fox-hunting] should have singled out an activity in which animals and humans, working in happy companionship, are fully and magnificently alive, and in which no suffering occurs that is not part of nature's due. Do the protestors trouble themselves, I wonder, over the factory farms, where pigs and chickens are grown like vegetables for the sake of their meat? One glance into these fermenting seas of misery would cure people of the illusion that they live on morally respectable terms with the rest of nature. ... Many who shout and scream at the hunt happily eat the tortured limbs of battery chickens. ... [Factory farmed pigs] are served in the restaurant of the House of Commons. And not one of those members who parade their tender conscience over fox-hunting has protested over the crime.

2. Annie is a line manager in an organisation with direct responsibility for about 20 staff. Although her team works relatively well, she feels that there is more she could do to improve its performance. She feels that the management training she has so far received is not enough to enable this improvement, so she is looking to learn more. Her own line manager is in the same situation and regards herself as largely self-taught. There are endless popular books on how to be a good (or 'great' or 'extraordinary') manager, but these tend to advocate a particular approach, she suspects that many are quite shallow, and how is she to know which of these she should be consulting? There are also a vast range of academic textbooks on the subject, but which should she choose? In her experience, different leadership styles and techniques will be effective in different situations (different types of organisation, different types of employees, and different types of leaders/managers etc.) so any answers she finds will need to involve decisions made by her on what methods to use in her particular context. This then suggests that she will need to find out as much as possible to allow her to make these decisions, but how does she go about this? With work and family commitments she does not have time to study for a part-time management degree, or to read immense amounts of academic literature, but without this depth of learning, she realises that she will be quite heavily reliant upon the authority of a range of authors and colleagues to steer her in the right direction.

Using some of the ideas and critical questions explored in this chapter, make some recommendations about how Annie should approach this problem.

NOTES

1 A modern advocate of this, drawing on Aristotle's and Seneca's ideas on virtues and rhetoric, is Alan Brinton, see, for example, Brinton (1986).

2 For example, Johnson and Blair (2006, pp. 168–72) have four; Douglas Walton (2006, p. 88) has six, and Christopher Tindale (2007, pp. 134–43) has seven.

3 *The Life Scientific*, BBC Radio 4, 28 July 2015.

4 Group selection is the idea that evolution works, at least in part, at the level of the adaptive fitness of groups rather than genes. Thus a group in which individuals are more cooperative and willing to self-sacrifice for the sake of the collective will fare better than one in which individuals are more selfish. The selfish gene theory, on the other hand, states that cooperative tendencies (reciprocal and kin altruism) are only selected to the extent that they benefit the individual and those who share their genes.

5 E. Pennisi (2011) 'Researchers challenge E.O. Wilson over evolutionary theory'. Available at: http://news.sciencemag.org/2011/03/researchers-challenge-e.-o.-wilson-over-evolutionary-theory

6 My analysis of these issues has been significantly influenced by Heather Battaly's article 'Attacking character' (2010).

7 *The Guardian*, 15 August 2015, p. 32, and available at: www.theguardian.com/politics/2015/aug/14/the-labour-party-stands-at-a-crossroads.

8 You know who you are!

9 See R. Mason (2014) 'Fiona Woolf resigns as chair of government's child abuse inquiry'. Available at: www.theguardian.com/politics/2014/oct/31/fiona-woolf-resigns-chairman-child-abuse-inquiry. (For other reasons, Lowell resigned (or was sacked) in 2016.)

10 Adapted from Walton (2006, p. 123) and Tindale (2007, p. 89).

11 Described and analysed in Hannah Arendt's book *Eichmann in Jerusalem: A Report into the Banality of Evil* (Harmondsworth: Penguin, 1965).

12 For an insightful discussion of this, and *ad baculum* arguments in general, see Woods (1995).

13 It should also be noted though that an alternative to this bargaining approach exists – 'principled negotiation' (Fisher and Ury, 1991). In this model the attempt to understand the other side's core commitments in order to find creative solutions is promoted in place of a more superficial haggling over positions.

14 For two excellent example of charismatic leadership (as well as a range of rhetorical techniques), see the character Andreas Wolf in Jonathan Franzen's novel *Purity* (London: Fourth Estate, 2015, p. 262), and Forest Whitaker's portrayal of Idi Amin in the film *The Last King of Scotland* (Kevin MacDonald, 2007), in particular the section where Amin is persuading the young Scottish doctor to be his personal physician (between approx. 24 and 36 minutes).

15 A very good book devoted to this subject is Miranda Fricker's *Epistemic Injustice* (Oxford: Oxford University Press, 2007).

16 See A. Hoffman (2011) 'Talking past each other? Cultural framing of skeptical and convinced logics in the climate change debate', *Organization & Environment*, 24(1), 3–33.

17 See http://uk.reuters.com/article/2013/07/25/uk-britain-church-lenders-idUKBRE96O0CG20130725.

18 *The Guardian*, 25 July 2015.

19 T. Stanley (2013). Blog. Available at: http://blogs.telegraph.co.uk/news/tim-stanley/100240034/mehdi-hasan-the-daily-mail-ralph-miliband-and-the-scary-moral-hypocrisy-of-the-left/

20 H. Rifkind (2015) 'Jeremy Corbyn is not an anti-Semite but he is reaping what he sowed'. Blog. Available at: http://blogs.spectator.co.uk/coffeehouse/2015/08/jeremy-corbyn-is-not-an-anti-semite-but-he-is-reaping-what-he-sowed/

21 For example, Discovery Channel's *Mythbusters*, and the *Fortean Times* column 'Mythconceptions'.

22 *The Guardian* view on the Tim Hunt affair: an explosive combination of science, sexism and social media (2015). Editorial. Available at: www.theguardian.com/commentisfree/2015/jun/30/the-guardian-view-on-the-tim-hunt-affair-an-explosive-combination-of-science-sexism-and-social-media

23 See O. Payne, *Inspiring Sustainable Behaviour* (London: Earthscan, 2012), pp. 97–9.

6

CAUSAL ARGUMENTS, GENERALISATIONS, ARGUMENTS FROM CONSEQUENCES AND SLIPPERY SLOPE ARGUMENTS

Since we are all such absolutists by instinct, what in our quality as students of philosophy ought we to do about this fact? Shall we espouse and endorse it? Or shall we treat it as a weakness of our nature from which we must free ourselves if we can? I sincerely believe that the latter course is the only one we can follow as reflective men.

(William James, 'The will to believe', 1967)

Generalisations ... never right, always fun.

(Henry Rollins, *Talk is Cheap*, vol. 3)

When decisions are made, they are often justified in term of the consequences they will bring about: making these changes to the criminal justice system will decrease reoffending, making these cuts to renewable energy subsidies will help reduce the budget deficit, introducing goal-line technology in football will not impede the flow of the game, eating less processed meat will make us healthier, and so on. But we of course – and those we are trying to convince – need to have reasons for believing these consequences will occur. Sometimes these reasons take the form of arguing for the causal relationship between various phenomena, and this involves two kinds of reasoning:

1. Establishing the likely causes of events that have happened in the past.
2. Generalising from those events to future events, or to aspects of the world that have not been directly observed or studied.

So, in deliberations about policies or everyday courses of action consequences, causes and **generalisations** are intimately linked. In this chapter we will investigate each of these, beginning with causal arguments and ending with a common, but usually problematic, type of reasoning from consequences called the **slippery slope argument**. Establishing cause and effect is basic to scientific and historical research and thus knowledge of the methods these disciplines employ, and analyses of the strengths and weakness of these methods, are fundamental to the students' and practitioners' ability to think critically in these areas. Critical thinking as a subject will explore the basic forms of this kind of reasoning, and sometimes discuss its association with the philosophy of science (see the end of this chapter for recommended reading along these lines). A philosophical or critical thinking perspective seeks to do more than provide a general introduction to scientific and academic methods though. By teaching us (or reminding us) about some fundamental features and assumptions, it aims to refresh our thinking and make us more open-minded in our approach to knowledge. In accordance with the themes of this book there is particular emphasis on the kinds of errors we tend make when reasoning about causes, generalisations and consequences, and their relationship to rhetoric, psychology and dialogues. From these insights we can hopefully gain a better reflective understanding of ourselves as deliberators and the dispositions that can assist or impede these aspects of critical thinking.

6.1 CAUSAL ARGUMENTS AND CAUSAL FALLACIES

When I bought my first MP3 player and read the instructions for turning it on, it said: 'Hold down the button for 2–3 seconds and it will switch on.' I did this, but nothing happened for about 6 or 7 seconds. Because I've not always had the best experiences with technology I assumed that (typically) my MP3 player was a bit slow. It otherwise worked fine though, so this was not much of a problem, and I would learn to love it anyway. I just developed the habit of holding the button down for this length of time. Several months later I was distracted by something while going through this ritual and let go after a couple of seconds. When I looked back at the screen a few seconds later I was surprised to see that it was on. The penny dropped. I had been assuming that turning it on meant that something needed to appear on the screen, but clearly that is not the case; holding down the button for 2–3 seconds is indeed enough to activate it, but nothing actually appears on the screen until after 6 or 7 seconds.

Apart from a need to reassess my relationship with technology, what this illustrates is how the quick assumptions we make about cause and effect can be both erroneous and habit-forming. Establishing the cause of something can be very difficult indeed, and of course attempts to do this are basic to the theoretical work of the natural and social scientific disciplines and to the work of historians. Each discipline will have distinctive criteria for establishing the strength of causal claims, and they will share some general principles as well.

In the natural sciences a causally closed system is assumed in which all phenomena adhere to the physical principles governing the behaviour of matter. In the social sciences, explanations range from the physical to the cultural and are entwined with philosophical debates about the nature of the mind's relationship with the brain and the meaning and existence of free will. How, for example, can a thought – conceived of as a non-physical thing – cause changes to the physical world? If the mind is essentially a physical thing, and thus part of a chain of cause and effect, is free will possible? How are reasons for acting in certain ways different in kind from the mechanical causes of natural phenomena?

These are metaphysical questions, but more closely associated with critical thinking are epistemological puzzles. As David Hume ([1748] 2008) pointed out, we do not directly observe the cause of an event; the process by which X brings about Y. We observe that my golf club making contact with the ball is perfectly correlated with the ball moving (even if not always the distance and direction I want it to go), but the physical laws that we assume determine this are inferred rather than evident to the senses. Kant ([1781] 1929) argued that the very possibility of having experiences requires certain necessary conditions, including causality, but that the actual basis of our experience of causation is itself unknowable.

It is this limitation on our knowledge, combined with the complexity of the world, and combined with what Kahneman (2012, pp. 74–8) suggests is an innate tendency to 'see' causes where they do not exist, that makes causal reasoning particularly vulnerable to error. The causes of phenomena like climate change, educational attainment, and criminal behaviour; or of particular events like the Reformation, the American Civil War, and the fall of apartheid in South Africa are complex, intertwined and hard to establish with certainty. As we have seen, we have a tendency to jump to conclusions about straightforward cases of cause and effect, and with complex phenomena an added problem is of over-simplifying our explanations.

The specialisation of academics can present us with a variation of this problem, and increasingly collaboration between disciplines to improve accuracy in establishing causes is encouraged. For example, the current obesity epidemic in parts of the developed world falls into the domains of (among others) health and nutrition, sociology, politics, psychology and economics. Similarly, practitioners from a range of professions (social work, medicine, mental health, education) will work together to implement solutions for child abuse prevention, community and clinical care for people with mental health problems, or managing end of life care.

Everyday reasoning presents similar challenges. What caused Aunt Eliza to divorce Uncle Vance? Were they 'simply' growing apart? Was it the influence of her sister-in-law? Was she never truly able to forgive him for what happened in Brussels? Was it all of these things combined, or some of them, or something else entirely? This is clearly not a matter for a research project or a team of practitioners, but concerned friends and family will often be mulling over causal explanations and presenting arguments to one another in an analogous fashion.

It is outside the scope of this book to delve further into the subtleties of the causal explanations that different situations present or that different disciplines trade in. It is, however, important to survey some general principles of causal reasoning. The aim here is to seek to clarify these through the description and analyses of causal reasoning errors. After this, I will explore the dispositions and psychological vulnerabilities that help explain what makes these errors so prevalent.

An initial distinction to make is between cases in which we have:

1. Multiple instances of one event being correlated with another (such as tea being more flavoursome and it being made with near-boiling water rather than slightly cooler water; or a patient's belief in the effectiveness of a drug and an increase in the speed of their recovery). In such cases natural and social scientific methods can usually be employed to observe or recreate conditions in which the cause and effect underlying the correlation can be adequately demonstrated.

2. Unusual or highly distinctive cases where causation needs to be argued for more indirectly (such as world wars, or the extinction of dinosaurs). In particular instances like these, we can normally still find historical precedents or comparisons with subsequent events (for example, the causes of the 2008 financial crisis shared some features with the 1929 crash, and the causes and consequences of the 13 November 2015 shootings in Paris are not entirely dissimilar to other terrorist attacks), and thus we find that inductive arguments from analogy (see Chapter 7) are often employed to help establish the causes.

With this distinction in mind we can formulate the general structure of causal arguments:

P1: (Either through direct observation or analogy we have confidence that) X is correlated with Y.

P2: The ways in which a causal relationship can be confused with a mere correlation have been acknowledged and discounted to an extent that is reasonable through appropriate methods.

C: Therefore it is probable that X causes/caused Y.

CAUSAL FALLACIES

When attempting to establish the cause of a happening, we can be presented with two broad kinds of relationship between it and its possible causes. On the one hand, it can be clearly preceded by an event that could plausibly cause it to happen (and the more times we observe this temporal sequence, the greater the chance of the prior event having something to do with the event's causation). On the other hand, we may be looking at two or more happenings that occurred around the same time, but with no clear temporal ordering.

In both cases, causality will not be known without further investigation, but where there is a clear temporal relationship, the specific fallacy known as *post hoc ergo propter hoc* (or *post hoc* for short) is a risk. This Latin term mean 'after this, therefore that because of this', and captures the assumption that because one event has followed another, then the second event has been caused by the first.

Without a clear sequence of events the direction of causality (if indeed there is a causal relation at all) can also be questioned. I find myself in a grumpy mood and blame the kids' bad behaviour, but can I be sure that it was their bad behaviour that caused my grumpy mood rather than my grumpy mood that caused their bad behaviour? To further complicate things, once initiated the causal link can work in both directions in a mutually reinforcing fashion. But what if the two things are entirely unrelated and I'm being too quick or too lazy in my hypothesising? If I reflect, then perhaps it was Uncle Vance's email about the divorce that put me in a bad mood, and come to think of it, the kids were already behaving poorly when I arrived home from work.

The main fallacies associated with causal reasoning fall under the headings of coincidence, direction of cause, shared cause, multiple cause, placebo effect, and mistaking cause for correlation (the Sod's law fallacy). These apply to either one or both of the types of correlation outlined in the previous two paragraphs.

COINCIDENCE

If two events regularly occur together but are not causally related, the chances are that they have a shared cause (see below). With singular or unusual events, there is a strong possibility of mistaking mere coincidence for cause. My belief about my MP3 on button is an example of this, as are many superstitions. Every so often in the news we hear about 'super-centenarians'; people who have lived past 110. 'What is their secret?' is often asked, but no one knows and the replies are clear cases of coincidences pretending to be causes. In a brief article on the subject in the *Fortean Times* various super-centenarians told us their secrets:[1] Besse Cooper (116 years) said, 'I mind my own business and I don't eat junk food'; ex-postman Jiroemon Kimura (also 116) put it down to 'the sun', but on other occasions said it was caused by his diet (e.g. steamed fish), exercise, and early rising. Magomed Labazanov (122) claimed it was 'abstaining from alcohol, tobacco and women'. Maybe some of these can contribute to a given individual living past 110, but even if they do it would be prohibitively difficult to test these causal beliefs.

At the other end of life, our youngest child was a week overdue so we found ourselves being fed, and occasionally looking for, advice on how to induce labour: raspberry leaf tea, bumpy rides, pineapple, walks, sex, curry. Having no other pressing engagements my wife (and I) spent an afternoon doing lots of these things, and the next day she went into labour – AMAZING! Like the long-livers, these recommendations are largely anecdotal; *no one knows*.

One other example is more serious because it identifies a particular type of mistake made in formal scientific reasoning. Below we'll look at the placebo effect as the basis of a discrete category of causal reasoning error, but it's also possible to infer a **placebo effect** where none exists. The phenomenon known as **regression to the mean** predicts that an extreme measurement for any phenomenon will typically be followed by a less extreme one. As hard-to-please cricket pundit Geoffrey Boycott was keen to point out, getting too excited about young England batsman Ben Stokes' record-breaking 258 runs in the Second Test against South Africa in January 2016 is premature; he has to consistently score high to really prove his self. In terms of everyday causal reasoning, regression to the mean is particularly problematic when trying to understand pain and other symptoms. These tend to occur in cycles – severe → less severe → severe, and so on – and there's a reasonable chance that people will seek medical intervention when their symptoms are at, or close to, their worst. If pain relief or other medication is then supplied, this will typically correlate with a reduction in symptoms, and consequently in the belief that it was the medication that caused this reduction. For this reason clinical trials need to control for, not just the placebo effect, but for regression to the mean as well.

DIRECTION OF CAUSE

As indicated, correlated events observed on repeated occasions are likely to be linked in some respect, and the mistake is to jump to unwarranted conclusions about the nature of this link. However plausible a causal connection seems, it is worth reversing it to see if there is another possibility. In fact, the more plausible the direction of cause seems, the more revelatory a reversal can be. Group psychotherapist Irvin Yalom (1980, p. 394) describes the case of Eve, who was reluctant to fully engage with the other members of the group, or to discuss herself except in the vaguest of terms. Finally she was confronted with the negative effect this was having on the others, and Yalom encouraged her to take more of a risk by making more honest and direct comments. At this point she revealed that she was an alcoholic, and said that the shame that this led her to feel was the reason for keeping herself hidden. Yalom, however, proceeded to reverse her causal argument, suggesting, 'She did not hide herself because she drank, she drank because she hid herself.' Yalom's theory about Eve was that her underlying loneliness, created by an inability or unwillingness to connect with others, caused her drinking. Primarily, the drink was a means of coping with her isolation, rather than her isolation resulting from the shame associated with her drinking.

SHARED CAUSE

A third type of mistake in causal reasoning is to overlook a cause that is shared by the correlated events. If religious people are happier on average than non-religious people, this could be because religion leads to greater happiness, but it could also be that a third variable – for example, religious families being more stable – results in both the happiness and the religious commitment.

In a contrasting example some recent research into the relationship between teenage goths and mental illness[2] was widely reported in the news as 'Goths three times more likely to suffer depression or self-harm.' Although this headline does not necessarily state that being a goth causes or contributes to depression, this is what is implied (presumably because it makes for a better story). Read on and the issue of direction of cause is usually mentioned in press coverage, and the article itself, though very cautious about causation, suggests that identifying with the goth sub-culture does increase vulnerability to depression and self-harm (rather than a reversal in which mental health issues make it more likely that a person identifies as a goth). However, the authors readily acknowledge that they are not in a position to rule this out and, importantly, nor do they rule out **shared causes** such as 'stigma and social ostracism' (a key aspect of the article that was sometimes overlooked in the news). In other words, rather than 'peer contagion' (hanging out with other goths) being the sole, or even contributing, cause of these mental disorders, both the disorders and the goth identification could have a shared cause in underlying conditions such as social exclusion and bullying.

The visibility of the variables in question – in this case mental disorders and being a goth – and the simplicity of certain causal explanations, perhaps combined with certain stereotypes, is prime **System 1 candy**. Shared causes are far less obvious and require more imaginative hypothesising, and thus we are vulnerable to overlooking them.

MULTIPLE CAUSES

System 1's fondness for jumping to conclusions is abetted by a dislike of complexity. What has been called the 'narrative fallacy' (see below) is explained by a desire for coherence in our understanding of the world, and this is achieved by ignoring gaps in our knowledge. Unfortunately few interesting things have simple causal stories, and so critical thinking must alert us to the fallacy of **over-simplification of causes**. For example, there is a widely held belief that it was the Great Fire of London in 1666 that ended the bubonic plague epidemic in England that had started the previous year. Current thinking on the issue, although still not settled, is that the full picture is more complicated. Although the fire did kill many of the black rats that carried the plague fleas, the plague was on its way out anyway. Theories suggest that this was partly because black rats were being displaced by the relatively non-plague-transmitting brown rat, and that the cold weather that autumn (the fire happened in September) killed off the remaining fleas.

Once again the availability of the fire and the plague, and the rough plausibility of one destroying the other, is no doubt at least partly responsible for the myth's perpetuation. But whether or not that is the case, the attraction of simple causal stories is again demonstrated. Further examples include the cause of the American Civil War (which was not just about slavery), and it is interesting to note that many researchers into environmental communication and behaviour change cite the inherent complexity of the causes and effects of climate change as a reason why the public often fail to engage with the issue.[3]

THE PLACEBO EFFECT

The **placebo effect** can be defined as someone's expectation that an intervention (such as a drug) for a certain condition will work causes the condition to improve, rather than the intervention itself being the cause of the improvement.

Mistaking a placebo's effect for the intervention's effect forms a separate category of causal reasoning error because it is not a coincidence, nor a mistake in the direction of cause, nor an overlooking of a shared cause, and nor does it have to be part of a multiple cause. Instead the cause is very much connected with the mistaken cause, but in a way that is peculiarly indirect. I say 'peculiarly' because the actual cause (the patient's expectation) is of a different order to the supposed cause (a directly physiological one). With non-peculiar cases of causation, an indirect cause is typically part of a chain of cause and effect, and the error would be to miss a link in the chain, but overlooking a placebo effect is to overlook a different chain altogether that has its own beginning in the patient's psychology.

In medicine, the placebo effect is a well-recognised (if not well-understood) phenomenon that clinical trials need to be conscious of in their design. For example, if half the patients in a trial are taking a new drug and half the same drug as before, although all participants will be told they taking part in a trial, it is crucial not to tell them which group they will be in.

It is also important that trials are 'double-blind', which means that not only are the participants unaware of whether they are in the intervention or placebo group, the experimenters are also unaware of who's who. The reasons for this are that:

- This knowledge can unconsciously bias the way experimenters observe and interpret results.
- Experimenters' expectations can be communicated unknowingly to participants, which can then influence their experiences and behaviour.

This latter phenomenon is known as a 'self-fulfilling prophecy', which itself shares features with the placebo effect. Examples of this are the 'pygmalion effect' and its opposite, the 'golem effect'. In their book *Pygmalion in the Classroom* ([1968] 2003) Robert Rosenthal and Lenore Jacobson demonstrated how teachers' expectations about children's abilities would unconsciously affect these children's educational attainment. Take two groups of school pupils of equal ability, tell one teacher that their group is predicted (by a fictitious test) to make an intellectual 'spurt'; tell the other teacher nothing, and at the end of a school year the performance of the first group will tend to be significantly better than the control. One suggested reason for this is that teachers with high expectations are more likely to praise the effort children put into their work, reinforcing the belief that effort pays off, and thus encouraging persistence. In contrast, teachers with lower expectations focus more on correcting negative elements of pupils' work. The absence of feedback about effort leads to these students attributing success and failure to ability rather than effort, thus discouraging persistence (Cooper, 1979).

What overlooking the placebo effect and overlooking self-fulfilling prophecies share is a failure to account for the psychological influence of actors within particular contexts. As a culture we are reasonably familiar with these phenomena now, but we can nevertheless be surprised by the potency of unconscious processes in affecting physical and social change. For this reason, and perhaps because of their relative invisibility, they are easy to overlook or dismiss.

MISTAKING CAUSE FOR CORRELATION (SOD'S LAW FALLACY)

We are often motivated to jump to conclusions and affirm causal relationships between phenomena without sufficient reasoning or evidence. However, we can also be motivated to do the reverse and **mistake cause for correlation**. This could take the form of a rationalisation in a situation where we want to avoid having to take responsibility. For instance: 'When I drove at 50 in a 30 mph zone, *that's* when I ran over a dog. Sod's law I suppose.' Sod's law means that things tend to go wrong at the most inconvenient time, and is essentially about bad luck. It's Sod's law that my boiler breaks down the very month that my car and house insurance are due for renewal, and all those things in Alanis Morissette's song *Ironic* are examples of Sod's law (rather than being ironic). In the driving example, it's not Sod's law that you ran someone's dog down, it was because you were driving too fast and could not stop in time. To make yourself feel better, you infer an unfortunate coincidence of events rather than accepting a causal relationship between your speed and the accident occurring.

A somewhat different set of motivations lie behind this next example. In October 2015, the singer and activist Charlotte Church appeared on the live UK political debate show *Question Time*, and among other things suggested that climate change was partially responsible for the Syrian crisis. A few days later *The Sun* (the UK's best-selling tabloid newspaper) found this hilarious, mocking the statement under the sub-header, 'Charlotte on … Syria'. On the face of it, this does seem far-fetched, and coming from someone perceived as a political non-expert, it can easily be portrayed as silly or naïve. However, she was referring to a serious piece of research that indicated a plausible connection between these things. It is known as the 'food shock' argument and connects a food shock in 2011 (extreme weather such as droughts leading to globally significant food shortages which have a disproportionate effect on poorer places, especially those reliant on imports), to civil unrest in the Middle East and the Arab Spring. This is then causally connected with the rise of IS and the devastating effects of the Syrian civil war. 'In a sense what we're living with IS today came out of a spark that came from food price rises,' says Professor Tim Benton of the UK Global Food Security

Program and the University of Leeds. The link to climate change is that it is making food shocks far more frequent than they were (a one-in-one-hundred-year event to a one-in-thirty-year phenomenon, and potentially a seven-in-ten-year phenomenon in 2070), and perhaps more to the point in terms of Church's message, this kind of humanitarian disaster serves as a synecdoche (meaning a small part of something representing the whole) for the kinds of impacts climate change will have.[4]

CRITICAL QUESTIONS FOR CAUSAL ARGUMENTS

The critical questions that can be applied to causal arguments correspond to the headings above:

Q1: Has a correlation been identified? [Acceptability]
Q2: If so, how convincing is the causal reasoning that attempts to explain the phenomenon in question? [Sufficiency]

This second critical question can then be answered in accordance with the headings above:

Can the correlation be explained by coincidence?
Can the causal relationship be reversed?
Can the correlation be explained by a shared cause?
Have multiple causes been overlooked?
Can the correlation be explained by psychological phenomena such as the placebo effect or a self-fulfilling prophecy?
Are there reasons for thinking that the possibility of a causal relationship (rather than a mere correlation) has been dismissed too quickly or for the wrong reasons?

CAUSAL ARGUMENTS: PSYCHOLOGY AND RHETORIC

Errors in causal reasoning are exacerbated by several features of our psychology:

• We like to have explanations rather than remaining uncertain about why things happen.

- The explanations we come up with, or more readily believe, will typically be consistent with our present assumptions about how the world is.
- As we have seen, seeking coherence is a fundamental motivator of **System 1 thinking**, making it all the more likely that we will jump to roughly coherent, but incorrect conclusions.

When this year's Halloween pumpkin began to rot, the first thing that happened was the jaw collapsed, closing up the mouth and making it appear more round again. My 4-year-old reasoned that it 'wants to be a pumpkin again', i.e. rejecting the grotesque face I'd carved. And like many kids of his age he has surmised that the clouds rain in order to water the plants. The need for causal explanations is evidenced by kids' constant 'why' questions, but abstract scientific reasoning is not available to their cognition, in which case they attempt to make sense of the world in accordance with what they do understand − conscious intentions.

Two areas of research that make particularly interesting contributions to our understanding of causal reasoning errors are the psychology of superstition, and what's been termed the **narrative fallacy**.

SUPERSTITION

In his investigations in to trial and error learning ('operant conditioning') in rats and pigeons, behavioural psychologist B.F. Skinner conditioned superstitious behaviour. Most of Skinner's experiments investigated animal learning in situations in which there is a causal relation between behaviour and a reward; a pigeon must learn to peck a button when a light comes on in order to receive food, for example. In his studies of superstition, however, this causal connection was absent. Food was presented to the (hungry) pigeons at regular intervals, and nothing the birds did could alter this. Despite this it was observed that in most cases an action randomly performed just prior to the food arriving would then be repeated. If the repetition coincided with the next scheduled delivery of food, then that behaviour − turning around in a certain direction, a 'pendulum motion of the head and body', for instance − would be learned.[5]

Correlation is confused with cause, and the pigeons' behaviours have the appearance of a ritual.

In the pigeon's case, it cannot fathom the underlying causal features of the situation, but as a species humans have, as we know, become increasingly good at this. Nevertheless we are extremely superstitious, suggesting an adaptive advantage to being sensitive to correlations, which in turn causes a negative emotional response to the interruption of routines. System 2 knows that the colour of your socks has no effect on how well you will perform in the exam, but this will not make System 1's anxiety at the prospect of wearing blue rather than black go away without a fight.

In his book, *Caveman Logic* (2009), Hank Davis examines the widespread nature of superstitious beliefs and behaviours, and his evolutionary explanation is that interpreting causality on the basis of too little evidence had greater survival prospects than its reverse (i.e. being overly conservative in such judgements). Why is this? One answer is simply the value of heuristics as discussed in Chapter 1; inheriting and being disposed to learn a range of intellectual short-cuts rather than a bias towards the slow analysis of causal relationships seems to have been more adaptively advantageous for our ancestors. Another answer – one that is directly pertinent to superstition – is that feeling in control of situations that we are in fact not in control of is beneficial to us. Several reasons have been suggested for why this is, including the idea that the confidence this inspires, although resulting in some mistakes, also has beneficial side-effects. One of these is being motivated to put more effort into our endeavours, so that when we can in fact influence outcomes, those outcomes are all the more impressive.

THE NARRATIVE FALLACY

The coherence of a causal explanation – for example, that it is consistent with known truths – is a necessary but far from sufficient condition for the truth of that explanation. It is easy to concoct multiple alternative explanations for a phenomenon but the difficult part is establishing which, if any, of these is true. Here again we encounter our dislike of uncertainty, and our resulting tendency to jump to unwarranted conclusions.

The narrative fallacy is a term coined by risk scholar Nassim Taleb in his book *The Black Swan* (2007). It refers to our attraction to, and confidence in, coherent but simple explanations at the expense of an appreciation of complex and unknown factors. Our desire to make sense of the world rather than acknowledge the limitations of our understanding leads us to invent (or readily accept), and then act upon, straightforward, but inaccurate, causal stories.

One of Taleb's examples is especially revealing of the entrenched and automatic nature of this way of thinking. After hearing Taleb speak at a conference, a fellow academic congratulates him on his theory (as presented in an earlier book) but also reveals his frustration because he had been planning to write a book on the same subject. He then proceeds to hypothesise that Taleb would not have had the idea had he been brought up in a Protestant country where outcomes are so firmly linked to individual efforts rather than luck and circumstance. According to Taleb's theory, of course, there will be a multiplicity of causes of how he came by this theory and of its subsequent success, many of them unknown. This learned admirer, however, manages to reduce this to a simple narrative, and therefore commit the very fallacy he is discussing. If this is not ironic enough, for a short while Taleb finds himself actually agreeing with him (ibid., p. 63).

CAUSAL ARGUMENTS, DISPOSITIONS AND CONSTRUCTIVE DIALOGUES

The narrative fallacy provides psychological insight into all of the causal fallacies explored in this chapter, which share two essential features: seeing causes where they do not exist, and overlooking complexity. For the most part we like to be able to control or at least predict our environments, but there are an awful lot of things that affect us that are unknown. Combine this state of affairs with our deep-seated tendency to see causal connections where they do not exist, or to overlook complexity, and you can see how vulnerable we are to false claims about how buying this product, performing this behaviour, or voting for this party, will make us happier. To protect ourselves, we need to do the following:

- work towards greater clarity about what we can and cannot know, control or predict;
- develop meta-cognitive awareness of the conflict between *how things are* in terms of what we can control and predict, and how we'd *like them to be*;
- develop meta-cognitive awareness of our proneness to superstition and the narrative fallacy.

We need to learn to tolerate uncertainty and be more like Juror 8 in *Twelve Angry Men* (see Chapter 2). The illusion of control, like other self-serving biases, is in opposition to modesty, understood as a realistic perception of our attributes and abilities. From a dialogical perspective, encountering over-confidence in others can be demotivating and lead to antagonism. Moreover, jumping to conclusions has an unfortunate self-fulfilling tendency. The principle of **commitment and consistency** (see Chapter 1) predicts that once we have taken a position (such as 'the defendant is guilty'), especially where this is made public, it is hard to go back on. Being consistent is very important, implying as it does dispositions such as wisdom, trustworthiness and not being unduly influenced by peer pressure. If a conclusion is prematurely declared, therefore, retracting it this can come at a cost. If this cost is (consciously or unconsciously) seen as too high, then (consciously or unconsciously) we may choose to dig in rather than go where the evidence should be taking us.

Dialogues will often be more productive if firm conclusions are avoided too early on. It is far better to declare oneself as currently agnostic until the issue has been further discussed, or to qualify one's position so that a change of mind does not lead to embarrassment (or worse): 'I'm inclined to this view on the matter, but this isn't a firm conviction and I'm open to being persuaded otherwise'; or 'I think this is probably true, but I'm not entirely sure and would like to know more before reaching a conclusion.'

6.2 GENERALISATIONS

Causal arguments are often **generalisations**, but not all generalisations are causal arguments. Another type involves arguing from qualities that characterise a particular class of things (aircraft, politicians, pandas, scientific theories, vegetables, and so on) to the expected qualities of individual instances of that class (the 737 I'm currently sitting on, Hillary Clinton, Ling Ling, string theory, runner beans). Perhaps the most recognisable version of a generalisation is the reverse of this; arguing from a single instance or a sample of something to claims about those things as a whole: string theory is tough to understand, therefore all scientific theories are tough to understand.

In a similar fashion to causal arguments, generalisations are fundamental to scientific reasoning. A significant proportion of the methodological knowledge and skills of scientists is about the legitimacy of generalisations: what constitutes a large enough and representative sample; understanding the degree of strength that a generalisation holds, and the statistical methods appropriate for finding these things out. At the end of this chapter you will find recommendations for critical thinking textbooks which go into detail about generalisations, often with a philosophy of science perspective, but you should also bear in mind that texts on natural and social scientific research methods are also an important (and often overlooked) critical thinking resource.

Generalisations are most commonly classified into two kinds: absolute (also known as 'universal', 'strict', or 'hard'), and non-absolute (also known as 'non-universal', 'inductive' or 'soft'). Absolute generalisations are those that claim that all of a certain type of thing are a certain way (like 'all countries have flags'), and non-absolute generalisations claim that 'most' or the majority of a type of thing are a certain way (like 'most countries have land borders with other countries'). Non-absolute generalisations can be subdivided into statistical and non-statistical forms. The latter will use vague terms like 'most', while the former quantify probabilities in terms of percentages and other fractions.

The statistical/non-statistical division has relevance to a third type of generalisation that aligns with **plausible arguments** (see Chapter 4). As characterised by Douglas Walton (2006, pp. 17–19), a **defeasible generalisation** (full name: a 'presumptive defeasible generalisation') is an attempt to apply a generally accepted belief to a particular instance. Unlike absolute and non-absolute generalisations, they do not typically involve qualifiers like 'all' or 'most', and they certainly never involve statistics. As with all plausible arguments, their most important feature is their practical and contextualised nature. They are saying that prior personal experience and common knowledge have established the right to presume X about situation Y in circumstances where more rigorous investigation is not practical; 'meat that is before its sell-by date and which has been stored in the fridge is edible', for example.

Like all defeasible arguments, there is a background assumption that there are very likely to be exceptions to the rule, but that the burden of proof falls to those who want to claim an exception in this instance. Defeasible generalisations, however, are vulnerable to stereotyping; to being derived from 'common knowledge' that is in fact inaccurate, and personal experience that is skewed by the **confirmation bias**. This will be addressed under 'sweeping generalisations', below.

The general formal structures of arguments employing a generalisation are these:

From a specific instance to the whole:

P1: All (or most) observed instances of X have characteristic Y.
C: Therefore all (or most) instances of X will have characteristic Y.

From the whole to a specific instance:

P1: The class of things X typically exhibit characteristic Y.
C: Therefore Z (which is a member of class X) will typically exhibit characteristic Y.

The remainder of this section will explain and discuss the main fallacies associated with generalisations: **hasty generalisations** and **sweeping generalisations**.

HASTY GENERALISATION

In her research into everyday argumentation, Deana Kuhn studied people's reasoning on a couple of topics, including why people fail at school. One participant illustrated a certain pattern of reasoning when, after explaining failure in terms of laziness and peer pressure, gives this response to the question: 'How do you know this is the cause?':

> [Because] I see it around me, you know. I have friends who fail. They figure it's the right thing to do, and, you know, they just get lazy or want to hang out with their friends.

(1991, p. 74)

This is a case of generalising from too few examples to a conclusion about the whole, and as in many cases of this (we're all guilty), the 'too few examples' come from our own particular experiences. It is understandable why we do this; our experiences are vivid and concrete and thus collude with the availability heuristic. They exaggerate the relevance of the pattern in question, prompting us to jump to a conclusion.

Hasty generalisations are also known as the 'fallacy of insufficient statistics' or as a 'sampling error'. In social science, generalising from a sample to a whole population is basic to its methodology. Since testing or observing the whole population is usually too time-consuming and costly, sampling and statistical methods have been devised which are quite reliable in their predictions. In the hands of those suitably trained, generalisations in these academic and applied contexts (such as market research and opinion polls) are not fallacious when appropriately derived and when their limitations are known and accounted for. Where this is not the case, hasty generalisations can occur. These take two general forms: too small a sample, and an unrepresentative sample.

The previous example is problematic in both of these respects: the people this person knows who have failed at school will not be a large enough sample to base a prediction about the whole of America on (although an appropriately sized sample is far smaller than we would typically imagine – 1000–2000 people); and it is highly unlikely that they would be representative in terms of the demographics they represent (age, sex, race, region, social class, and so on).

A variation of unrepresentative samples is what is known as **cherry picking**. This means that information or examples that conform to your hypothesis or that present your position in a particularly flattering light are presented as evidence, while non-conforming or unflattering data is ignored or supressed. We can cherry pick in a non-deliberate way (unconsciously driven by the confirmation bias), but it can also be a deliberate attempt to misrepresent the available data. The main difference between an unrepresentative sample and cherry picking is that with cherry picking a more complete set of information is available but not shared, whereas with an unrepresentative sample only a partial data set exists.

Superficial and one-sided communications such as advertisements, company annual reports, CVs, or social media personal profiles will cherry pick like there is no tomorrow. This might be undesirable, but is at least something that we expect to happen. In other contexts it is more troubling. It's a common tactic of organised corporate and political denial of the health risks from smoking and global environmental issues, and, as Ben Goldacre argues, is commonly used in research carried out by advocates of alternative therapies and, in particular, nutritionism.[6] All reporting of research findings is at risk from cherry picking, though, but in theory at least avoiding it is relatively straightforward. It involves what is called a 'systematic review', which puts in place rules for unbiased selection and questions to guide assessment of previous research on a subject. The 'traditional' method was open to bias caused by non-rigorous searches or a lack of open-mindedness on the part of the researcher. Crucially, although the original research of the scientist is always peer-reviewed in academic journals, the review part of it (i.e. a summary of the research findings to date) was not. The systematic review approach insists on peer review of this aspect and thus requires transparency with respect to the scientist's method of selection and evaluation.[7]

SWEEPING GENERALISATION

The other topic Deana Kuhn used to study people's everyday reasoning skills was criminals re-offending. In one example a participant accounts for re-offending in the following way: 'Human beings are very much creatures of habit, and I don't think that there's such a habit as committing a crime, but everything that leads up to committing a crime is probably habit.' Asked how they know, the participant replies, 'I'm not certain, but it just seems pretty obvious from all other spheres of life, people are so set in their ways' (1991, p. 60).

In cases like this, a broad assumption about a phenomenon is used to predict the cause of a specific instance: human beings are 'creatures of habit' therefore re-offending will be the result of habit. As the beginning of a process of hypothesis-forming, there is nothing wrong with this – habit is a major component of human behaviour and it is reasonable to assume that it plays a part in re-offending – but should this be the only cause suggested, then the arguer runs the risk of presenting a sweeping generalisation.

An example of sweeping generalisation in ethics might be: 'Killing people is always wrong.' In the hands of a pacifist, this is defensible, but more usually in a conversation it's the work of System 1 and is in need of qualifying. (There are many examples of killing that can be argued to be morally acceptable, such as combatants in the theatre of war, euthanasia, capital punishment, social revolution, and self-defence.)

We refer to a generalisation as 'sweeping' when the context requires us to know about a particular instance rather than the class was a whole. My knowing that Nissans are reliable cars has limited value when deciding whether or not to buy this particular ten years-old-with-three-previous-owners Nissan. Knowing that philosophy graduates tend to be better than average critical thinkers does not mean an employer should assume this is the case for the philosophy graduate they are about to interview. The very notion of a stereotype encompasses this kind of problem. Generalisations are important and useful in all sorts of ways, but in the wrong context they become over-simplifications that, in the case of social categories such as race and gender, can be highly offensive.

'Stereotype' also refers to generalisations that are inaccurate in the first place. As we saw above, **defeasible generalisations** run the risk of being simply off the mark. It is one thing to be open to exceptions to the rule (which is crucial to the correct presentation and dialogical handling of plausible arguments), but quite another for the rule to be wrong in the first place. To say that people from the Home Counties of England (the areas surrounding London) are posh Tories might be intended as a defeasible generalisation, but is in fact implausible because it is based on a gross over-simplification of the people who live in this region. Stereotype therefore means two things: reducing an individual to a generalised truth about a category to which she belongs; and over-simplifying and therefore distorting the nature of the category in the first place. The first of these is a form of sweeping generalisation, and the second is a hasty generalisation.

CRITICAL QUESTIONS

In light of the above discussions, the main critical questions that can be applied to arguments involving generalisations are these:

For absolute and non-absolute generalisations

Q1: Is the generalisation made based on a large enough sample? [Sufficiency]

Q2: If so, is the generalisation made based on a representative sample? [Relevance]

For defeasible generalisations

Q3: Is the generalisation plausible? [Acceptability]

For all generalisations

Q4: Is this a context in which applying a generalised truth is appropriate? [Relevance]

GENERALISATIONS: PSYCHOLOGY AND RHETORIC

It seems that we are fond of generalising; they render a complex, probabilistic and hard-to-predict world seem a simpler place. For philosopher and psychologist William James we are 'absolutists by instinct',[8] and in his *Rhetoric,* Aristotle observed how generalisations appeal to prejudicial tendencies in audiences. We like to make quick leaps from particulars to the general, and in persuasive communication he identifies the maxim as especially effective for providing generalised legitimacy to the audience's limited experiences. Maxims are broad truths communicated in a single sentence, and, if spoken by the right person, they carry a kind of moral wisdom. Among Aristotle's examples are: 'He is no lover that not always loves', and 'Do not, thou mortal, harbour deathless anger'. Although leaving us pretty cold, these would have been familiar to Athenian audiences, and familiarity is crucial for their effectiveness. In modern Anglophone cultures we recognise expressions like 'Actions speak louder than words' and 'All things in moderation' (or better still, Oscar Wilde's 'All things in moderation including moderation').

As cognitive-behavioural therapy (CBT) demonstrates, generalisations do not necessarily lose their appeal even when they work against the individual. For CBT, unhappiness and mental disorders are caused and maintained by people's inaccurate (or 'inefficient') beliefs. Originator Aaron Beck identified 'basic errors' of thought in patients such as over-generalisations and black-and-white thinking, and among the 'irrational beliefs' listed by Albert Ellis are absolutes and generalisations like:

One should be loved by everyone for everything one does.

One should be thoroughly competent, intelligent and achieving in all respects.

Because something once affected one's life, it will indefinitely affect it.

Because I had bad luck once, I will always have it.[9]

CBT seeks out unrealistic and inflexible patterns of thought that have become automatic responses to situations and guides to behaviour. In a therapeutic context the aim is to help people replace these with healthier (for the most part, more accurate) ways of thinking, and the relative success of this form of intervention is evidence of the broad benefits of critical thinking.

Of particular interest to CBT are causal generalisations. Harmful assumptions such as bad luck always being with us involve erroneous beliefs about the nature of luck, and, on the whole, people suffering depression tend to wrongly attribute negative events to features internal to them (such as personality traits), and positive events to external causes. It is easy to see how biased generalisations of this kind will take a cumulative toll on an individual's self-esteem.

GENERALISATIONS, DISPOSITIONS AND CONSTRUCTIVE DIALOGUES

Generalisations are, then, strangely satisfying, and when not creating the kind of problems CBT confronts, they are also quite entertaining.

Spoken word artist and comedian Henry Rollins observes how they are 'never right, always fun';[10] a particularly good line since it is itself a generalisation that is not accurate (since some generalisations can be right, and are, as we've just seen, not necessarily fun). Humour is full of generalisations, and no doubt this is in part because we enjoy the fantasy of a simplified world and the momentary release it affords. But journalism and many other forms of communication are also full of generalisations, and where the genre in question is not just entertainment, then our liking for how they represent the world can be a serious impediment to critical thinking.

Towards protecting ourselves against this tendency much of the discussion in the equivalent section under 'Causal arguments and causal fallacies' is pertinent. In addition, however, over-generalisations are a form of excess that we need to moderate and so temperance is also very important. Like Oscar Wilde (and Uncle Vance) I would suggest that a life without moments of excess is unfulfilling for many of us, but there is a time and a place, and in most respects an excess of generalisations, tempting though they are, is not amenable to the pursuit of truth.

Comments made in the causal arguments section about declaring your position too soon and the premature closing down of dialogues are also relevant to generalisations. Making absolutist statements can force us into having to defend them even when we come to realise their problems (a single counterexample is enough to defeat them). Probabilistic statements, on the other hand – especially vague or 'soft' ones containing words like 'most', 'many', 'the majority', 'usually', and so on – allow for flexibility in the positions we can arrive at without appearing inconsistent.

A form of defence we can be pushed into as a result of an ill-thought-through generalisation is the 'no true Scotsman' fallacy. Also referred to as an 'ad hoc rescue', it involves changing the definition of the class of things in question in order to avoid an absolute generalisation being defeated by a counterexample. The name comes from philosopher Anthony Flew's original example of a Scotsman reading about a brutal crime committed by an Englishman in the paper and proclaiming that no Scotsman would do such a thing. The next day he reads about a worse crime committed by a man from Aberdeen (in Scotland), but instead of acknowledging the inaccuracy of his generalisation, he insists that this person is no 'true' Scotsman.

In an *ad hoc* fashion (meaning that it is created in order to deal with a particular problem rather than part of the original planning), he has changed the definition of a Scotsman from a (presumed) geographical one to one that specifies certain traits or behaviours (Flew, 1985, p. 49). The desperation of such a manoeuvre is pretty clear, but in technical terms the arguer has re-established the validity of the argument by arbitrarily changing the definition of what he is arguing about.

In an article about conspiracy theories,[11] Matthew Dentith makes the point that sometimes they are true, but that they have come to be defined as something that is not true. He is arguing against this 'no true Scotsman' attitude, and is concerned that we will miss uncovering real conspiracies as a result:

> Conspiracy theories sometimes turn out to be warranted, although many deny this by saying: 'Ah, but then it's not really a conspiracy theory, is it?' ... We have been told that conspiracy theories are bunk, and so we treat them as such.

> (2015, p. 39)

6.3 ARGUMENTS FROM CONSEQUENCES AND SLIPPERY SLOPE ARGUMENTS

Causal arguments and generalisations are basic to many deliberations because they help us to determine the consequences of our decisions. Decisions can be argued for because of the positive consequences they will bring about, or they can be argued against because of foreseen negative consequences. In both instances, judgements are often based on relative positive and negative consequences: we should do X because it will bring greater benefits than Y; or we should not do P because it will bring worse consequences than Q.

Thus, the basic structure of an argument from consequences is this:

Positive form:

P1: Deciding X will bring about consequence Y.
P2: Consequence Y is better than the consequences that will arise from alternatives to X.
C: Therefore we should decide X.

Negative form:

P1: Deciding X will bring about consequence Y.

P2: Consequence Y is worse than the consequences that will arise from alternatives to X.

C: Therefore we should not decide X.

The **critical questions** applicable to arguments from consequences are these:

Q1: Is this a situation in which the consequences of a decision are the appropriate standard of evaluation? [Relevance]

Q2: How sure are we that deciding X will actually bring about Y? [Acceptability]

Q3: Is consequence Y clearly good/bad in the way that is being claimed? [Acceptability]

Q4: If so, is it better/worse than consequences arising from alternative decisions? [Acceptability]

Q5: If so, is the right degree of certainty established in order for us to make a decision to encourage/allow/prevent consequence Y from occurring? [Sufficiency]

On the subject of the use of drones in attacks on terrorist suspects, the following negative argument from consequences is made:

> If targeted drone strikes become legitimized in this context, the need to try other means first to quell the threat may be diminished. The risk becomes that military leaders will bypass nonlethal alternatives, such as apprehending alleged terrorists and continued surveillance, and move straight to extrajudicial killing as the standard way of dealing with the perceived threat of terrorism.[12]

The context of the discussion is 'just war theory', and one of the criteria for deciding if waging a war is just is whether it is a 'last resort'. If drone strikes are considered 'actions short of war', then their becoming acceptable could corrupt the 'avoiding violence' impetus behind this criterion. The negative argument from consequences concerning this use of drones can satisfy Q1 and Q3, and there is possibly a case for Q2. However, because there are a number of other arguments for and against drone strikes and their relationship to just war theory (e.g. greater precision leading to fewer civilian casualties, but also less likelihood of surrender since the enemy do not feel that they are fighting a real enemy), then Q4 is complicated to assess. We should be aware though that if, on balance, Q4 does not weigh against drone strikes, then greater certainty is needed in response to Q2.

SLIPPERY SLOPE ARGUMENTS AND THEIR RELATIVES

A type of argument from negative consequences that has received a lot of attention from scholars of informal logic is the **slippery slope argument**. A number of authors and textbooks will refer to this as the slippery slope fallacy (e.g. Johnson and Blair, 2006; Bowell and Kemp, 2010; Lunsford and Ruszkiewicz, 2010), but as Douglas Walton (2015) and others have argued, slippery slope arguments are not necessarily weak.

They share the general structure of arguments from negative consequences, but with these features:

- They claim that by bringing about an initial, relatively inconsequential (and possibly benign) occurrence (such as a policy change), a series of hard-to-stop consequences will follow.
- This series is hard to stop for two reasons: we have little or no control over its unfolding once it begins; and (in some instances because of the incremental nature of the change) there is a significant degree of indeterminacy about when this loss of control will actually occur.
- Once underway, this sequence will then eventually lead to a final serious (or catastrophic) negative consequence.

Slippery slope arguments are quite common in deliberative reasoning, and perhaps most conspicuously in debates about drug legislation and euthanasia. In both of these cases it is claimed that small changes to legislation that might, on the face of it, be acceptable (such as legalising cannabis or voluntary euthanasia) should not be enacted because this will lead to a cascade of uncontrollable consequences, the end point of which is highly unacceptable. In the case of drug laws, it is claimed that the links between cannabis and harder drugs (links that are not there with alcohol) will result in a greater number of heroin addicts. In the case of euthanasia, incremental changes in social attitudes towards death and the rights of the dying (including greater pressure perceived by the elderly to agree to terminate their lives even though it is not what they really want) will result in cases of involuntary euthanasia, and the public acceptance of non–voluntary euthanasia.

Communicating the seriousness of climate change is impeded by its complexity and the fact that many of its impacts will not affect us for a number of decades. It also has the form of a slippery slope argument. Under the heading 'Increasing magnitudes of warming increase the likelihood of severe, pervasive, and irreversible impacts', the IPCC's 5th Assessment (2014, p. 15) states:

> Some risks of climate change are considerable at 1 or 2°C above preindustrial levels (as shown in Assessment Box SPM.1). Global climate change risks are high to very high with global mean temperature increase of 4°C or more above preindustrial levels in all reasons for concern (Assessment Box SPM.1), and include severe and widespread impacts on unique and threatened systems, substantial species extinction, large risks to global and regional food security, and the combination of high temperature and humidity compromising normal human activities, including growing food or working outdoors in some areas for parts of the year (*high confidence*). The precise levels of climate change sufficient to trigger tipping points (thresholds for abrupt and irreversible change) remain uncertain, but the risk associated with crossing multiple tipping points in the earth system or in interlinked human and natural systems increases with rising temperature (*medium confidence*).[13]

At the moment, carrying on as we are has relatively minimal direct impact on the quality of life of western industrialised nations, and it of course avoids the 'inconvenience' that mitigating measures will bring for many. However, as the passage claims, such inaction will likely result in tipping points, the timing of which is hard to predict precisely, but which will be irreversible and lead to a range of very serious final consequences.

The critical questions associated with slippery slope arguments share the ones for arguments from negative consequences, except that Q2 will need to be applied to every step in the sequence of consequences. Also, in order to evaluate the true slipperiness of the hypothesised slope a sub-question must be added:

Q2a: Are there good reasons for thinking that a loss of control over consequences will occur during the sequence of cause and effect? [Acceptability]

This could mean loss of control over purely physical events as in the climate change example, but also loss of control over subsequent actions of policy-makers, or changes in public attitudes.

Applying this to the climate change argument; although some commentators highlight the benefits of climate change (such as Arctic shipping lanes opening up), most of us will accept that the predicted consequences of anything above 2°C rise will be very serious indeed. The argument thus satisfies Q3, and it also satisfies Q1. Q4 can be in some doubt in so far as sceptics have argued that mitigation policies are harmful to developing economies, but since the consequences of climate change will almost certainly be worse economically speaking, and since the concessions made by developed countries at the Paris conference in 2015, this does not seem to pose a threat to the argument. In response to Q2, the findings of the IPCC show that it is highly likely that not cutting emissions will lead to catastrophic outcomes, and it is of course very important that the passage quoted makes reference to the details of the research which confirms these predictions. With respect to Q2a, we are, ominously, told that tipping points are involved (the nature of which is also explained in the details of the research), and these are by definition 'irreversible'. When they will occur is uncertain, such that continuing to emit greenhouse gasses to the extent that we are is running a significant risk. In light of the devastating consequences brought about by these tipping points, the cautionary principle seems the only logical one to apply (Q5), and thus the continued lack of coordinated international action is the wrong policy.

The following example, from an article about the Scottish Independence referendum of 2014 appears to be less successful. The passage below is from a section subtitled 'What good will devo max do?' 'Devo max' is short for 'devolution maximum', which here refers to more powers (such as setting income tax rates) being awarded to the Scottish government by the UK government in Westminster.

> If the Scots decide to vote against independence, David Cameron is already promising that more powers will be devolved to the Scottish parliament. Many have interpreted these additional powers as equating to devo max. But what would be the likely outcome of the Scots being granted devo max as a concession following a no vote? ... Does anyone believe for a split second that a Scottish government run by the Scottish National Party devoted to extricating the Scots from the British state would be placated with devo max? Once the Scots have it, what's to stop them, just like any good negotiator, from continually asking for additional powers and threatening to separate if they don't get them? Wouldn't Scotland and England continue to grow further apart within the UK until all that would be left to say is that they are the two largest national components of one excessively decentralised state? What good does this do for England, Wales and Northern Ireland? The English must know that in the long term, offering devo max is a disastrous policy fraught with dire consequences for the union.[14]

The author is describing how, once a short-term gain is made (preventing independence), a sequence of cause and effect will occur over which Westminster would have little control, and which would end badly for them. This does appear to be a slippery slope argument, in which case we can apply the relevant critical questions.

The consequences of a decision like this are certainly relevant to its evaluation (Q1); and the loss of the union's integrity (and the eventual Scottish independence possibly implied by this) is not a good outcome as far as a Unionist UK Government is concerned (Q3). Q4 is tougher to answer because if devo max had not been on the table, then the UK could have lost Scotland in 2014. More critical for the strength of the argument, however, is the plausibility of the series of consequences that the author suggests (Q2 and Q2a). A Nationalist government in Scotland might well negotiate in the way claimed, but since this is a situation in which the no vote has (currently) won the day, how confident can we be that the Scottish people who are not wanting independence will not see the potential for this slope themselves? If they do, then any party with this agenda (most obviously the Scottish National Party) risks their majority being weakened or being voted out of the Scottish Parliament.

So, even though you could argue that offering devo max places the UK government in a weak position in any future negotiations (and thus the unfolding sequence is out of their control) (Q2a), whether the necessary forces will be at work in Scotland that would lead to such negotiations is debatable. We can conclude then that this is a relatively weak slippery slope argument. For the arguer there seems to be no doubt that this move will end in disaster, whereas at best it is a possible outcome that a Unionist UK government might be prepared to risk (Q5).

RELATIVES OF THE SLIPPERY SLOPE ARGUMENT

Care should be taken when labelling something a 'slippery slope argument', as other argument forms and fallacies bear a resemblance to it. These are important (or important to know about) in their own right, but differ from slippery slopes in important respects.

Complex causal sequences

Arguments from negative consequences that involve chains of causation but not loss of control are not slippery slope arguments. The consequences of climate change without the tipping points would be just such an argument. And we should note that the difference is not trivial since policy-makers and other deliberators need to know whether and at what points an unwanted series of events can be halted. To label a situation a slippery slope is to set off alarm bells, and although in some cases this might be the aim, to misapply the label can lead to misplaced fear or panic.

Argument from precedent

An argument from precedent is one in which it is said that we should not do X, because if we did, we would have to allow Y and Z, etc. to happen as well. The most common example is legalising gay marriage; a move whose detractors often claim will open the legal door to practices like marrying animals, cars and siblings. This, however, is more obviously a form of **argument from analogy** (see Chapter 7) rather than a slippery slope argument. In the case of gay marriage, the analogy is weak, in which case there is no reason to suppose that social and legal systems will have to allow these undesirable consequences to happen. If it were a strong analogy though, the detractor presumably sees something inherently troubling in the initial step, in which case it is some distance from the basic structure of a slippery slope argument (where the consequences of the initial step are unproblematic or positive). From the perspective of some of those opposing gay marriage, it really is as wrong as incest.

The continuum fallacy

The continuum fallacy is related to the *sorites* paradox. '*Sorites*' means 'heap' in Greek, and the paradox identifies the contrast between ideas that we confidently use in natural language, but which on analysis turn out to be unquantifiable. We can intuitively distinguish between a heap of sand and a non-heap (perhaps a 'pile' or a 'mound'), but the process of adding single grains of sand to the non-heap and trying to establish the point at which it becomes a heap appears to be impossible. One grain is not going to be the difference, but this means that no matter how many single grains we add (or take away if we are talking about moving from a heap to a non-heap), the non-heap can never become a heap.

Nevertheless we do still want to maintain that there is a meaningful difference between a non-heap and a heap, just as (sadly) there is a difference between bald and non-bald (adding or subtracting single hairs creates the same kind of problem). We make this distinction through (1) acknowledging the inherent vagueness of these concepts; and (2) rejecting the idea that vagueness makes concepts meaningless or impractical. So, the fallacy is to conclude that because this incremental process cannot define where the line is drawn, there is in fact no line at all; no real difference between the concepts in question. There are countless examples of this kind of vagueness, including what counts as reasonable flexibility around a designated bedtime ('please, just five more minutes'), saplings and trees, or, more seriously (for versions of the abortion debate), the point at which a zygote becomes an embryo, or an embryo a foetus.

The relevance of the *sorites* paradox to slippery slope arguments should be clear. If used to argue against the justifiability of rules, then it is usually a fallacy; allowing five minutes flexibility around bedtime does not mean that six is acceptable. Despite the vagueness, agreement can be reached both on the basis of roughly where the line should be drawn, and, very importantly, on the basis that a line *has to be drawn*. The drink driving limit in Scotland is 50 milligrams of alcohol in every 100 millilitres of blood. No doubt we are no less safe at 55 milligrams, but quite understandably the law cannot see it this way, and someone caught will be banned whether they have 55 mg or 155 mg.

Stronger *sorites*-type slippery slope arguments are found in situations where rules are not enforceable. My wife and I are always up early because of work and the children, but when the latest series of *The Walking Dead* or *Game of Thrones* is released on DVD, we face a problem. We say we will limit ourselves to one or two episodes a night, but often end up watching three or four. 'Just one more?' when this is 40 minutes less sleep is hard to resist, but the cumulative effect is the problem. This is without doubt a slippery slope, and because it is so addictive, we sometimes just have to not step onto it and leave the box set until Friday night.

Insensitivity to small, incremental changes kills frogs (if put in boiling water, they jump out, but when placed in very gradually boiling water, or so some claim, they do not notice and fail to escape) and causes sleep deprivation in humans like me. But it also has its benefits. In what behavioural therapists call 'systematic desensitisation', phobias are cured through incremental exposure to the fearful object. Someone with arachnophobia cannot get close to spiders, but if they can tolerate being on the other side of a large room as a contained spider, this can be the start of a process of counter-conditioning. The person is encouraged to move closer and closer to it – one step at a time if necessary. The lid comes off the container and they get closer still, until finally the beast is running across their hands. At each stage the small step must be accompanied by a manageable level of fear, and it is maintaining this level that is made possible by the relatively painless incremental exposure.

I recently gave up taking sugar in coffee, not quite one grain at a time, but pretty close. In a lengthy but painless process, avoiding the cold turkey of total abstinence, I succeeded in turning a heap into a non-heap and a non-heap into nothing.

SLIPPERY SLOPE ARGUMENTS: PSYCHOLOGY AND RHETORIC

In different respects, slippery slope arguments and their relatives can be seen as being too persuasive or not persuasive enough. Their power comes from the severity of the end point and the fear it provokes, and from the anxiety caused by the loss of control that results in this end point. (For more on fear, see *ad baculum* **arguments** in Chapter 5.) We should note though that a slippery slope argument in support of the status quo (such as not changing the laws concerning drugs or euthanasia; Scotland remaining part of the UK) is far more likely to be successful than one requiring quite radical changes that are perceived as undesirable. Despite the evidence for anthropogenic climate change and its negative consequences being overwhelming for two decades, the burden of proof in terms of the need for social change has remained with the climate scientists and their supporters. Under these circumstances the complexity of a slippery slope assists our deep-seated desire to ignore the problem, or rationalise it away.

Applied to rhetoric then, there appears to be a simple message: if campaigning to keep things as they are, the fear and anxiety provoked by slippery slope arguments could well work in your favour. But if campaigning for change, their complexity can provide an excuse for many to disengage. Also, since they are a quite a well-used and well-known argument form in public debates, the simple appearance of a slippery slope argument (including its relatives) could lead to an automatic dismissal of the issue or your stance on it.

SLIPPERY SLOPE ARGUMENTS, DISPOSITIONS AND CONSTRUCTIVE DIALOGUES

Because of their complexity, slippery slope arguments are often presented in a shortened (or 'compressed') form. We might hear, for example:

> In theory, freedom of speech is a good thing, but allowing any form of extremist religious or political views – whether or not they advocate violence – will eventually lead to more of our teenagers and young adults joining IS.

This is a controversial and emotive topic, and you can imagine this argument against the preaching of extremist beliefs having some support in countries facing terrorist threats. Before assessing it though we would need to hear more from its source to gain a clear picture of what they think would happen to these young people if we continue to tolerate non-violent extremist views. Thus the skills of constructive dialogue and argument reconstruction are required to fill in the various steps. Only once this effort is made, can the argument be properly evaluated.

We have seen that although many slippery slope arguments do not stand up to scrutiny, some do, and because they deal in severe negative consequences, then we need to be careful about what we dismiss. Notwithstanding the preciousness of our time and our developing ability to read signs of unreliability in sources, we need to be suitably open-minded, persistent in our focus, and inquisitive in the presence of proposed slippery slopes. Although we are unlikely to have direct access to the evidence for the steps in question, we can at least adopt a provisional stance on their plausibility which can then shape our subsequent attitude to the issue.

EXERCISE

1. The passage below is from Martin Luther King's *Letter from Birmingham Jail* (see Chapter 1 for context and background). Many of the argument forms discussed in this chapter can be found in it. Attempt to identify and reconstruct some of these and, using the appropriate critical questions, assess its strength as best you can. Taking into consideration King's audiences (white Southern clergy, politicians and the American public in general), you might also want to evaluate its rhetorical power.

If this philosophy [of nonviolent direct action] had not emerged, I am convinced that by now many streets of the South would be flowing with floods of blood. And I am further convinced that if our white brothers dismiss as 'rabble-rousers' and 'outside agitators' those of us who are working through the channels of nonviolent direct action and refuse to support our nonviolent efforts, millions of Negroes, out of frustration and despair, will seek solace and security in black nationalist ideologies, a development that will lead inevitably to a frightening racial nightmare.

Oppressed people cannot remain oppressed forever. The urge for freedom will eventually come. This is what has happened to the American Negro. Something within has reminded him of his birthright of freedom; something without has reminded him that he can gain it. Consciously and unconsciously, he has been swept in by what the Germans call the *Zeitgeist,* and with his black brothers of Africa and his brown and yellow brothers of Asia, South America, and the Caribbean, he is moving with a sense of cosmic urgency toward the promised land of racial justice. Recognizing this vital urge that has engulfed the Negro community, one should readily understand public demonstrations. The Negro has many pent-up resentments and latent frustrations. He has to get them out. So let him march sometime; let him have his prayer pilgrimages to the city hall; understand why he must have sit-ins and freedom rides. If his repressed emotions do not come out in these nonviolent ways, they will come out in ominous expressions of violence. This is not a threat; it is a fact of history. So I have not said to my people, 'Get rid of your discontent.' But I have tried to say that this normal and healthy discontent can be channelled through the creative outlet of nonviolent direct action.

2. Over the next few days pay particular attention to the use of causal fallacies, hasty and sweeping generalisations, and slippery slope arguments in your own thoughts and conversations, and in other sources (notably the media). Make a note of some of them, including such things as the contexts in which they arise, their degree of emotionality and automaticity, and the effect they had on you and other people.

FURTHER READING

CAUSAL ARGUMENTS

- Deanna Kuhn's book *The Skills of Argument* (1991) is a very interesting investigation into how people formulate causal arguments and associated generalisations. In it, she theorises four stages of sophistication in causal reasoning.
- Hank Davis' *Caveman Logic* (2009) is primarily an argument for the dangers of heuristic reasoning, but has a particular focus on causal reasoning errors.

GENERALISATIONS

- A very readable and insightful discussion of generalisations (including prejudice and stereotyping) can be found in Michael Scriven's excellent book *Reasoning* (1976, pp. 196–210).
- Within the context of critical thinking books, one of the most comprehensive treatments of generalisations and their relationship to scientific method is Chapter 10 of Robert Ennis' book *Critical Thinking* (1996a).

ARGUMENTS FROM CONSEQUENCES AND SLIPPERY SLOPE ARGUMENTS

- For a good recent overview of slippery slope arguments, see Anneli Jefferson (2014) 'Slippery slope arguments', *Philosophy Compass*, 9/10, 672–80. And for a more advanced history and analysis, see Douglas Walton (2015) 'The basic slippery slope argument', *Informal Logic*, 35(3), 273–311.

NOTES

1 *Fortean Times*, Sept. 2013.
2 L. Bowes *et al.* (2015) 'Risk of depression and self-harm in teenagers identifying with goth subculture: a longitudinal cohort study', *The Lancet*. Available at: www.thelancet.com/psychiatry, Vol. 2.
3 See, for example, Kollmuss and Agyeman (2002) 'Mind the gap: why do people act environmentally and what are the barriers to pro-environmental

behaviour?' *Environmental Education Research*, 8(3), 239–60. See, in particular, p. 254.

4 M. McGrath (2015) 'Global warming increases food shocks threat'. Available at: www.bbc.co.uk/news/science-environment-33910552, and R. Bailey *et al.* (2015) 'Extreme weather and resilience of the global food system'. Available at: www.foodsecurity.ac.uk/assets/pdfs/extreme-weather-resilience-of-global-food-system.pdf

5 B.F. Skinner (1948) '"Superstition" in the pigeon', *Journal of Experimental Psychology*, 38, 168–72.

6 See B. Goldacre (2008) *Bad Science* (London: Fourth Estate, pp. 97–9, 165–70).

7 For a good overview of systematic reviews in medicine, see P. Hemingway (2009) 'What is a systematic review?' Available at: www.medicine.ox.ac.uk/bandolier/painres/download/whatis/syst-review.pdf.

8 'The will to believe', in *Selected Papers on Philosophy* (New York: Dutton, 1967), p. 110.

9 M. Mahoney and A. Freeman (eds) *Cognition and Psychotherapy* (New York: Plenum Press, 1985).

10 *Talk is Cheap*, Volume 3 (audio recording, 2004).

11 *Fortean Times*, February 2015.

12 D. Brunstetter and M. Braun (2011) 'The implications of drones on the just war tradition', *Ethics and International Affairs*, 25(3), 337–58.

13 IPCC (2014) *Climate Change 2014 Impacts, Adaptation and Vulnerability: Summary for Policymakers*. Available at: www.ipcc.ch/pdf/assessment-report/ar5/wg2/ar5_wgII_spm_en.pdf

14 B. Glass (2014) 'Wise up England, you'd be better off without Scotland'. Available at: http://theconversation.com/wise-up-england-youd-be-better-off-without-scotland-28621

7

ARGUMENTS FROM ANALOGY

> Argument by analogy is often the most powerful and compelling type of argument we can use.
>
> (Michael Scriven, 1976, p. 210)

An **analogy** is an attempt to illuminate, explain or make an argument about a certain thing (or situation, event, etc.) by comparing it with something that shares relevant features with that thing (situation, event, etc.). Analogies are extremely common in communication.

A letter to the UK's *Sun* newspaper (29.9.10) uses an analogy to argue against slipping standards in the long-running soap opera *Coronation Street* (or 'Corrie'):

> The unpleasant sight of Kevin and Molly naked in bed before the 9pm watershed shows how Corrie's standards sink lower all the time. Clark Gable and Vivien Leigh sustained over three hours of passion in *Gone with the Wind* without once getting their kit off. Corrie should learn from this.

The argument is that the programme should not need to use explicit sex scenes to facilitate romantic plotlines, and the reason it gives is that *Gone with the Wind* (GWTW) did not need to. Regardless of how strong this comparison is (which is the kind of question that will be dealt with in the rest of this section), the argument stands a chance of being persuasive to the degree that GWTW will be known to, and liked by, many readers of the paper. The success of many analogies is dependent on the audience's familiarity with them: what people know, and perhaps have strong feelings about. The familiar case guides the understanding – provides a way into the issue in question – and so presenting an analogy can be seen as a form of **framing** (see Chapter 1).

Metaphors are very similar to analogies, but tend to be briefer comparisons which have a more literary purpose. They illuminate some aspect of the world in a way that grabs the audience's attention and stirs the imagination. As we will see, that analogies can also have this effect is relevant to understanding their persuasive potential, but primarily they should be understood as having an informational rather than poetic function. When used as explanations or arguments, the relationship between the items being compared needs to stand up to analytical scrutiny. If not, then the explanation will mislead, or the argument will be weak.

7.1 STRUCTURE AND CRITICAL QUESTIONS

An argument from analogy is one which claims that, because a certain state of affairs is true about idea or situation Y, so it is likely to be true of idea or situation X because X, in relevant respects, is comparable to Y.

The most basic way of representing the structure of an argument from analogy is this:

P1: X is comparable to Y.
P2: Z is true of Y.
C: Therefore Z is also true of X.

A more detailed version is this:

P1: Y has features a, b, c, etc.
P2: X is comparable to Y with respect to features a, b, c, etc.
P3: Z is true of Y.
P4: Z is linked with features a, b, c, etc.
C: Therefore Z is also true of X.

The film *The Last King of Scotland* (Keven MacDonald, 2007), set in the 1970s, is about a young Scottish doctor (Nicholas) who, when volunteering in Uganda, ends up becoming the President (Ide Amin's) personal physician. Initially he is reluctant to accept Amin's offer because his motivation for coming to Uganda is to help ordinary people, but Amin persuades him by arguing, initially, that by helping the President he will be helping the people (for example, by having a role in setting up a national health service). Nicholas politely refuses. Amin's second argument is an analogy that can be reconstructed like this:

P1: I had no personal desire to become President, but the people wanted it.
P2: You have no desire to become my physician, but the people will benefit from it.
P3: Through a sense of duty I became President.
P4: Doing one's duty is relevant to cases where taking on an important position, whatever one's personal feelings, is something that will benefit the people.
C: Duty dictates that you should serve as my personal physician.

The whole of this sequence (between approx. 24 and 36 minutes into the film) is worth watching and analysing as an excellent example of persuasive communication, and this particular dialogue serves as an example of an argument from analogy.

Terminology tends to differ slightly between different books and theorists, but for our purposes the issue or entity that the conclusion refers to (that the argument is essentially about) is known as the primary case (in this instance, whether Nicholas should become Amin's physician); what it is being compared with is the analogue case (Amin's decision to become President), and the relevant feature of the analogue case that the argument wants to claim is also true of the primary case is called the target feature (the decision being based on duty rather than personal preference).[1]

Just how arguments from analogy should be categorised has been the subject of a lot of debate among philosophers and other academics in recent decades. One important and generally accepted distinction (first identified by Aristotle (1991, Chapter 2.20) is between these two types:

- Real–life (or historical) analogies, where the comparison is with empirical truths or historical events that the audience is familiar with. These are commonly referred to as **inductive analogies**.
- **Hypothetical analogies**, where the comparison is with an invented situation that draws out, in a clear (and often vivid) way, the target feature of the primary case.

Extended inductive analogies can sometimes form the entire structure of lengthy books and documentaries. For example, Joel Bakan's *The Corporation* (2004) argues that the problem with large, publicly traded companies is that by law they have no option but to behave like psychopaths, whose symptoms and influence are systematically analysed and applied to corporate behaviour. Just as psychopathic behaviour is socially discouraged and legally neutered, so too should the modern form of the corporation. As the title suggests, Andrew Jennings' *Omertà! Sepp Blatter's FIFA Organised Crime Family* (2014) argues that the corruption in football's governing body is best understood in terms of the Mafia, and thus the appropriate alarm, moral disgust and responses we have towards such organisations should rightfully be directed towards Blatter's FIFA (as it subsequently has been).

The history of philosophy is full of analogies used as arguments and explanations. In one of the most famous contemporary examples, Judith Jarvis Thomson argued that legally or morally denying the right to an abortion in the case of rape is akin to a person being surgically attached to a famous violinist against their will for nine months because their blood and kidneys are the only thing that can keep him alive. If we agree that this violates the person's rights, so the argument goes, we should also accept the right to an abortion.[2]

Another hypothetical analogy, well known in philosophy and theology, is William Paley's 'watchmaker' argument for intelligent design (published in 1800). In it he states that on encountering a watch for the first time (in comparison to a stone), its complexity and evident function would give us every reason for believing that it has been designed and constructed by an intelligent being for a particular purpose. That being the case, he draws an analogy between what we believe about the origins of the watch and what we should believe are the origins of nature as a whole:

> Every indication of contrivance, every manifestation of design, which existed in the watch, exists in the works of nature; with the difference, on the side of nature, of being greater and more, and that in a degree which exceeds all computation. I mean that the contrivances of nature surpass the contrivances of art, in the complexity, subtlety, and curiosity, of the mechanism; and still more, if possible, do they go beyond them in number and variety: yet, in a multitude of cases, are not less evidently mechanical, not less evidently contrivances, not less evidently accommodated to their end, or suited to their office, than are the most perfect productions of human ingenuity.
>
> (Paley, [1800] 2009, p. 19)

The most reasonable belief, he concludes, is that nature is the product of intelligent design – the work of God.

The critical questions we can apply to arguments from analogy are these:

Q1: Is what is said of Y actually true (or plausible)? [Acceptability]

Q2: Are there relevant similarities between X and Y? [Relevance]

Q3: Are there dissimilarities between X and Y that undermine the similarities? [Sufficiency]

Q4: Can convincing counter-analogies be found (or in the case of hypothetical analogies, be hypothesised?) [Sufficiency]

Q5: Is the conclusion drawn from the comparison of the appropriate strength? [Sufficiency]

Prior to these, a question it is wise to ask ourselves is whether the analogy is actually intended to serve as an argument, rather than to explain or illuminate the primary case.

In his *Dialogues Concerning Natural Religion* (published in 1779, two decades before Paley's book), David Hume employed these questions to good effect against design arguments. We can grant that someone coming across a watch for the first time (in contrast to a stone) would rightly believe that it is not a random occurrence (Q1). (Note that with hypothetical analogies we can challenge the belief that is assumed in the analogue – so in Thomson's analogy we might want to claim that we do not have the right to disconnect our self from the violinist as she thinks we would – but in real-life analogies the facts of the analogue can be challenged *as well as* our supposed attitude towards those facts). Arguably there are relevant similarities between the watch and the workings of nature (Q2), but Q3 begins to reveal weaknesses in the argument. Despite their complexity and functionality, living organisms and their component parts are noticeably different from man–made artefacts, and in many respects (irregularities, shapes, textures, and so on) share more with the contrasting stone than with watches and other devices. Also, a simple dissimilarity is that we can observe watches and other machines being designed and built, but have no such empirical evidence for the origins of nature. Q4 is problematic for design arguments since an alternative analogy for the creation of nature is the creation of living organisms as a result of procreation. A designer is not an observable or necessary feature of the continuation of animal and vegetable species, so why should it be for the world as a whole? In Hume's words,

> The world plainly resembles more an animal or a vegetable, than it does a watch or knitting-loom. Its cause, therefore, it is more probable, resembles the cause of the former. The cause of the former is generation or vegetation. The cause, therefore, of the world, we may infer to be something similar analogous to generation or vegetation.
>
> ([1779] 1990, Part VII, p. 87)

Of course, Hume's argument would have been greatly strengthened had he been writing after Darwin's *Origin of Species* had been published; in the *Dialogues* he can only assert that we have no conclusive evidence either way. Without this evidence, to make a firm assertion on the basis of either the machine or generation analogy is unwarranted (an example of a **circular argument** (see Chapter 8)). A further argument of Hume's against the design argument, therefore, is a variation of Q5. Applying this to Paley, we can say that he concludes too much from his analogy.

7.2 PSYCHOLOGY AND RHETORIC

Analogies have the potential to be highly persuasive. In a benign sense they are persuasive precisely because they motivate us, through the familiarity of the analogue or the inventiveness and narrative features of the hypothetical scenario, to engage more fully with the topic. In this respect, analogies have an educational function. Less benignly though, they can be distracting, play to our prejudices, and lead us to accept conclusions that we should not accept. The clever persuader will employ analogies and other forms of figurative language that have emotional resonance for the audience in question. When making an argument from analogy, our choice of comparison can be partly determined by this consideration. For example, in *An Inconvenient Truth*, Al Gore did not have to choose Hurricane Katrina (and later in the film, 9/11) to make his point about preparedness and responses to global warming, but he knew that these appropriately memorable and moving events would aid the US audience (in 2006 at least) to engage with his message.

Even where figurative language is not directly used as part of an argument, its presence can still influence audiences. Aristotle (in *The Art of Rhetoric*) and modern research (see Sopory and Dillard, 2002, for a review) provide us with the following two criteria to evaluate the persuasive power of analogies and metaphors.

THEY SHOULD BE UNFAMILIAR, AND YET LEAD TO IMMEDIATE RECOGNITION

Used in non-fiction prose, the appeal of novel metaphors needs to be balanced with their clarity of meaning. They should, in Aristotle's words, 'name things without name, which on being spoken immediately reveal their affinity' (1991, p. 220). This is a real art; effectively knowing what is on the tip of your audience's tongue, and then finding the right word or image to capture it. When Marx said in the *Communist Manifesto*, 'You have nothing to lose but your chains', there was little doubt about what he meant, and the word 'chains' serves to dramatically crystalize the 'affinity' between the conditions of the working classes and slavery. Even if this connection is understood abstractly, the power of this imagery can be the difference between inaction and revolutionary action.

Metaphors are of course basic to poetry because they have the potential to be beautiful (or moving in some other respect). Part of the art of persuasion through metaphor is to know what will be pleasing to the audience in question. This can be in a poetic sense, but also something which has the right kind of emotional resonance which, when associated with the primary case, adds to its appeal. For many years now the Automobile Association in the UK (the AA) has used the strapline 'the fourth emergency service', something which is not literally true, but which borrows connotations of security, reliability and selfless deeds that many associate with responses to 999 calls.

THEY SHOULD BE SITUATED SO AS TO MAXIMIZE MESSAGE COMPREHENSION

It is important to get the positioning as well as the content of metaphors right. The effect of using a *single metaphor* rather than multiple ones, and of *employing the metaphor early on* in the message can help to provide a clear frame for engaging with the overall argument. This process is explained by the 'superior organisation' theory which sees metaphors as facilitating our understanding and memorising of the arguments presented by providing a 'structure' to link them together that is more effective than literal language. In other words, well-situated metaphors allow us to make better overall sense of what we are hearing or reading than if this stylistic feature were absent (Sopory and Dillard, 2002, p. 387).

If this potential for enabling audiences to structure the arguments they are hearing is to be actualised, then the metaphor must be carefully selected. As well as being aesthetically pleasing and novel (but recognisable), it should be consistent with the message and rich enough to illuminate as many of the arguments within it as possible.

A number of these criteria, including using a single metaphor, are exemplified by two recent and well-received political speeches: President Obama's moving and sympathetic address in Newtown, Connecticut, shortly after the Sandy Hook school shooting in December 2012; and ex-UK Prime Minister Gordon Brown's fiery pro-union speech in Glasgow just prior to the Scottish independence referendum in September 2014.[3]

The only metaphor Obama used in his speech referred to the anguish all parents face when confronted with the impossibility of protecting their children from all eventualities: 'someone once described the joy and anxiety of parenthood as the equivalent of having your heart outside of your body all the time, walking around'. This is a vivid metaphor for vulnerability; something we care about more than anything is continually exposed to circumstances beyond our control. It would lead to immediate recognition by any parent, and serves to structure the central argument of the speech – how the nation must do more to provide the protection that parents cannot (alluding, among other things, to gun laws).

In Brown's speech, his only metaphor referred to the risks of an independent Scotland in terms of an 'economic minefield', and an 'economic trapdoor down which we go from which we might never escape'. These images chimed with the fear appeal that was central to the ultimately successful 'No' campaign, and which was a central theme of this address.

From these examples, we can see that the lone, carefully selected metaphor helps keep messages coherent and memorable. Further use of figurative language would risk creating linguistic clutter that would interfere with this aim. In both speeches, however, the metaphor appears closer to the middle of the speech than the beginning, and in both cases the reason is that unrelated content was (for good reasons) positioned prior to this. In the Obama case, the speech naturally begins with condolences rather than arguments, and in the Brown case other arguments (concerning, for example, national (British) pride) were more appropriate as openers. If a metaphor functions as a joker, it makes sense that Brown would choose to play his on the economic theme.

7.3 DISPOSITIONS AND CONSTRUCTIVE DIALOGUES

If there is a disposition with particular significance for arguments from analogy, then it is having a good imagination. Hughes, Lavery and Doran (2010, p. 213) describe these as 'probably the most creative form of reasoning', and Christopher Tindale asks us to 'note how much this argument scheme requires us both to delve into the context and to use our imaginations' (2007, p. 198).

Imagination is important both for formulating appropriate analogies for our own arguments and for formulating counter-analogies when questioning other people's arguments (see Q3). This imaginative aspect makes arguments from analogy unusual. It contributes to their persuasive potential, but it is also part of what makes them difficult (and risky) to generate. In particular, it is hard to come up with convincing analogies in the heat of the moment. Producing counter-analogies is, however, less tricky since we can usually follow the lead of the other arguer's analogy. Someone attempting to justify the Iraq War, for example, might draw an analogy with the successful (but also, technically, illegal) humanitarian intervention in Kosovo in 1999. But once faced with this form of argument, it is relatively easy to find counter-analogies in other unsuccessful and less well-motivated wars such as Vietnam (wasteful, futile, a national embarrassment to the USA) and the Crusades (self-righteous, militarist and imperialist folly).

As the design argument example demonstrates, arguments from analogy tend not to be particularly strong. Where hypothetical analogies have creative qualities, however, they are effective for generating discussion and catalysing stronger arguments and deeper understanding. There is a cognitive reason for this, concerning stimulation of the imagination, and a motivational reason as well. A number of literary philosophers (such as Søren Kierkegaard, Jean-Paul Sartre, Iris Murdoch and Martha Nussbaum) have written about the importance of stories (including allegories) for de-personalising topics; their aesthetic distance provides an engaging focus while helping to avoid some of the emotional distortion that political and ethical debates can generate and that

> frequently impede our real-life deliberations. Since the story is not ours, we do not find ourselves caught up in the 'vulgar heat' of our personal jealousies or angers or in the sometimes blinding violence of our loves.
>
> (Nussbaum, 1990, p. 48)

Hypothetical analogies can function in a similar way. Bruce Waller says that Judith Jarvis Thomson's 'famous violinist' analogy, is

> effective because it starts with a case sufficiently different from our everyday experiences that our preconceptions do not distort our view; thus we can think about what principles we hold without the heat and passion and entrenched doctrines that swirl around the question of abortion.
>
> (2001, p. 215)

A lot of this section has emphasised the role of familiarity in effective analogies, but here Waller makes a good case for the important function of *unfamiliarity* in many hypothetical analogies. Rather than insight into what an audience knows and has strong feelings about, the imagination that goes into the production of these analogies is an example of philosophers (and other academics) at their most creative.

FURTHER READING

Three sources on arguments from analogy that will help develop your understanding of the subject and of some of the disagreements within it are these:

- Bruce Waller (2013) 'Classifying and analysing analogies', *Informal Logic*, 21(3), 199–218.
- Christopher Tindale (2007) *Fallacies and Argument Appraisal*, Chapter 10.
- Trudy Govier (2013) *A Practical Study of Argument*, Chapter 11.

EXERCISES

1. There are a number of examples of brief and extended analogies in this chapter (such as the film *The Corporation*, and Thomson's 'famous violinist') which have been explained or cited, but not analysed. This you could do by applying the critical questions and the criteria for the persuasiveness of figurative language in the 'Psychology and Rhetoric' section. You can of course, find your own examples as well – this is easy to do once you start tuning in to them.

2. Apply the critical questions to Dale Jamieson's intriguing argument from analogy found in his book *Reason in a Dark Time:*[4]

   > A revealing example of elite scientific ignorance was on display in the Supreme Court during the oral arguments in *Massachusetts versus EPA*. After being gently corrected for confusing the troposphere with the stratosphere, Justice Scalia replied, 'Troposphere. Whatever. I told you before I'm not a scientist.' As laughter swept the courtroom, Scalia added, 'That's why I don't want to have to deal with global warming,

to tell you the truth.' Justice Scalia's scientific ignorance is sad but not surprising. What is truly disturbing was his indifference to his ignorance, and his stated desire to ignore an important problem because it has a scientific dimension. Even worse, Scalia was correct in surmising that his attitudes would be widely and sympathetically shared among his audience of lawyers, students, journalists, and others. Imagine a Supreme Court justice expressing comparable ignorance and attitudes toward problems centering on religion, politics, or economics: 'Supply and Demand. Whatever. I told you before, I'm not an economist. That's why I don't want to have to deal with monopolies, to tell you the truth.' Were a justice to say that, I doubt that it would be viewed as a charming eccentricity.

NOTES

1 The choice of terminology is closest to Trudy Govier's (2013), but 'target feature' is Hughes, Lavery and Doran's phrase (2010, p. 215).
2 J.J. Thomson (1971) 'A defence of abortion', *Philosophy and Public Affairs*, 1(1), 47–66.
3 Both of these speeches are easily located for viewing online.
4 Oxford: Oxford University Press, 2014, pp. 62–3.

8

FURTHER FALLACIES

> The European Union is something you're either for or against. Personally I'm somewhere in between.
>
> (Sacha T. Burnstorm, pers. comm.)

The previous three chapters have been about argument forms (and their associated fallacies) that warrant extended analysis and exploration. The focus of this chapter is a selection of fallacies and rhetorical techniques that could not be located among these analyses, but that are also important to know about. These are **affirming the consequent** (and denying the antecedent); **circular arguments**; **false dilemmas**; the **perfectionist fallacy**, and **red herrings** and **equivocations**.

8.1 AFFIRMING THE CONSEQUENT (AND DENYING THE ANTECEDENT)

There is a type of argument – sometimes known by the Latin *modus ponens* – that has this form:

P1: If X, then Y.
P2: X.
C: Therefore Y.

So, for example:

> P1: If a celebrity is responsive to her fans and treats them with respect, then she will remain popular.
>
> P2: Taylor Swift is responsive to her fans and treats them with respect.
>
> C: Therefore Taylor Swift will remain popular.

This is a form of valid deductive argument (see Chapter 4) that includes what is known as a 'conditional statement' or 'conditional premise' – if X is the case, then Y will also be the case.

The logic of this argument is easy to follow, but we are also quite easily led to accept as valid a non-deductively valid version of it that goes like this:

> P1: If X, then Y.
>
> P2: Y.
>
> C: Therefore X.

So,

> P1: If a celebrity is responsive to her fans and treats them with respect, then she will remain popular.
>
> P2: Taylor Swift will remain popular.
>
> C: Therefore Taylor Swift is responsive to her fans and treats them with respect.

In this version the information provided in P1 and P2 cannot ensure the truth of the conclusion because there will be other reasons for a celebrity remaining popular other than being responsive to their fans and treating them with respect. The first clause in a conditional statement is known as the 'antecedent', and the second clause is the 'consequent'. In the *modus ponens* argument form, the second premise should affirm the antecedent, so the fallacious version is known as 'affirming the consequent'.

In a radio interview in 2015, Carlo Rovelli, discussing his book about science theories, said (with some slight paraphrasing), 'Science is beautiful … The theory of relativity is a work of art. This is because, like Shakespeare or the Sistine Chapel, it makes us emotional.'[1] This appears to be an example of affirming the consequent:

P1: If something is a work of art, then it makes us emotional.
P2: The theory of relativity makes us emotional.
C: Therefore the theory of relativity is a work of art.

Many things can make us emotional in the way that Rovelli seems to mean – like walking in a mountainous landscape, or contemplating the night sky, or watching our team win an important match – but these are not works of art.

A similar argument to *modus ponens* is *modus tollens*, which has this structure:

P1: If X, then Y.
P2: Not Y.
C: Therefore X.

If X is the case, then Y must also be the case; therefore if Y is not the case then X cannot be the case.

P1: If you like all forms of music, then you must like scat.
P2: You don't like scat.
C: Therefore you don't like all forms of music.

The fallacious version of *modus tollens* is known as 'denying the antecedent':

P1: If you like all forms of music, then you must like scat.
P2: You don't like all forms of music.
C: Therefore you don't like scat.

As unlikely as it seems, someone not claiming to like all forms of music could still like someone singing improvised impressions of jazz instruments (i.e. scat). A *modus tollens* argument should deny the consequent rather than deny the antecedent.

8.2 CIRCULAR ARGUMENTS

A circular argument (otherwise known as 'begging the question') is when the conclusion of an argument is required in order to establish one or more of the premises. A circular argument is expressed in this dialogue:

> *Jesse*:   I have psychic powers.
> *Simone*: Really? How do you know?
> *Jesse*:   My psychic aunt told me, and only a psychic can tell if you're psychic.
> *Simone*: How do you know your aunt's really a psychic?
> *Jesse*:   Well, because I'm psychic of course.

Jesse is trying to argue that he is psychic on the basis of his psychic aunt's insight, but he can only know that his aunt is psychic on the assumption of his own psychic powers. The trouble is his psychic powers can only be established if the aunt is psychic, and so round it goes. In a circular argument no grounds for accepting a premise are offered beyond what is stated in the conclusion of the argument – a conclusion that is, by its nature, reliant upon that very premise for establishing its own truth.

We tend to recognise circular arguments when we encounter them, but articulating them can sometimes be difficult. Setting them out in a formal structure is slightly tricky as well, but Bowell and Kemp (2010) achieve this by joining two separate arguments together like this:

P1: I have psychic powers.
P2: Only a psychic can tell if someone else is psychic, and I know my aunt is psychic.
C1: My aunt is psychic.
P3: My aunt says I have psychic powers, and only a psychic can tell if someone else is psychic.
C2: Therefore I have psychic powers.

Circular arguments are fairly common, and if you get the scent of one it's worth pursuing it even if it takes some trial and error to pin it down. If someone tries to prove God's existence using the Bible, for example, persistence can pay off because it's probably circular:

> X: How can we rely on the word of the Bible?
> Y: Because the Bible is the word of God.
> X: But how do we know God exists?
> Y: Because it says so in the Bible.

Some independent grounds are needed to prove either the existence of God or the veracity of the Bible, just as an independent justification is needed for the psychic powers of either Jesse or his aunt.

A more subtle version of a circular argument – the sort of thing I see in student essays occasionally – is seen in this example: 'If all of the issues were to be correctly considered, it would be seen that abortion is wrong.' The word 'correctly' signals the circularity. Imagine setting out reasons why abortion is wrong, and then adding a premise to the effect that anyone who understands these reasons correctly must conclude that abortion is wrong. Someone who concludes otherwise cannot have reasoned correctly. The idea of 'correct' here is therefore defined in terms of leading to the conclusion that abortion is wrong, and the conclusion that abortion is wrong is only supported by this 'correct' reasoning.

8.3 FALSE DILEMMAS

A false dilemma is an argument in which a range of options are presented that either deliberately or accidentally under-represent those that are actually available. It is sometimes known as a '**false dichotomy**', the difference being that 'dichotomy' means only two choices are presented, whereas 'dilemma' can mean two or more. Also, however, a dilemma indicates that the alternatives are unsatisfactory; that we would rather not have to choose between them because each has significant drawbacks. Better state health care and education provision typically comes at the cost of higher taxes (and vice versa); and as a pretty poor golfer, if I tee off with a wood instead of an iron I'll be sacrificing accuracy for distance (and vice versa). If I am offered tea or coffee, it is not usually a dilemma (aside from the fact that having one means that I cannot, right now, have the other), but we might call it a '**false choice**' if hot chocolate is also available but has not been presented as an option.

The basic argument has this structure:

P: Situation X allows for only these beliefs/courses of action.
C: Therefore your decision must be one of these beliefs/courses of action.

But quite often this forms a sub-conclusion towards a further (possibly implicit) conclusion:

P2: Of the options available, these beliefs/courses of action should be rejected.
C2: Therefore you should choose the remaining belief/course of action.

We need to ask ourselves two critical questions:

Q1: Are the beliefs/options offered genuine alternatives? (For example, are some not real or feasible, or if they are, are they really incompatible with one another?) [Acceptability]
Q2: Are the outcomes/options listed really the only ones available? [Acceptability]

As Taeda Tomić (2013) points out, taking a critical stance towards arguments that present dilemmas not only allows us to consider further alternatives, but to think creatively in terms of how apparently incompatible options might be synthesised into a previously unconsidered theory or solution.

False dichotomies play squarely into our tendency to see situations in black and white, especially if strong emotions are involved. We hear quite often in the TV talent show *The X Factor* how it's 'all or nothing' or 'Now or never' for those auditioning, whereas in many cases it does not actually come down to a choice between superstardom and working at McDonald's. News media will typically simplify stories in this way as well, making us all the more vulnerable to thinking that issues present us with more clear-cut choices than they usually do. In his handbook, *How to Win Campaigns* (2010, pp. 181–2), former Greenpeace Strategic Adviser Chris Rose recommends that campaign messages are framed in binary ('either/or') terms because of the clarity and emotional engagement this brings. While this makes sense from the point of view of rhetoric and the practicalities of initiating social change, as critical thinkers our aim is both engagement *and* truth.

We should be aware though that the reverse of the false dilemma is used in argumentation as well; denying that an issue is black and white when in fact it is. In *This Changes Everything* Naomi Klein argues that we really do have a clear choice between the continuation of unregulated capitalism and catastrophic climate change (a 'battle between capitalism and the planet'). She is critical of the 'fetish of centrism – of reasonableness, seriousness, splitting the difference' (2015, p. 22); in other words, believing that we can have both.

The implication of this and similar arguments is that it can be convenient to think that two or more things that we want are not incompatible with one another. Moreover, to complicate the choice by arguing for a false dilemma seems plausible and delays actions towards radical change. Klein might not be right, but the point stands that many situations do indeed present us with a limited number of incompatible choices. The important thing is to determine precisely what these choices are, but wanting to arrive at this insight too soon makes us susceptible to false dilemmas.

8.4 THE PERFECTIONIST FALLACY

The perfectionist fallacy has similarities with the false dilemma. In both cases, lazy, black and white thinking plays a role in making us vulnerable to some quite extraordinarily weak arguments. The perfectionist fallacy, in particular, is one that **System 2** will recognise as absurdly poor, but that seems to be such sweet temptation for **System 1**'s 'instinct to absolutise'.

The basic structure is:

P: Response X to problem Y will not provide a perfect solution.
C: Therefore response X should be rejected.

If this seems pretty dumb, that is because, in the vast majority of cases, it is. For example, after mass shootings in the USA, we usually hear a variation on this argument:

P1: If the USA changes its gun control laws, then people will still be able get hold of guns.
P2: If people can get hold of guns, then shootings and massacres will be a possibility.
C: Therefore there's no point in the USA changing its gun control laws.

Implicit here – the assumption being made – is that

> P3: There's no point in making changes unless those changes will solve the problem completely.

What a strange thing to think, and yet it's remarkable how readily we do think this kind of thing across a range of situations. On the gun law issue, words of wisdom come from rock musician and supporter of guns, Johnny Van Zant (of Lynyrd Skynyrd): 'I would like to see more rules on owning guns. People could still get them underground, man. But you gotta start somewhere.'[2] Yes, you do have to start somewhere, and even if some lives are saved by a modest change in the law, surely this is worth it. In a similar fashion I have heard it suggested that there's no point in lowering the speed limit in the UK to 50 mph because 'people will still die on the roads'. Yes, *but not as many*. There might be some good reasons for not lowering the speed limit, but this is not one of them.

On a less life-and-death note, a now-retired pundit on BBC's football highlights programme *Match of the Day* would regularly argue that 'Even if we introduce video technology for penalties and goal line decisions, referees will still make mistakes with off-sides, late tackles and so on, so what's the point?' The point is that *fewer errors are better than more errors*.

Life is such a thing that perfect solutions are rarely feasible, and this is something that System 1 seems to struggle with. A motivation-based explanation for this tendency is suggested by moral philosopher Jonathan Glover. In a discussion of how the individual should respond to global problems when the difference their actions will make is so minimal, he says,

> In many of the cases where it is used, the argument from the insignificant difference can be dismissed at once. If I can rescue a single person from death or misery, the fact that there are many others I cannot rescue is irrelevant to the moral worth of doing this. Huge problems sometimes produce an irrational paralysis of the imagination. It is so terrible to think of the poverty and starvation that will still exist in the world whatever I do, that it is tempting to despair and do nothing.
>
> (1986, p. 126)

8.5 RED HERRINGS AND EQUIVOCATIONS

If you hear the term '**red herring**' in relation to someone's argument (or your own) it means: (1) it is not relevant to the main point being debated, but (2) has the appearance of being relevant such that it is liable to shift the focus of the debate. In a way that is analogous to straw man arguments, this can happen by accident – in the moment the arguer feels that the point is relevant – or it can be a deliberate ploy to divert or obscure proceedings.

In 2010, the cap on university fees was raised from £3,000 to £9,000 per year for English and Northern Irish students studying in the UK. The government minister responsible for universities at the time was asked a question in a radio interview along the lines of 'What do you say to students who start university next year and who have to pay three times the fees of students this year?' His response was 'But you must remember that the monthly amount they will be paying back will in fact be less than students have to pay now.' Somewhere along the line this point might have some relevance to the general debate on higher education fees, but it is some distance from the matter at hand. The interviewer's question is perhaps unfair, but nevertheless the minister's response seems to be a deliberate attempt to move the discussion to a place where he is more comfortable.

A common way in which red herrings succeed in diverting the argument away from its proper focus is through **equivocation**. This is a fallacy linked to **ambiguity**, where an alternative meaning of a word or phrase is deliberately or accidentally employed across premises and conclusions in a way that leads the argument off track. In all cases a very poor argument is the result, but it can be one that stalls the argumentation process because equivocations can be tricky, or at least time-consuming to unpick.

After a bad run of games in 2013, the then Chelsea manager José Mourinho responded to a question in a press conference asking if there was a crisis at the club by saying, 'Crisis at Chelsea? What crisis? Syria is a crisis, we've just suffered two bad results.'[3] By employing the **contrast effect** and the impression of an unexpectedly worldly answer from a football manager, Mourinho, true to form, managed to deflect the question, but it is a clear case of equivocation. The type of crisis the questioner is referring to and the one that Mourinho invokes are radically different. If we are to accept his argument, then 'crisis' is a word that could never legitimately be used in the context of sport, but that is not the case; it simply has a different meaning to 'crisis' as referring to fatally serious, urgent, on-going and large-scale humanitarian situations.

EXERCISES

1. The 'perfectionist fallacy' assumes that a perfectionist argument will always be weak, but can you think of situations in which reasoning in this way constitutes a strong argument? If so, in what ways are these situations different from fallacious examples?
2. Choose a topical issue and construct two versions of an argument in relation to it; one that employs a false dilemma, and one that employs a true dilemma. A good model for this is Gore's *An Inconvenient Truth* documentary. Towards the end he dispels some false choices (such as environment vs. the economy), but of course the entire debate around climate change hinges on some very real choices.

FURTHER READING

Most textbooks on informal logic and critical thinking will discuss these fallacies. Some good examples are Bowell and Kemp (2010), Johnson and Blair (2006), and Hughes, Lavery and Doran (2010).

NOTES

1 *Today*, BBC Radio 4, 28 September 2015.
2 *Classic Rock*, December 2015, p. 22.
3 B. Jefferson (2013) 'José Mourinho: Chelsea losing to Basel and Everton isn't a crisis, Syria is a crisis.' Available at: www.express.co.uk/sport/football/430957/ Jose-Mourinho-Chelsea-losing-to-Basel-and-Everton-isn-t-a-crisis-Syria-is-a-crisis

CONCLUSION

I want people who can think, who can paint pictures and communicate ...,
and be prepared to have discussion and debate and dialogue and
argument.

(Construction Sector, Departmental Manager)[1]

What would Davis do?

(Sacha T. Burnstorm, pers. comm.)

As stated in the Introduction, the aim of critical thinking is to make
us better deliberators and decision-makers through a frame of mind
and a set of knowledge and skills that:

1. help us to identify, reconstruct and assess the arguments of
   others;
2. help us to construct, assess and improve our own arguments;
3. educate us in the pitfalls associated with reasoning in terms of:

   i. fallacies and their associated psychological biases;
   ii. features of unconstructive dialogues;
   iii. dispositions that make us prone to fallacious reasoning and
   unconstructive dialogues.

The aims of assessing the arguments of others and improving our own arguments are closely related. This is partly because a significant part of putting forward a position is to demonstrate its strength in comparison to rival positions, but it is also because we should assess our own arguments by the same standards that we assess the arguments of others. There is an understandable tendency when learning critical thinking to concentrate on reconstructing and evaluating other people's arguments at the expense of our own, and for this reason it is this reflexive application that I would like to emphasise in the book's concluding pages.

In the opening chapters, the relevance of critical thinking to self-knowledge is quite apparent, and in this respect a book like this brings us close to the spirit of philosophy as represented by Socrates. Fundamental to the search for truth is to understand the strengths and weaknesses of the very thing that is doing the searching – the human mind. Generalised discussions about cognitive biases and the dispositions that can help us transcend or manage them take us so far, but the examples and chapter exercises provided are also designed to encourage individual self-reflection. On the one hand, this is part of the process of deepening our understanding of these ideas. Through appreciating their relevance to our particular strengths and weaknesses as revealed through our own particular contexts, we can understand all the better their power and prevalence. On the other hand, this reflection is valuable for the individual in and of itself. Self-understanding and the role it plays in improving our lives are also part of the spirit of philosophy.

The chapters on argument reconstruction and argument forms and fallacies are less obviously 'about you' in this sense, but they nevertheless are personal because, as stated, these skills and this knowledge apply equally as much to our own arguments as they do to the arguments of others. The continued focus on psychology, rhetoric, dispositions and dialogues may help to remind us of this, as should those exercises which are clearly reflexive in nature (such as the one asking you to reconstruct and evaluate arguments from your own essays or other assignments in Chapter 4).

In this spirit, I will make some final points about how the skills and knowledge of argumentation can act as a catalyst for self-reflection.

Specifically, will I set out, in the form of a list, ways in which you can apply this learning to the practices of academic and professional communication:

1. When constructing arguments, the guidelines for argument reconstruction and evaluation can be adapted so that we ask ourselves questions like: What is my conclusion? What are my reasons for supporting it? Are these acceptable, relevant and sufficient?

2. Be careful to make your language as clear and precise as possible; avoid ambiguity, vagueness and equivocation.

3. Be watchful of the tendency to allow absolutist premises and conclusions to appear in our arguments where they are not appropriate. Most of the time they will not be. In other words, *commit with care*. Lessons can be learned in this respect from the section on generalisations in Chapter 6, but also from the discussion of false dilemmas and the perfectionist fallacy in Chapter 8. System 1 likes to jump to conclusions of a somewhat black-and-white nature, but where this is undesirable we might try asking ourselves 'What would Davis do?' (Davis being the name of Juror 8 in *Twelve Angry Men*, something we only learn right at the end of the film.)

4. If you are going to use authorities to support your conclusions, apply the critical questions to them and make sure you are using them for the right reasons. In the end you must take responsibility for the positions you argue for.

5. Before evaluating other people's arguments, make sure you understand them. The disposition of open-mindedness and the technique of argument reconstruction (along with the principle of charity) are not peripheral but central to critical thinking. In the opening chapters an important distinction is made between critical thinking as a more detached evaluation, and critical thinking as the spontaneous asking of questions that is part of being absorbed in the ideas that one is reading or hearing (what Dewey calls 'wholeheartedness'). Since the confirmation bias is such a deep-seated tendency, we need to make a sustained effort towards being *better listeners*.

6. Ask questions that help to ensure open-mindedness, such as 'Is there anything important that I'm missing here?' and 'Have I

understood with sufficient depth the point of view of the people I am arguing against (or supporting)?' Get to know your particular biases so that you are better able to prevent them from undermining your objectivity in argumentation. Be your own devil's advocate.

7. Be on guard against over-confidence in the strength of your arguments. Because of our self-serving bias, we are inclined to think that we are less susceptible than other people to the various biases discussed in Chapter 1 (and throughout the book). But we are not. Whatever our self-serving bias tells us, we too are prone to the self-serving bias.

8. Become acquainted with the ways in which emotions can hinder (and help) argumentation. And notice the kinds of arguments that are especially emotive, such as *ad hominems* and slippery slopes.

9. Consider the communication needs and limitations of your audience. Make judicious use of enthymemes, take care with your vocabulary, and avoid alienating others through smart-arsery. Where permitted by the subject matter, choose authorities and analogies that will be recognisable and appealing to your audience.

10. If we listen carefully to the views of others, we might find that we agree about more than we think we do; that disagreements are caused by misunderstandings, or are superficial. To get there, we need to be willing to ask questions, and not with a view to tripping people up. Thinking critically about beliefs and courses of action means that our evaluations can be positive as well as negative. To be oriented to the negative is a bias, and at its worst it can make us 'argumentative'. Don't be argumentative, be a critical thinker.

NOTE

1 Quoted in G.W. Hinchliffe and A. Jolly (2011) 'Graduate identity and employability', *British Educational Research Journal*, 37, 563–84.

GLOSSARY

Abusive ad hominem argument: See **ad hominem argument**.

Ad baculum **argument (appeal to force):** An argument that involves a threat, such as: 'Accept X, or I will ensure that negative consequence Y will occur.'

Ad hominem argument: An argument that attacks the arguer rather than their argument. A negative feature of the arguer – such as their character (**'direct'** or **'abusive'** ad hominem), behaviour that is inconsistent with what they are advocating (*'tu quoque'*), a biased perspective (**'circumstantial'** ad hominem), or some association with people or institutions of questionable character, bias, etc. (**'guilt by association'**) – is given as a reason for us to reject their argument (no matter how strong that argument otherwise is).

Ad populum **argument:** An argument that claims that, because the majority of people hold a certain belief or behave in a certain way, we should also hold that belief or behave in that way.

Affect heuristic: Basing a judgement or decision on how we feel about a particular person, situation, etc., rather than on a more reflective consideration of relevant factors.

Affirming the consequent: A fallacious version of a valid deductive argument known as *modus ponens*, which runs: 'P1: If X, then Y; P2: X; C: Therefore Y.' The invalid version makes the mistake of affirming the consequent (Y) rather than the antecedent (X) of the first premise, leaving us with 'P1: If X, then Y; P2: Y; C: Therefore X.'

Ambiguity and vagueness: An ambiguous sentence is one that has two or more possible meanings. In argument reconstruction, one meaning must be settled before a sentence can constitute a premise or conclusion. A vague sentence is one that is imprecise. In argument reconstruction if this vagueness is problematic when interpreting the meaning of a sentence, then it should be made more precise.

Analogy: An attempt to illuminate, explain or make an argument about a certain thing (or situation, event) by comparing it with something that shares relevant features with that thing (situation, event). Where a comparison is being made with a real-life event or other state of affairs, it is known as an **inductive analogy**, and where the comparison is with an invented situation, it is known as a **hypothetical analogy**.

Anchoring: This is the biasing effect of being exposed to prior relevant information when making a judgement. For example, if I am asked to guess the age of an actor I recognise but know little biographical detail about, such as Daniel Craig, my answer will be affected by the framing of a previous age-related question, such as 'Is he older or younger than 30?' or 'Is he older or younger than 40?' I am liable to guess lower after being presented with the first question, than if presented with the second one, because my estimate is anchored by this prior number.

Appeal to emotion: A form of argument in which a particular emotion (such as fear, pity or guilt) is instrumental in establishing the conclusion. In strong forms of these arguments the emotion is usually an appropriate response to the argument's subject matter. In weak forms, the emotion has a distorting effect on the audience's understanding and assessment of the argument.

Argument: A claim we make that we want others to accept as true, combined with reasons supporting this claim. The claim is known as the **conclusion**, and the reasons are called **premise**s.

Argument forms: Commonly used types of argument (such as arguments from analogy, ad hominem arguments, causal arguments, argument from consequences, and so on) that share a general structure and are often associated with particular types of fallacy. They are sometimes known as 'argument schemes'.

Argument from analogy: An argument in which a situation (X) is compared with a supposedly similar situation (Y). In the case of Y, we know, or would believe, that Z is the case, and because of Y's similarity to X, it is concluded that Z is also true of (or likely to be true of) X.

Argument from authority: An argument in which we are encouraged to accept the **conclusion** on the basis that a relevant authority (such as an expert) endorses that position.

Argument from consequences: An argument of the form, 'If X happens, then consequence Y will occur.' (The consequence can be positive or negative.)

Argument reconstruction: The practice of extracting the essence of an argument from the everyday language in which it is expressed or implied, and formulating it in terms of appropriately ordered **premises** and **conclusions**.

Argumentation: The exchange of arguments in dialogues.

ARS criteria: The assessment of arguments in terms of the *accuracy* of their premises; the *relevance* of their premises to the conclusion, and whether the premises are *sufficient* for establishing the conclusion. See also **critical questions.**

Assumptions: An assumption, in the context of an argument, is a belief that has relevance to the argument, but which has not been defended.

Availability heuristic: The quick rule by which we judge the likelihood of an occurrence on the basis of how readily it comes to mind.

Base rate neglect (or sometimes 'background' rate neglect): A fallacy referring to situations in which, when making a judgement about a particular person or event, we overlook relevant background information. So, if judging whether a shy person is more likely to be a librarian or a salesperson, the relative number of people employed in these jobs needs to be taken into consideration. See also **representative heuristic**.

Burden of proof: If a belief is taken to be generally established, the norm among a group of people, or an agreed default position, then this tends not to be a position that requires defending if challenged. Instead, the burden of proof falls to the challenger, and should they fail to convince those holding the established view, then the matter is closed.

Causal arguments: Arguments that claim that correlated events (X and Y) have a particular causal relationship (such as X causes Y).

Causal fallacies: A range of arguments in which a mistaken claim is made about a causal relationship; such as overlooking a shared cause, misunderstanding the direction of cause, or overlooking multiple causes.

Cherry picking fallacy: Information or examples that conform to the arguer's hypothesis or that present their position in a particularly flattering light are presented as evidence, while non-conforming or unflattering data is ignored or suppressed.

Circular argument (begging the question): An argument in which we must accept the **conclusion** in order to accept one or more of the **premise**s. This is to argue 'in a circle' because, of course, the conclusion can only be established once the truth of the premise is established.

Circumstantial ad hominem argument: See **ad hominem argument**.

Coercive power: The social influence someone has resulting from their ability to punish the actions of others (through violence, insults, fines, detentions, and so on). Note that one does not need to have **legitimate power** in order to have coercive power.

Cognitive dissonance: The discomfort experienced as a result of an (often unconscious) inconsistency between one's beliefs, or between one's beliefs and one's behaviour. See also **commitment and consistency**.

Commitment and consistency: A heuristic based on the need for beliefs and behaviours to be consistent with prior commitments. It is especially powerful when commitments are publicly declared.

Conclusion: See **argument**.

Confirmation bias: The largely automatic tendency to seek out, attend to or remember information that confirms existing beliefs, at the expense of information which disconfirms them.

Constructive dialogue: A dialogue is a discussion between two or more people, and dialogues that aim to establish truth, solve a problem or resolve a dispute can be carried out in ways that are constructive or unconstructive. A constructive dialogue is guided by a set of (often implicitly held) rules that help ensure the dominating presence of critical thinking. Examples include participants being willing to defend any claims that they make, and the dialogue not being considered complete until all parties have been able to express their views, and these views are given due consideration.

Contrast effect: The effect that nearby comparators with contrasting qualities have on our perception and interpretation of information. For example, if you are trying to impress someone with your singer-song writer abilities, do not do it after that someone has just been listening to Bob Dylan.

Critical questions: The questions which are important to ask in order to establish the strength of an argument.

Critical thinking disposition: See **disposition**.

Deductive argument: An argument in which the conclusion follows logically (or necessarily) from the premises, so that if the premises are true, the conclusion must also be true.

Defeasible generalisation: A type of **generalisation** that attempts to apply a generally accepted belief to a particular instance in the context of a **dialogue**. They typically do not employ qualifiers such as 'all' or 'most', but they are regarded as provisional and form premises in **plausible arguments**.

Dialogue: See **constructive dialogue**.

Direct ad hominem argument: See **ad hominem argument**.

Direction of cause: Where two events appear to occur simultaneously there is a danger of mistaking the direction of cause; in other words, determining which event is the cause and which event is the effect.

Disposition: A tendency in a person that inclines them to think, feel and act in a certain way (similar to an attitude, character trait or virtue). A **critical thinking disposition** is one that inclines a person to be a good critical thinker.

Ego defences: Ways in which we distort reality in order to keep painful truths away from full consciousness. See also **rationalisation**.

Enthymeme: An argument with a missing premise or premises, usually for the sake of brevity, with the arguer confident that the audience is well aware of what has been omitted.

Equivocation: This is a fallacy linked to ambiguity, where an alternative meaning of a word or phrase is deliberately or accidentally employed across **premise**s and **conclusion**s in a way that leads the argument off track. See also **red herring**.

Ethotic power (ethotic authority): The social influence of someone who is regarded as a broadly 'good' or 'virtuous' person (like Barack Obama or Oprah Winfrey, for some).

Expert power (expert authority): The social influence a person has by virtue of their expertise (or perceived expertise) in a certain area.

Explanation: In contrast to **argument**s, with explanations it is agreed that something is true, and a person is then offering reasons to explain why it is true (for example, what has caused it). With an argument, it is not agreed that something is true, and the arguer presents reasons in order to convince the other person of what they believe to be true.

Fallacy: Fallacies are weak **argument**s of certain types that are used frequently and are liable to be convincing to those not thinking critically.

False dilemma/false dichotomy/false choice: A set of fallacies in which the options available in a particular situation have been misleadingly represented. 'False dilemma' indicates that the options offered and the implied pay-off between them are not fully accurate; 'false dichotomy' means that only two possibilities have been presented but that there are in fact more than this, and 'false choice' is a more general term that covers two or more options and does not imply a pay-off between them (as a 'dilemma' does).

Framing: In communication, framing refers to a way of looking at things; of putting an 'angle' or 'spin' on a particular issue. It involves emphasising some aspects of a concept, policy proposal, product, and so on, at the expense of others. The purpose can be to enable an audience's understanding of the thing in question, or to put it in a more favourable light, and to encourage certain forms of action in relation to it. For example, in response to calls for alcohol to be banned on planes after a series of 'air rage' incidents, comedian Doug Stanhope (on the *Deadbeat Hero* CD) suggests we consider all the air rage that has been *prevented* as a result of people being mellowed out by alcohol.

Generalisation (absolute and non–absolute): Absolute (also known as 'universal', 'strict', or 'hard') generalisations are those that claim that all instances of a certain category of a thing have a certain quality (e.g. 'all planets have a gravitational pull'), and non-absolute (also known as 'non-universal', 'inductive' or 'soft') generalisations are those that claim that only 'most' or 'the majority' of instances have this quality (e.g. 'most planets in our solar system are bigger than Mars').

Groupthink: A set of processes of social influence (such as collective over-confidence and **pluralistic ignorance**) that causes a group of otherwise rational and intelligent people to make very poor decisions.

Guilt by association: See **ad hominem argument**.

Halo effect: Our pronounced tendency to generalise known positive features of a person to other, unknown, aspects of them. If there is someone we find likeable at work, we tend to wrongly assume we would like them in other contexts as well; or if someone is kind to non-human animals, we might jump to the conclusion that they are also compassionate towards human beings. The opposite of this is the **horn effect**; illegitimately generalising negative characteristics.

Hasty generalisation: Where a general truth is assumed on the basis of insufficient evidence. A **sweeping generalisation** is one in which a generalised claim is accepted as true, but where relevant exceptions are overlooked.

Heuristic: A tool for quick decision-making; a rule of thumb that is applied to certain types of situation that, although lacking precision, makes better than chance judgements. See also **System 1 and System 2 thinking**.

Horn effect: See **halo effect**.

Hypothetical analogy: See **analogy**.

Inductive analogy: See **analogy**.

Inductive argument: In contrast to a **deductive argument**, the conclusion of an inductive argument does not necessarily follow from the premises, so it is possible for the **premises** to be true and the **conclusion** false.

Informal logic: The study of **argument**s and reasoning as employed in real-life contexts, and often viewed as synonymous with critical thinking.

Information power: The social influence a person has by virtue of the information they have access to (e.g., as a result of their job, or people they know). A sub-category of this is **witness**

testimony – the knowledge resulting from first-hand experience of an unusual event.

Legitimate power: The social influence a person has resulting from the position they hold, or moral and legal principles their decisions and actions uphold.

Meta-cognition: This can sometimes simply mean self-awareness, but a more specific usage refers to our awareness of the mental processes (e.g. thoughts and emotions) we are currently experiencing with a view to regulating these or the judgements, decisions or actions that might arise from them.

Mistaking cause for correlation: Otherwise known as 'Sod's law fallacy', in which a person overlooks a causal relationship between two events and instead declares them to be a coincidence. Where the effect is negative, it might be interpreted as the kind of bad luck that is typical of certain circumstances, hence being 'Sod's law'.

Narrative fallacy: This can be understood as a psychological basis of the **over-simplification of causes**, and refers to our attraction to, and confidence in, coherent but simple explanations at the expense of an appreciation of complex and unknown factors.

Necessary and sufficient conditions: A necessary condition is one that must be fulfilled in order for something to be the case (belong to a particular category, cause something to happen, and so on); and a sufficient condition (or set of conditions) is one that is enough to make something the case. A sufficient condition can also be necessary, but it does not have to be.

Overlooking shared cause: The fallacy of looking for a causal relationship between correlated events instead of considering the possibility that the correlation is the product of a shared cause.

Over-simplification of causes: The fallacy of assuming a more straightforward causal explanation for a phenomenon than is actually the case. In many cases multiple causal factors need to be taken into account. See also **narrative fallacy**.

Perfectionist fallacy: The claim that unless a perfect solution to a problem (such as gun crime or death on the roads) can be found, it is not worth intervening (through, for example, new policies on gun control or lowering speed limits).

Placebo effect: Beneficial medical outcomes resulting from a patient's belief that the treatment they are receiving will improve their health, rather than from any direct physical effects of the treatment itself.

Plausible argument: A style of argument employed in deliberations and other dialogues in which generally accepted assumptions act as the basis for reaching conclusions. They are recognised as provisional in nature, and can function as opening moves in what becomes a more systematic process of reasoning about the matter in hand. See also **burden of proof**, and **defeasible generalisation**.

Pluralistic ignorance: A socially based form of ignorance in which indecision or inaction results from the mutual misinterpretation of (often) non-verbal communication. One person's non-urgent or calm demeanour is seen by another as a sign of insight that a situation is under control, but in fact this demeanour is either the result of believing that similar body language in others has this same meaning, or that they do not want to appear to be anxious or out of their depth.

Position to know argument: An argument based on **information power** (but excluding **witness testimony**).

Premise: See **argument**.

Premise and conclusion indicators: When identifying and reconstructing **argument**s, certain words and phrases can help to indicate the presence of **premise**s and **conclusion**s. 'The reasons for this are', and 'this is so because' are examples of premise indicators; and 'thus', 'therefore' and 'in which case' are examples of conclusion indicators.

Principle of charity: When reconstructing arguments, the principle of charity is the best reasonable interpretation of ambiguous, vague or otherwise unclear sentences or arguments.

Proposition (statement): A sentence that (at least in theory) can be adjudged to be true or false. These are contrasted with, for example, sentences that are questions, or directives (orders). All premises and conclusions in an argument must be propositions, and sometimes argument reconstructions require the rewording of information originally presented in non-propositional form (such as rhetorical questions).

Psychology of persuasion: The study of the psychological principles underlying persuasive communication.

Rationalisation: To rationalise is to provide a reason why something happened, but one that is not the real reason – a fact that is only unconsciously known to us. Rationalisation is a form of **ego defence** in that it functions to protect us, at least temporarily, from an aspect of reality (such as unsavoury motivations) that we do not want to acknowledge.

Reciprocation: A **heuristic** linked to the norm of equitable exchange of favours, goods, and so on. If someone gives something to us, we feel strongly obliged to give them something in return.

Red herring: A fallacious argument with the potential to divert other arguers away from the issue being discussed because of its apparent relevance and often emotive content. It can be employed deliberately or accidentally. See also **equivocation**.

Referent power: The form of social influence held by a person or a group that we identify with. The sense of, and desire for, belonging make us likely to conform to the attitudes and behaviours of that person or group.

Regression to the mean: A phenomenon whereby outstandingly good or poor results or performances are typically followed by more average ones. Fallacious thinking can result from this if we base beliefs and decisions on a single extreme score.

Representative heuristic: A simple rule whereby quick answers to questions like 'What's the probability of individual X belonging to group Y', or 'What is the probability of event P being the cause of event Q?' are provided by making reference to what a typical member of group Y, or a typical cause of Q is like.

Reward power: The social influence someone has resulting from their ability to reward the actions of others (through gifts, treats, praise, bonuses, and so on). Note that one does not need to have **legitimate power** in order to have reward power.

Rhetoric: The art of persuasive communication.

Self-serving bias: An automatic and systematic tendency to overestimate those features of ourselves and the world that are core to our sense of self-esteem and our motivation to succeed.

Shared causes: See **overlooking shared cause**.

Slippery slope arguments: Arguments that share the general structure of arguments from negative consequences, but in which it is claimed that an initial, relatively inconsequential or benign consequence will lead to a series of further consequences that (1) are largely out of our control, and (2) will end in a disastrous final consequence.

Social proof: A **heuristic** in which the behaviour of other people is used as a guide to what to believe or how to act.

Straw man argument: An **argument** in which the position of an opponent is misrepresented in such a way that it makes it easier to argue against. This misrepresentation can be deliberate or accidental.

Sub-conclusions: Conclusions reached on the way to an overall conclusion in a larger **argument**. The conclusions of component arguments function as further **premise**s in the larger argument.

Sweeping generalisation: See **hasty generalisation**.

System 1 and System 2 thinking: System 1 is the 'fast thinking' that is employed in situations we are familiar with (or think we are familiar with) and which is reliant on heuristics. System 2 is the sort of 'slow thinking' that we associate with focused attention, problem solving and critical thinking.

System 1 candy: A term to characterise certain features of arguments or other persuasive messages that encourage System 1 (heuristics-based) decision-making in situations where System 2 ought to be employed.

Tu quoque: See **ad hominem argument**.

Vagueness: See **ambiguity and vagueness**.

Witness testimony: See **information power**.

SELECT BIBLIOGRAPHY

Aikin, S. and Casey, J. (2011) Straw Men, Weak Men and Hollow Men. *Argumentation*, 25, 87–105.

Aikin, S. and Casey, J. (2016) Straw Men, Iron Men, and Argumentative Virtue. *Topoi*, online: 1–10.

Aikin, S. and Clanton, J. (2010) Developing Group-Deliberative Virtues. *Journal of Applied Philosophy*, 27(4), 409–24.

Aristotle (1991) *The Art of Rhetoric*. London: Penguin.

Barnett, R. (1997) *Higher Education: A Critical Business*. Buckingham: Open University Press.

Baron, R. (2005) So Right It's Wrong: Groupthink and the Ubiquitous Nature of Polarized Group Decision Making. *Advances in Experimental Social Psychology*, 37, 219–53.

Battaly, H. (2010) Attacking Character: Ad Hominem Argument and Virtue Epistemology. *Informal Logic*, 30(4): 361–90.

Berrill, D. (ed.) (1996) *Perspectives on Written Argument*. Cresskill, NJ: Hampton Press.

Blass, T. (2000) *Obedience to Authority: Current Perspectives on the Milgram Paradigm*. Englewood Cliffs, NJ: Erlbaum.

Bohm, D. (2004) *On Dialogue*. London: Routledge.

Bowell, T. and Kemp, G. (2010) *Critical Thinking: A Concise Guide*, 3rd edn. London: Routledge.

Brady, M. (2013) *Emotional Insight*. Oxford: Oxford University Press.

Brinton, A. (1986) Ethotic Argument. *History of Philosophy Quarterly*, 3(3), 245–58.

Brown, R. (1986) *Social Psychology*. New York: Free Press.

Burns, J.M. (1978) *Leadership*. New York: Harper & Row.

Cialdini, R. (2007) *Influence: The Psychology of Persuasion*. New York: Harper Collins.

Cohen, D.H. (1995) Argument is War ... and War is Hell: Philosophy, Education, and Metaphors for Argumentation. *Informal Logic*, 17(2), 177–88.

Cooper, H. (1979) Pygmalion Grows Up: A Model for Teacher Expectation Communication and Performance Influence. *Review of Educational Research*, 49(3), 389–410.

Csikszentmihalyi, M. (2002) *Flow*. London: Rider.

Damasio, A. (2000) *The Feeling of What Happens: Body, Emotion and the Making of Consciousness*. London: Vintage.

Davis, H. (2009) *Caveman Logic*. Amherst, NY: Prometheus Books.

Descartes, R. ([1641] 1968) *Discourse on Method and the Meditations*. London: Penguin.

DeSteno, D., Petty, R.E., Rucker, D.D., Wegener, D.T. and Braverman, J. (2004) Discrete Emotions and Persuasion: The Role of Emotion-Induced Expectancies. *Journal of Personality and Social Psychology*, 86(1), 43–56.

Dewey, J. (1910) *How We Think*. New York: D.C. Heath & Co.

Eemeren, F. van and Grootendorst, R. (2004) *A Systematic Theory of Argumentation: The Pragma-Dialectical Approach*. Cambridge: Cambridge University Press.

Ennis, R. (1996a) *Critical Thinking*. Upper Saddle River, NJ: Prentice Hall.

Ennis, R. (1996b) Critical Thinking Dispositions: Their Nature and Accessibility. *Informal Logic*, 18(2–3), 165–82.

Facione, P. (2006) *Critical Thinking: What It is and Why It Counts*. Hermosa Beach, CA: Measured Reasons LLC.

Facione, P., Sanchez, C., Falione, N. and Gainen, J. (1995) The Disposition towards Critical Thinking. *The Journal of General Education*, 44(1), 1–25.

Festinger, L. (1957) *A Theory of Cognitive Dissonance*. Stanford, CA: Stanford University Press.

Fisher, R. and Ury, W. (1991) *Getting to Yes: Negotiating an Agreement Without Giving In*. London: Random House.

Fiske, S. (2005) What's in a Category? in A. Miller (ed.) *The Social Psychology of Good and Evil*. New York: Guilford Press.

Flew, A. (1985) *Thinking About Thinking*. London: Flamingo.

Freeden, M. (2005) What Should the 'Political' in Political Theory Explore? *Journal of Political Philosophy*, 13(2), 113–34.

French, J. and Raven, B. (1959) The Bases of Social Power, in D. Cartwright (ed.) *Studies in Social Power*. Ann Arbor, MI: Institute for Social Research.

Furnham, A. and Boo, H.C. (2011) A Literature Review of the Anchoring Effect. *The Journal of Socio-Economics*, 40(1), 35–42.

Gigerenzer, G., Todd, P. and the ABC Research Group (1999) *Simple Heuristics that Make Us Smart*. Oxford: Oxford University Press.

Gilbert, M. (1994) Feminism, Argumentation and Coalescence. *Informal Logic*, XVI(2), 95–113.

Gilbert, M. (1997) *Coalescent Argumentation*. Englewood Cliffs, NJ: Erlbaum.

Glover, J. (1986) It Makes No Difference Whether or Not I Do It, in P. Singer (ed.) *Applied Ethics*. Oxford: Oxford University Press.

Goldacre, B. (2008) *Bad Science*. London: Fourth Estate.

Goodwin, J. (2011) Accounting for the Appeal to the Authority of Experts. *Argumentation*, 25, 285–96.

Govier, T. (1988) *Problems in Argument: Analysis and Evaluation*. Dordrecht: Foris Publications.

Govier, T. (2013) *A Practical Guide to Argument*, 7th edn. Belmont, CA: Wadsworth.

Hamblin, C. (1970) *Fallacies*. London: Methuen.

Hanscomb, S. (2015) Assessments and the Self: Academic Practice and Character Attributes. *Journal of Learning Development in Higher Education*, 8.

Hargie, O. and Dickson, D. (2004) *Skilled Interpersonal Communication*, 4th edn. London: Routledge.

Hughes, W., Lavery, J. and Doran, K. (2010) *Critical Thinking*, 6th edn. Peterborough, ON: Broadview Press.

Hume, D. ([1779] 1990) *Dialogues Concerning Natural Religion*. London: Penguin.

Hume, D. ([1748] 2008) *An Enquiry Concerning Human Understanding*. Oxford: Oxford University Press.

Janis, I. ([1972] 1982) *Groupthink*, 2nd edn. Boston: Houghton Mifflin Co.

Jefferson, A. (2014) Slippery Slope Arguments. *Philosophy Compass*, 9/10, 672–80.

Johnson, R. and Blair, A. (2006) *Logical Self Defense*. New York: IDEA.

Kahneman, D. (2012) *Thinking Fast and Slow*. London: Penguin.

Kant, I. ([1781] 1929) *Critique of Pure Reason*, trans. N. Kemp Smith. Basingstoke: Macmillan.

Kant, I. ([1784] 1963) What is Enlightenment? in *On History*, ed. and trans. L. White Beck. New York: Macmillan.

Keltner, D., Oatley, K. and Jenkins, J. (2013) *Understanding Emotions*, 3rd edn. New York: Wiley Global Education.

Kierkegaard, S. ([1846] 1979) *Two Ages*, ed. and trans. H.V. Hong and E.H. Hong. Princeton, NJ: Princeton University Press.

King, M.L. (1963) *Letter from Birmingham Jail*. Available at: http://kingencyclopedia.stanford.edu/kingweb/popular_requests/frequentdocs/birmingham.pdf

Klein, N. (2015) *This Changes Everything*. London: Penguin.

Kuhn, D. (1991) *The Skills of Argument*. Cambridge: Cambridge University Press.

Larrick, R. (2004) Debiasing. In D.J. Koehler and N. Harvey (eds) *Blackwell Handbook of Judgment and Decision Making*. Oxford: Blackwell.

Lerner, M. and Simmons, C. (1966) Observer's Reaction to the 'Innocent Victim': Compassion or Rejection? *Journal of Personality and Social Psychology*, 4(2), 203–10.

Lunsford, A. and Ruszkiewicz, J. (2010) *Everything's an Argument*, 5th edn. London: St Martin's Press.

Makan, J.M. and Marty, D.L. (2001) *Cooperative Argumentation: A Model for Deliberative Community*. Long Grove, IL: Waveland Press.

McElroy, T. and Dowd, K. (2007) Susceptibility to Anchoring Effects: How Openness-to-Experience Influences Responses to Anchoring Cues. *Judgment and Decision Making*, 2(1), 48–53.

Melling, D. (1987) *Understanding Plato*. Oxford: Oxford University Press.

Milgram, S. ([1974] 2005) *Obedience to Authority*. London: Pinter & Martin.

Mill, J.S. ([1859] 1962) *Utilitarianism, On Liberty: Essay on Bentham*. Glasgow: Collins.

Morrow, D. and Weston, A. (2011) *A Workbook for Arguments*. Indianapolis: Hackett.

Narveson, J. (1993) Morality and Violence, in T. Regan (ed.) *Matters of Life and Death*, 3rd edn. New York: McGraw-Hill.

Newman, J.H. ([1852] 1982) *The Idea of a University*. Notre Dame, IN: University of Notre Dame Press.

Nussbaum, M. (1990) *Love's Knowledge*. Cambridge: Cambridge University Press.

Nye, A. (1990) *Words of Power: A Feminist Reading of the History of Logic*. New York: Routledge.

Oatley, K., Keltner, D. and Jenkins, J. (2006) *Understanding Emotions*, 2nd edn. Oxford: Blackwell.

Osman, M. (2004) An Evaluation of Dual-Process Theories of Reasoning. *Psychonomic Bulletin and Review*, 11(6), 988–1010.

Paley, W. ([1800] 2009) *Natural Theology*. Cambridge: Cambridge University Press.

Paul, R. (1984a) Teaching Critical Thinking in the Strong Sense: A Focus on Self-Deception, World Views, and a Dialectical Mode of Analysis. *Informal Logic*, 4(2), 2–7.

Paul, R. (1984b) Critical Thinking: Fundamental to Education for a Free Society, *Educational Leadership*, Sept., 4–14.

Paul, R. (1995) *Critical Thinking*. Santa Rosa, CA: Foundation for Critical Thinking.

Perelman, C. and Olbrechts-Tyteca, L. (1969) *The New Rhetoric: A Treatise on Argumentation*. Notre Dame, IN: University of Notre Dame Press.

Perkins, D., Jay, E. and Tishman, S. (1993) Beyond Abilities: A Dispositional Theory of Thinking. *Merrill-Palmer Quarterly*, 39(1), 1–21.

Peters, R. (1973) The Aims of Education, in R. Peters (ed.) *The Philosophy of Education*. Harmondsworth: Penguin.

Peterson, C. and Seligman, M. (2004) *Character Strengths and Virtues*. Oxford: Oxford University Press.

Petty, R. and Cacioppo, J. (1996) *Attitudes and Persuasion: Classic and Contemporary Approaches*. Boulder, CO: Westview Press.

Plato (1993) *The Last Days of Socrates*, trans. H. Tarrant and H. Tredennick. London: Penguin.

Plato (2004) *Gorgias*, trans. C. Emlyn-Jones and W. Hamilton. London: Penguin.

Raven, B. (1965) Social Influence and Power, in I.D. Steiner and M. Fishbein (eds) *Current Studies in Social Psychology*. New York: Holt, Rinehart, & Winston.

Rose, C. (2010) *How to Win Campaigns*, 2nd edn. London: Earthscan.

Rosenthal, R. and Jacobson, L. ([1968] 2003) *Pygmalion in the Classroom*. Carmarthen: Crown House Publishing.

Schultz, P., Nolan, J., Cialdini, R., Goldstein, N. and Griskevicius, V. (2007) Constructive, Destructive, and Reconstructive Power of Social Norms. *Psychological Science*, 18(5), 429–34.

Scriven, M. (1976) *Reasoning*. New York: McGraw-Hill.

Scruton, R. (1999) *On Hunting*. London: Yellow Jersey.

Seech, Z. (1993) *Open Minds and Everyday Reasoning*. Belmont, CA: Wadsworth.

Siegel, H. (1988) *Educating Reason*. New York: Routledge.

Slovic, P., Finucane, M.L., Peters, E. and MacGregor, D.G. (2007) The Affect Heuristic. *European Journal of Operational Research*, 177(3), 1333–52.

Smith, E., Mackie, D. and Claypool, H. (2014) *Social Psychology*, 4th edn. Philadelphia, PA: Psychology Press.

Solomon, R. (2003) Emotions and Choice, in R. Solomon (ed.) *What is an Emotion?*, 2nd edn. Oxford: Oxford University Press.

Sopory, P. and Dillard, J.P. (2002) The Persuasive Effects of Metaphor: A Meta-Analysis. *Human Communication Research*, 28(3), 382–419.

Sutherland, S. (2007) *Irrationality*. London: Pinter & Martin.

Tajfel, H. and Turner, J. (1986) The Social Identity Theory of Intergroup Behaviour. In S. Worchel and W.G. Austin (eds) *Psychology of Intergroup Relations*. Chicago: Nelson-Hall, pp. 7–24.

Taleb, N. (2007) *The Black Swan*. London: Penguin.

Taylor, S.E. and Brown, J.D. (1988) Illusion and Well-Being: A Social Psychological Perspective on Mental Health. *Psychological Bulletin*, 103(2), 193–210.

Tiberius, V. (2008) *The Reflective Life*. Oxford: Oxford University Press.

Tindale, C. (2007) *Fallacies and Argument Appraisal*. Cambridge: Cambridge University Press.

Tomić, T. (2013) False Dilemma: A Systematic Exposition. *Argumentation*, 27(4), 347–68.

Toulmin, S. (1958) *The Uses of Argument*. Cambridge: Cambridge University Press.

Tremain, R. (2000) *Music and Silence*. London: Vintage.

Tversky, A. and Kahneman, D. (1974) Judgment under Uncertainty: Heuristics and Biases. *Science*, 185(4157), 1124–31.

Tversky, A. and Kahneman, D. (1983) Extensional Versus Intuitive Reasoning: The Conjunction Fallacy in Probability Judgment. *Psychological Review*, 90(4), 293–315.

Waller, B.N. (2001) Classifying and Analysing Analogies. *Informal Logic*, 21(3), 199–218.

Walton, D. (1989) *Informal Logic*. Cambridge: Cambridge University Press.

Walton, D. (1992) *The Place of Emotion in Argument*. Philadelphia, PA: Penn State University Press.

Walton, D. (1995) *A Pragmatic Theory of Fallacy*. Tuscaloosa, AL: University of Alabama Press.

Walton, D. (1998) *The New Dialectic: Conversational Contexts of Argument*. Toronto: University of Toronto Press.

Walton, D. (2006) *Fundamentals of Critical Argumentation*. Cambridge: Cambridge University Press.

Walton, D. (2009) *Ad Hominem Arguments*. Tuscaloosa, AL: University of Alabama Press.

Walton, D. (2015) The Basic Slippery Slope Argument. *Informal Logic*, 35(3), 273–311.

Walton, D., Reed, C. and Macagno, F. (2008) *Argumentation Schemes*. Cambridge: Cambridge University Press.

Weber, M. (1978) *Economy and Society*. Berkeley, CA: University of California Press.

Willard, C.A. (1990) Authority. *Informal Logic*, 12(1), 12–22.

Woods, J. (1995) Appeal to Force, in H. Hansen and R. Pinto (eds) *Fallacies*. Philadelphia, PA: Penn State University Press.

Woods, J. (2013) *Errors of Reasoning: Naturalizing the Logic of Inference*. London: College Publications.

Worth, L. and Mackie, D. (1987) Cognitive Mediation of Positive Affect in Persuasion. *Social Cognition*, 5(1), 76–94.

Yalom, I. (1980) *Existential Psychotherapy*. New York: Basic Books.

INDEX